Four Voices
The Great Manitoulin Island Treaty of 1862

Shelley J. Pearen

© Shelley J. Pearen 2012
All rights reserved
Printed on acid-free paper

ISBN 978-0-9880865-0-0 (paperback)

Library and Archives Canada Cataloguing in Publication

Pearen, Shelley J.
    Four Voices : The Great Manitoulin Island Treaty of 1862 / Shelley J. Pearen.

Includes bibliographical references and index.
ISBN 978-0-9880865-0-0

    1. Canada. Treaties, etc. 1862 Oct. 6. 2. Ojibwa Indians–Treaties. 3. Ottawa Indians–Treaties. 4. Ojibwa Indians–Land tenure–Ontario. 5. Ottawa Indians–Land tenure–Ontario. 6. Manitoulin Island (Ont.)–History. I. Title. II. Title: Great Manitoulin Island Treaty of 1862.

KE7749.O45P42 2012   346.7104'32089973330713135   C2012-904337-0
KF5662.O45P42 2012

Cover design by Crystal Migwans.

Four Voices
The Great Manitoulin Island Treaty of 1862

iii   Preface

v   Notes

vii   Introduction

xi   Foreword

1   Chapter 1: Great Manitoulin Island and the Honorable William McDougall
    William McDougall
    Recommendations and Negotiations
    The Treaty and the Government

25   Chapter 2: *Odawa Minising* and *Ogimaa* Itawashkash
    Sasso Itawashkash
    Rumours and Resolutions
    The Treaty and the *Ogimaag* of *Odawa Minising*

55   Chapter 3: *L'Ile Manitouline* and Père Jean-Pierre Choné
    Jean-Pierre Choné
    Threat and Action
    The Treaty and the Jesuits

75   Chapter 4: Manitoulin Island and Reverend Peter Jacobs
    Peter Jacobs
    Acceptance and Publicity
    The Treaty and the Protestants

93   Chapter 5: Reaction to the Treaty
    The Reaction of the Press
    The Reactions of the *Anishinaabeg*, the Government and the Missionaries

127   Chapter 6: Repercussions in the Fishing Industry
    Enforcement or Harassment
    Manitoulin Returns to the Headlines
    William Gibbard's Troubled Waters

| **139** | Chapter 7: The Aftermath
Renewed Protests
Reunification of the Bands
Resettlement |
|---|---|
| **165** | Appendix 1: Transcription of the 1862 Articles of Agreement and Convention for the Surrender of the Great Manitoulin Island and the Islands Adjacent |
| **169** | Appendix 2: Transcription of the 1836 Provisional Agreement for the Surrender of the Manitoulin Islands and the Islands on the North Shore of Lake Huron |
| **171** | Selected Bibliography |
| **175** | Index of Names |
| **179** | Endnotes |

Illustrations between pages 92 and 93:

Signatories to the Great Manitoulin Island treaty of 1862
Map of Manitoulin Island in 1862-63
Manitowaning, Manitoulin Island
Wikwemikong, Manitoulin Island
William McDougall (1822-1905)
Sasso Itawashkash (?-1882?)
"Indian Village of Wikwemikong Great Manitouline Island"
Jesuit missionary at Wikwemikong, August 1856
Peter Jacobs, Jr. (c1832-1864) (attributed)
Jean-Baptiste Assiginack (c1770-1866)
Amable Assiginack (c1788-1878)
Antoine Makons (c1819-1859)
Jean-Baptiste Atagiwinini (c1792-1867)
Michel Bemakinang (c1798-1878)
Wahcowsai (c1809-?)
William Gibbard (1818-1863)
The steamship *Ploughboy*, at Collingwood

Preface

My great-great grandfathers Donald McKenzie and Jabez Waters Sims settled on Manitoulin Island with their families before non-Native settlement was legal or encouraged. They witnessed the turbulent period of *Anishinaabe* resettlement that followed the 1862 treaty.

McKenzie and Sims were diametrically opposite in character and vocation. McKenzie was a big, jovial, Scottish-Presbyterian trader who settled his family in Wikwemikong in the mid-1850s. Sims was a petite, studious, English missionary who was sent to Manitoulin to serve the *Anishinaabeg* in 1864. Neither family would have survived without its *Anishinaabe* neighbours.

My interest in the history of my own family led to my research into the history of Manitoulin. In 1972, 110 years after the treaty, I began researching the history of the island and its people. In 1992 some of my research resulted in my book *Exploring Manitoulin*.

But all my research led back to the treaties of 1836 and 1862. In 2002, I decided to focus my research on the 1862 treaty. Regrettably, the 1862 Manitoulin treaty was not a unique action: the government repeatedly settled non-Native people on Native land, and then persuaded the Native population to accept smaller parcels of land in exchange for annuities or payments. Nor is Manitoulin unique in that unanimous agreement among the Native people was not obtained to relinquish their land. What is perhaps unique is that there is a prodigious paper trail left by the parties who were involved in, and affected by, the Manitoulin Island treaty. This trail can still be followed, one hundred and fifty years later.

The 100th anniversary of the treaty in 1962 was commemorated in the local press as "one hundred years of friendship and progress," rather than a celebration of the treaty itself. *The Manitoulin Expositor* newspaper covered the anniversary extensively through a series of articles culminating in a special treaty edition. There was a clear tone of regret that such a major event in Manitoulin Island's history had been so impudently concluded a century earlier.

The 150th anniversary of the Manitoulin Treaty in 2012 should also be observed as "one hundred and fifty years of friendship and progress." If you are reading this book anywhere in North America, you are doing so on land acquired from Native people. Granted, a lot of land was acquired under more forceful, brutal and bloody circumstances than Manitoulin experienced, but that is because peaceful people were involved in the deed, not because of the negotiators or the government. The island was surveyed, sold and resettled, and the *Anishinaabe* bands were enumerated, merged and established on reserves.

The treaty of 1862 produced the land allocation and appearance of today's Manitoulin Island. Today, you will have to look closely to find signs of acknowledgement of ownership beyond the actual First Nation settlements and the names of a few island townships and villages. Village streets bear the names of government functionaries or politicians—Vankoughnet, Dupont, Walcot—rather than the names of *Anishinaabe* leaders—Itawashkash, Maishegonggai, Paimoquonaishkung. The most genuine statement describing the Manitoulin treaty of 1862 is that the land was acquired peacefully from intelligent, generous people who repeatedly trusted the Crown and its agents to deal with them fairly and share the land and resources. History cannot be changed, but it must be acknowledged.

I would like to acknowledge the encouragement and assistance of my husband Gordon Fulton who has explored Manitoulin with me for decades.

I would especially like to say *chi-miigwech* to my friend Alan Corbiere for his ongoing support, and *merci beaucoup* to my friend Father William Lonc, S.J. Together, we three friends have transcribed, translated, compared and made sense of countless barely legible nineteenth-century documents written in Ojibwe, French and English.

Notes

The terms *Anishinaabeg* (*Anishinaabe* singular), Indians, Natives and aboriginals all refer to the same people in this book. *Anishinaabeg* means the First or Original People, or the Good Beings, in the dialects of the Algonquian language spoken by the Odawa, Ojibwe and Potawatomi. In the nineteenth century, Manitoulin residents referred to themselves as *Anishinaabeg* or *Otawag* and *Odjibweg* of *Odawa Minising*, while officials used the term Indians. The titles of agreement, indenture, treaty, surrender or cession were used to describe the Manitoulin documents in the nineteenth century. "First Nation" describes a band, and often replaces the nineteenth-century term "Reserve" when referring to *Anishinaabe* land. A council refers to an assembly of *Anishinaabeg* convened to discuss issues, and can involve one band or a grand council of many bands. The terms Père (Father) and Reverend designate Jesuit and Protestant missionaries respectively in this book. The North Shore is the local name for the northern mainland shore of Lake Huron.

The spelling of *Anishinaabeg* names in the historical documents on which this book is based is very irregular. The names were typically written as they sounded to non-Native ears. In addition, French- and English-speaking writers heard and transcribed the names differently: for example, the French-speaking Jesuits referred to Debassige whereas the English-speaking government officials referred to Taibosegai when writing about the grandson of Oga, the renowned warrior and chief. Both spellings reflect the sound of the name (Dai-BOSS-i-gai). To lessen confusion, I have used a standardized spelling for these names in the text (and in the index to names), except when quoting one of the source documents; in these cases I have retained the original author's spelling.

The *Anishinaabe* and Jesuit documents were written in Ojibwe or French. Their nineteenth-century translations have been quoted when available, in order to provide the same perspective the English-speaking public and officials had in the 1860s.

Introduction

For thousands of years, Manitoulin Island (*Mnidoo Minising* or *Odawa Minising*, the "Island of Manitou" or the "Island of the Odawa") has been the home of *Anishinaabeg*, the First or Original People.

This triangular-shaped 2,700-square-kilometre island with more than 80 inland lakes is the world's largest island in a freshwater lake. Manitoulin Island has fascinated non-Native visitors since the seventeenth century. Its isolated location in Lake Huron protected it from many of the conflicts that affected much of North America following the arrival of Europeans.

As Canada evolved from a land of Native peoples to Nouvelle France, to Quebec, Rupert's Land and Indian Land, to Britain's Province of Canada, its Native peoples evolved from independent organized nations to trading partners and war allies to isolated peoples who the government decided to assimilate. Concurrently, they became known collectively as Indians. Manitoulin's residents and others who spoke the dialects of the Ojibwe language continued to call themselves *Anishinaabe*.

The government persuaded Natives to transfer their land to the Crown through agreements or treaties. The Native people agreed to share—or, according to the government, to relinquish—their land for payment, usage rights and reserve land. Gradually, they ceded most of what forms present-day Canada. Their lands were surveyed, sold and settled by others.

In 1836, the *Anishinaabe* proprietors of Manitoulin signed an agreement with the government in which both parties agreed to withdraw their claims to the islands, making "them the Property (under your Great Father's Control) of all Indians who he shall allow to reside on them." Subsequently, many members of the Three Fire Confederacy—the Odawa, Ojibwe and Potawatomi peoples—moved to, or returned to, Manitoulin Island.

The *ogimaag* (chiefs) who signed the agreement in 1836 believed the government was acknowledging and affirming their title to Manitoulin and the adjacent islands; they were agreeing to share it, forever. The government was merely acquiring land on which to collect them, and accepted the agreement as one of several dozen major agreements, treaties or surrenders signed between the Crown and the Native peoples since Britain's assumption of control of North America.

Twenty-five years later, in 1861, Manitoulin Island's *Anishinaabeg* met new government representatives who claimed that the *Anishinaabeg* had not populated Manitoulin sufficiently, so a new treaty should take place. An offer to allow 25 acres for each *Anishinaabe* family, plus non-Native settlement on the balance of Manitoulin, was flatly rejected by the *ogimaag*.

The following year, in October 1862, senior government officials brought a revised offer to Manitoulin. Some of the *Anishinaabeg* succumbed to persuasion and signed a new agreement or treaty in which most of the island was surrendered. They subsequently claimed that they had been threatened and frightened into surrendering the land, and requested cancellation of the treaty. Their protests were disregarded; they were assigned to specific land reservations, and the unreserved land was surveyed, sold and resettled.

This book provides a first-hand look at the treaty of 1862 from the viewpoints of four people intimately associated with each of the main protagonists: the government, the *Anishinaabeg*, the Roman Catholic Church and the Anglican Church. Each individual played a key role in the story, and the perspective of each is presented, for the most part, in his own words: the Honorable William McDougall speaks for the government; Chief Sasso Itawashkash speaks for the *Anishinaabeg*; Père Jean-Pierre Choné speaks for the Roman Catholic Church; and the Reverend Peter Jacobs relays the Church of England's perspective. The stories of the protagonists and the treaty are followed by their post-treaty interactions.

William McDougall signed the treaty on behalf of the government, as superintendent general of Indian Affairs and commissioner of Crown Lands. Though his predecessor had initiated the treaty process, McDougall renewed the negotiations and finalized the treaty within months of his appointment as superintendent. McDougall was the ultimate envoy; he was persuasive and persistent, with a commanding presence and voice. After acquiring Manitoulin Island he participated in the Confederation of Canada and acquisition of the vast Hudson's Bay territory from Britain.

Ogimaa Sasso Itawashkash of Sheshegwaning was the eldest son of the renowned orator and war chief Jean-Baptiste Assiginack. Itawashkash signed the 1836 treaty and was the spokesperson for the *Anishinaabeg* at the 1861 and 1862 treaty negotiations. When rumours of land surrender reached Manitoulin Island, he and many island residents met in council and agreed to preserve Manitoulin for their children. But during the negotiations in October 1862, sometime between the Saturday evening adjournment and the Monday morning resumption, four chiefs were persuaded to surrender. Some witnesses alleged that Itawashkash was persuaded while under the influence of alcohol. On 7 October 1862 (dated 6 October on the document), he and seventeen others signed the "Deed of Cession." They later regretted signing, and attempted to cancel the treaty. After the cession, most of the *Anishinaabeg* living on the ceded lands were relocated from their waterfront settlements to inland lots.

Père Jean-Pierre Choné was a very experienced Jesuit priest who had worked with *Anishinaabeg* on Manitoulin Island and the north shores of Lake Huron and at Lake Superior since 1844. By 1862 he was one of four priests based at Wikwemikong. He was well known to the staff of the government's Indian Department for his advocacy on behalf of the *Anishinaabeg*. Choné attended the treaty council on Saturday, 4 October 1862, at the request of his superiors, who had been informed by the Indian Department of the negotiations. He returned to Wikwemikong Saturday evening in order to conduct the Sunday services, confident that a land surrender would once again be rejected by the people. Two days later, he was astonished to learn that a treaty had been concluded. He immediately criticized the treaty and encouraged the *Anishinaabeg* to object as well.

Reverend Peter Jacobs was the sole Church of England missionary stationed on Manitoulin. The son of a well-known *Anishinaabe*, he had been educated at a residential school. In 1862, 29-year-old Peter Jacobs was a naïve newlywed in fragile health who was eager to expand his mission. He had been convinced that isolation and protection of the *Anishinaabeg* had not been successful, so a surrender that would surround the *Anishinaabeg* with honest, hard-working settlers was necessary.

While the protagonists' stories are mostly in their own words, some conversational details have been invented in order to provide links between the quotations.

I have combed the archives for written records; I leave it to others to tell the story of the Manitoulin treaties through contemporary oral history.

I invite you to listen to these four voices, reflect and reach your own conclusion about the Great Manitoulin Island treaty of 1862.

x

Foreword

For the *Anishinaabeg, Odawa Minising*—Manitoulin Island—is a sacred place. In fact, Odawa Chief Assiginack declared that the Creator had placed the Odawa on the actual site of creation, *Odawa Minising*. Then, oddly, incomprehensibly, Chief Assiginack signed the 1862 treaty that ceded the western portion of the sacred island. Assiginack had actually wanted to sign a treaty a year earlier, when the terms of surrender were even worse! In this modern age, with the privilege of hindsight, we can judge (and condemn) those who signed the treaty—even if we do not fully understand their motives or the pressures to which they were subjected.

I believe that Shelley Pearen's book will shed light on what transpired, and help us understand these motives and pressures. I consider myself well read on Manitoulin history, and can confidently state that Shelley has compiled the most archival and published sources I have seen regarding the 1862 Manitoulin treaty.

I presume that the majority of people who write a foreword to a book are invited to do so. I actually asked to write this one a couple of years ago because of Shelley's generosity. In 2002, Lewis Debassige and I were quoted in a newspaper article about the *Anishinaabe* name for the island's "Cup and Saucer" limestone bluff. Shelley showed up a few days later, introduced herself and handed over a large manila envelope. "I read that you are researching Manitoulin history, so here you go," she said. In the envelope I saw many familiar documents, all in chronological order—she had handed me years of her research, just like that! I was dumbfounded. We immediately hit it off, and started swapping sources and documents. Anything I had she was welcome to, and vice versa.

Meanwhile, a whole new source of materials had become available to me with the translation and publication of letters written by the Jesuits who had been stationed at Manitoulin Island in the nineteenth century. Father William Lonc, S.J. had co-translated and published Lorenzo Cadieux's *Lettres des Nouvelles Missions du Canada* as *Letters from the New Canada Mission*. Another manuscript by Cadieux and Robert Toupin, "Les Robes Noires à l'Île du Manitou 1853-1870," was in French and therefore inaccessible to me. I had tried (unsuccessfully) to rope colleagues and friends into translating this manuscript into English so that I could continue my research. I gave a copy to Shelley, along with another collection of Jesuit letters called "Missionaliss Canadensis," and she applied her French translation skills to them. I then introduced her to Father Lonc, and together they started to crank out translations of Jesuit documents, in the words of another colleague, "faster than Harlequin romance novels."

Shelley combed the Archive of the Jesuits in Canada, Library and Archives Canada and the Archives of Ontario, diligently transcribing and translating handwritten letters, reports and petitions. As we compared finds, we discovered that some of the documents existed in all three languages, though not necessarily filed together, or translated well. Many had been written in Ojibwe, then translated into French, and then sometimes translated into English. I would frequently fire off a nineteenth-century French document I had found, and she would counter with an Ojibwe petition she had found for me to work on. Gradually, we both expanded our knowledge—and our pile of papers.

The story of the Great Manitoulin Island treaty is a microcosm of the story of Canada. The treaty process was, in Canada's eyes, honed here. Earlier "mistakes" or "anomalies," such as the 1836 Bond Head treaty and the 1850 Robinson treaties, were treated by the government as lessons learned as the treaty process moved westward with colonization. The colonization process sought not only to remove the property of *Anishinaabe*, but also to erase the traces of their occupation and land use by removing them from the most valuable lands (such as those deemed to be potential mill sites) and supplanting their place names.

Non-Native people commemorate others (usually men) with street names, state names and even city names. After the Manitoulin treaty was signed there was a proposal to have all the new townships on the island named after the signatory chiefs. This idea fell through—except for Chief Assiginack and his fellow deposed chief and signatory, Tehkummah, who had a township and a town named after him. It is fitting that these two chiefs, both deposed from Wikwemikong, would be commemorated by non-Native people by having a town and a township named after them.

The story of this treaty is compelling. The manner in which Shelley has decided to tell it, through "four voices," lends itself to a greater appreciation of the pressures each party faced. Adopting this "four voices" format allows the reader to better comprehend motivations and pressures, and sheds new light on the decisions made. This book brings to light a long concealed chapter in the history of Manitoulin Island—and Canada—that will fascinate and enlighten residents, visitors, schoolchildren and, hopefully, future generations.

Alan Ojiig Corbiere
Bne n-doodem, M'chigeeng ndoojibaa.

Alan Corbiere is an Ojibwe *Anishinaabe* from M'Chigeeng First Nation, Manitoulin Island, who has studied *Anishinaabe* language, history and culture for many years. He served as the Executive Director of the Ojibwe Cultural Foundation for four years.

Chapter 1
Great Manitoulin Island and the Honorable William McDougall

William McDougall
Thursday, 2 October 1862 was a grand autumn day in Toronto. It was grand not only in terms of the weather, but in terms of the future of a well-dressed man standing alone on the railway platform.

He stood out among his fellow travellers. His erect and commanding figure, clad in an impeccably cut suit, marked him as a man to be noticed. William McDougall (1822-1905) was on top of the world. The 40-year-old attorney-turned-journalist-turned-politician was the new commissioner of Crown Lands in John Sandfield Macdonald and Louis-Victor Sicotte's Reform government. McDougall had been elected as the Member of the Legislative Assembly for North Oxford four years earlier. Some criticized his ambition in joining the Reform government, but most admitted he was active and effective. Since entering political life he taken advantage of every opportunity to make himself heard by voters and colleagues. His clear and sonorous voice and skilful delivery of speeches meant that members of the press frequently quoted him verbatim. As a result, when he spoke, thousands heard his message.

McDougall was also forthright, and considered himself well versed in almost every topic that arose in parliament. He had little respect for members who served invisibly, including his predecessor, George Sherwood. He admired men like the previous commissioner, Philip Vankoughnet, who added the department of Indian Affairs to his portfolio in 1860 when Britain transferred the department to the Province of Canada. Vankoughnet was known to be a man of action. He promoted northwest expansion and railways while overseeing public lands, surveys, roads, fisheries, forests and mining.

Knowing what Vankoughnet had achieved, it was no wonder that McDougall felt optimistic. Within weeks of his appointment as commissioner, the pro-Reform party press was praising McDougall's actions. That very day, as McDougall was standing on the station platform, the *Huron Signal* quoted the *London News* that the "Honorable Mr. McDougall is indefatigable in performing the duties of his responsible office, and spares neither time nor pains to bring the business connected with his department to a speedy and satisfactory conclusion."[1]

McDougall was on the cusp of an important acquisition. He was travelling to the Great Manitoulin Island, where he intended to conclude a treaty with the Indians[2] and obtain the island for non-Native settlement. Though the previous government had failed in this task one year earlier, McDougall was confident his attempt would be successful. He based his confidence on that of his deputy superintendent, William Spragge, who assured him he knew not only why the first attempt had failed, but how to achieve success this time.

Spragge was already on board the train, no doubt reading his briefing notes for the negotiations or fine-tuning the surrender documents. McDougall had complete confidence in Spragge. Fortunately, Spragge likewise had complete confidence in McDougall. Both men were anxious to resolve the Manitoulin issue. A surrender and subsequent land sale would illustrate their capability.

William Prosperous Spragge, though deputy superintendent general of Indian Affairs for just six months, was a 33-year veteran of the Crown Lands Department. Well connected, he was a member of a prominent Upper Canadian family and married to Martha Ann Molson of the Montreal brewery family. Spragge was nevertheless determined to achieve success in the civil service on the basis of his intelligence and not his family connections: he was reputed to have rejected a lucrative brewery job, advancing instead from governmental clerk to superintendent of land sales to his current deputy superintendent position.[3]

Within days of his appointment, Spragge learned from Manitoulin's local superintendent that some Manitoulin Indians were favourable to ceding the island. Spragge acted immediately. He prepared a report about Manitoulin Island that explained the failure of the 1861 treaty negotiations and proposed a revised offer. Spragge presented his plan to his newly installed superior, William McDougall. The essence of the plan was to make a more liberal offer than had been made in 1861. This new offer reserved a larger portion of land for the Indians, as well as a share of the proceeds after the land was sold to non-Native settlers.

McDougall knew that voters wanted land. His former newspaper partner, Charles Lindsey, had launched a campaign to surrender Manitoulin Island in 1859, and had participated in the 1861 surrender attempt. McDougall embraced Spragge's Manitoulin proposal and presented it as a memorandum "relative to negotiations for surrender" of the Great Manitoulin Island to the government. The Legislative Council approved the plan on 12 September 1862.

And so Spragge and McDougall were together at the railway station early on that fine autumn day in October 1862. They were heading northwest by rail and then by steamboat to Manitoulin Island. They were so confident of success that they had invited a few friends and relatives and one special guest to witness and record their triumph.

McDougall knew how to manoeuvre the press. In fact, this was the reason he was standing on the platform. He was waiting for his carefully chosen guest, a special correspondent who he intended to witness, endorse and promote the project.

William McDougall's prized guest promptly arrived at the station. Clearly, he did not want to miss this opportunity to travel in style and in elevated company. Samuel Phillips Day was probably as excited about a free trip to Canada's hinterland as McDougall was anxious to have him.

Day was a 44-year-old British journalist writing about North America for England's *London Morning Herald*. His original mandate was to cover the

American Civil War, but his interest had expanded to embrace the entire continent. Day's affiliation with the *Morning Herald* had opened many doors for him in North America, and his articles had attracted a lot of attention. Some of his writing was very contentious: Day's reports from the southern United States were so pro-Confederate that Union camps refused to let him visit. By the time his controversial book *Down South* was published in 1862, he was safely ensconced in Canada. Day embraced the Manitoulin excursion as both a source of text for immediate release in newspaper columns, and as potential material for a book about Canada.

Day immediately set to work. "Our party," he wrote, "consisted of the Honourable William McDougall, Superintendent-General of Indian Affairs; the Honourable D. Reesor, M.L.A., Mr. Spragge, Deputy-Superintendent of the Indian Department, and one or two others who, like myself, had received invitations from the Commissioner to accompany him."[4]

Most of the small group of select travellers already knew each other. The Honourable David Reesor was William McDougall's brother-in-law. He was also a journalist, the publisher of *The Markham Economist* and a member of the Legislative Council of Upper Canada. Among "the others" were William's 22-year-old brother John Henry McDougall, from St. Marys, Canada West. John was one of William's numerous younger siblings. Another young relative, "Mr. Reesor Junior,"[5] was also introduced to Day.

Francis Assiginack, who was a clerk in the Indian Affairs Department and the son of a Manitoulin chief, accompanied the superintendents as their interpreter. Day later discovered that the placid young man would have been a more informative guide than his hosts. Assiginack, who considered himself "a warrior of the Odahwahs," was reputedly able to shoot a robin on the wing with a bow and arrow or hit a bull's eye with a rifle.

The party travelled in style. The Northern Railway had generously provided a special saloon carriage that had recently been built for vice-regal service. McDougall and his guests reclined on comfortable green-velvet sofas and easy chairs set on rich carpets and surrounded by elegant mirrors. An attached carriage provided the travellers with well-equipped dressing rooms.

The 95-mile trip from Toronto to Collingwood took less than six hours. Day made extensive notes on the towns, industries and geographical features, clearly intending to profit from this opportunity. The superintendents supplied facts and figures. They knew the power of the press, and wanted this correspondent to have all the facts they thought important, on the conviction that no one in possession of the facts could—or would—criticize the treaty they were about to conclude.

When the train reached Collingwood, the travellers boarded Captain Smith's steamboat *Clifton* for a side trip to Owen Sound. The new town plot of Brooke, formerly the Newash settlement, across the bay from Owen Sound was noted by the travellers. Just four years earlier, the site had been an Indian village that the government obtained by surrender and sold for the benefit of the tribe. The implication was that Manitoulin Island could prosper like Brooke, if it too was surrendered. After refreshments in a local hotel, the travellers boarded the steamboat *Ploughboy* to complete the final leg of their voyage. The *Ploughboy*, a two-decked paddle-wheeler, was equipped with staterooms for the overnight excursion to Manitowaning on Manitoulin Island.

Recommendations and Negotiations
Conversation resumed onboard the *Ploughboy*. The open water dispensed with the distractions of towns and industries and permitted the travellers to focus on the subject of Manitoulin Island. Day learned the island's history from McDougall and Spragge's point of view: "The Indians inhabiting this region, however, have claimed exclusive title to the entire island, by virtue of a treaty made with them in August, 1836, by Sir Francis Head, Governor of Upper Canada. Previous to that arrangement, Manitoulin was in the possession of a few Indians belonging to the Ottawa and Chippewa tribes." Day also learned their justification for a treaty: "The territory in the hands of the Indians, as a matter of course, remained uncultivated and useless. The interests of civilization, therefore, absolutely required that this obstacle should be removed, without in any way trespassing upon the rights of justice or humanity."[6]

Naturally, the issue of Manitoulin Island and the Indians had required William Spragge's attention upon his promotion to deputy superintendent of Indian Affairs. He had been interested in the country's Indians for six or seven years and had heartily approved of the transfer of Indian Affairs from Britain to Canada's Department of Crown Lands in 1860. This treaty would be the culmination of six months work on his part, though several others had laid the groundwork.

The department's man on Manitoulin, Captain George Ironside, had concluded or assisted in several important treaties on the mainland just north of Manitoulin, and was discussing additional treaties of these North Shore lands with several of Manitoulin chiefs.[7] Ironside, in fact, had been approaching chiefs and their bands about surrendering Manitoulin for almost two years. Spragge confided to Day that Ironside was a surrender advocate, but whether he believed treaties benefited Indians or viewed treaty negotiating as a means of land promotion was unknown. Spragge did not know or care his reasons. He seized the opportunity to illustrate what could be achieved with the Indian people by reciting Ironside's biography.

George Ironside was the son of George Ironside, Sr. and Vocemassussia, or Isabella, the reputed sister of famed Shawnee leaders Tecumseh and The Prophet. George, Jr. was raised at Amherstburg, the location of a military fort, naval yard and Indian Department headquarters at the mouth of the Detroit River on Lake Erie. George, Sr. was the chief clerk to Indian Department superintendent Matthew Elliott at the time of the War of 1812. Elliott's American Revolutionary War connections and Ironside's Shawnee relations were crucial to British success in the area. George Ironside, Sr. replaced Elliott as superintendent at Amherstburg after the war. George, Jr. took over as clerk and later replaced his father as superintendent. In 1845, George Ironside, Jr. succeeded Thomas Anderson on Manitoulin Island as the local superintendent of Indian Affairs.

Ironside's involvement in surrenders was ironic, considering his lineage. Fifty years earlier, his maternal relatives, Tecumseh and The Prophet, the former a brilliant war chief and the latter a powerful preacher, united to resist land surrenders and to create an Indian territory. The Prophet urged all Indians to retain their lands, which he insisted were held in common and could not be divided, sold or traded. Tecumseh mobilized warriors for the British side in order to regain Native lands in the United States. The two leaders were responsible for winning several battles. George must have witnessed the respect they received from both Indians and soldiers—though they never regained their lands or obtained an Indian territory. George Ironside, Jr. chose to follow his father's path as an agent for the Indian Department rather than his uncles' quest for independence.

McDougall interrupted his commentary, briefly, and then noted that most people knew him as *Captain* Ironside, referring to his leadership of three or four dozen Indians at the time of the 1837 rebellion, though his position simply granted him the title of "superintendent."

He then noted that, unfortunately for Ironside, by the time he arrived on Manitoulin Island in 1845, the government was reducing its investment in the settlement efforts it had begun at Manitowaning in 1836. Over the next decade, Manitowaning declined in population and prosperity. By the mid-1850s Ironside was discouraged.[8]

Nevertheless, Ironside worked hard on behalf of the Indian Department. He had done such a thorough job of promoting surrender that the Indians refused to participate in the 1861 provincial census, as they believed it was actually a treaty. Though every resident of the province was to be enumerated at his or her place of residence on the night of Sunday, 13 January 1861, it took Ironside more than six months to compile a very incomplete census. He complained that the "Indians have been made to believe, most implicitly, that there is a design on the part of the Government to deprive them of their Island—that I am working secretly for that end, and that the present Census taking is merely a prelude to the act."[9]

It was noted that their non-compliance was a mistake, since Manitoulin's population was actually rising and had increased by about ten percent between 1857 and 1861, from 1,287 to 1,443—though more than half the residents were less than 21 years of age.[10] In fact, Spragge explained, their population growth served to increase the quantity of land to which they would be entitled under his plan. He noted that most of the residents lived in one of the dozen settlements on the island's shores. Wikwemikong was by far the largest village, with a population of 650, but most of the other settlements had only 50 to 100 residents each.[11]

Day had followed the census controversy in the newspapers. In the twenty years since Upper and Lower Canada had united under a single parliament, Upper Canada's population had increased dramatically and its residents were demanding "representation by population" in parliament. The growth fuelled the perception that there was a lack of available affordable land.

McDougall paused and asked Day if he had any questions about the proceedings so far. Day indicated that he did not, without raising his eyes or pen from his notebook. Despite the generous supply of documents, Day preferred to take notes. McDougall continued his monologue.

While Ironside was working on the census, the Indians were reacting to rumours of a land surrender. He had reported that "the Indians having been informed that the Island was to be surveyed immediately and that, most likely, they would lose it, a Paper was in consequence, drawn up to be signed by all the Head men binding themselves to object to a sale, should a proposition for a purchase of the Island be made."[12] Ironside also reported that two Wikwemikong chiefs, Tehkummah and Mocotaishegun, had refused to sign the document and "had been deposed most unjustly by their brethren" due to their refusal and their participation in the delegation that met the Prince of Wales" when he visited in 1860. Ironside commented that aged and infirm Chief Cainooshimague had signed the paper only after "being threatened with the loss of office and other indignities."[13]

Ironside blamed the island's Jesuit priests for inciting the Indians. He reported that Father Choné, one of the leaders of the island's Jesuits, had criticized the government's wood harvesting regulations and accused Ironside of being "the cause of [Manitoulin Island's Indian] Brethren at the Sault St. Mary, and other places above, parting with Lands and rendering them landless and poor."[14]

Indian Department officials had responded sympathetically to Ironside, but did not recommend any action. The department was in transition. Richard Pennefather, the former superintendent general of Indian affairs, departed in March 1861, and Charles Walcot was left to manage the department under the direction of the commissioner of Crown Lands Philip Vankoughnet. Ironside was informed that "the Superintendent General of Indian Affairs entirely disapproves of the proceedings of the Indians towards their two chiefs [Tehkummah and Mocotaishegun], and he trusts that such conduct will not again be brought to his notice."[15] Neither Ironside nor his superiors denied the surrender rumours; apparently, their only concern was with the removal of the chiefs.

Ironside's actions prompted Manitoulin's residents to act in May 1861. They wrote two letters to the governor in which they recalled past promises and complained about their superintendent's actions. Ironside refuted their complaints and justified his conduct. He claimed that "during the last winter and spring reports having been circulated by designing persons, the Indians of Wequamikong were at last made to believe that, if not the whole, a part of the Manitoulin Island was to be taken from them by the Government and that they were then to be put on the same footing as the whites as regards Taxation."[16]

McDougall revealed that one of the Indian chiefs had also accused the priests of interference. Chief Tehkummah had complained that, in the summer of 1861,

> Father Choné told the Indians that the whiteman had already deprived their brethren above this, of their lands, and that they, the Indians, had become very poor in consequence—that the Government wished to treat them in the same manner with regard to this Island and men were even then working in an underhanded way to accomplish their object—that it was now necessary for them to be very watchful

else they too would be robbed of their land. After hearing this from the Priest the Weqwimekong Indians, made it a rule that thereafter no Chief, whether sent for or otherwise, should be allowed to go near the Superintendent without being accompanied by six Indians to hear all the conversations which might pass between them, and that the Chiefs should not be suffered to be out of their sight or hearing for a moment.[17]

Ironside had continued to encourage the Indians to surrender, approaching them quietly and individually. At the same time, in July 1861 he reminded them who was in charge when he forbade the Indians of Wikwemikong to sell wood to the steamboats from their own wharf. He insisted that all wood sales must go through him, with a tax paid to the government.

Parliament had been dissolved in June 1861. The government was re-elected in July and Philip Vankoughnet was reinstated as commissioner of Crown Lands and superintendent general of Indian Affairs. The election, census results, political representation by population, a union of all the British North American provinces, petroleum discoveries and the American Civil War dominated the news.

Philip Vankoughnet had been interested in Manitoulin since 1859, though he waited until Richard Pennefather, the former superintendent general of Indian Affairs, retired before taking action.[18] Manitoulin had come to the attention of the general public in September 1859 when *The Leader* newspaper in Toronto published the travel log of some "pleasure seekers." The "log" was essentially a trip to Manitoulin by an unnamed writer whose premise ("how many thousand people could thrive in the yet unimproved but promising and fertile wildernesses which may be found west of our present settlements and east of the Sault St. Marie") was quickly followed by statements suggesting that Manitoulin was underutilized and under populated. The three-day, six-column "log" was followed by a campaign led by *The Leader*'s editor (Charles Lindsey) to open the island to non-Native settlement. Even *The New York Times* picked up the story.

On 29 August 1861, Vankoughnet submitted a memorandum to the government in which he recommended assigning the Manitoulin Indians to 25-acre lots and selling the remainder of the land to non-Native settlers:

> The Commissioner of Crown Lands has the honor to report that the Island known as the Great Manitoulin Island was formerly claimed by the Crown, and the Ottawa and Chippewa band of Indians respectively.
>
> That on the 9th of August, 1836, an arrangement was made between His Excellency Sir F.B. Head and the then Chief of the Indians to the following effect:–
>
> The Crown "will withdraw its claim to these Islands (the Manitoulin Island and Islands on the North Shore of Lake Huron,) and allow them to be applied for the purpose of a place or residence for the Indians," the Ottawas and Chippewas agreeing to "relinquish their respective claims to these Islands and make them the property (under the control of the Crown) of all Indians" who shall be allowed by Government to reside on them.
>
> That the scheme has proved a failure, and the number of Indians now residing on the Island is in all about 1250; that the Island embraces about an area of 650,000 acres, and as far as he can learn is well adapted for settlement, and that very little has been done in the way of cultivating the soil by the few Indians who at present

reside thereon; very little more than six acres being cultivated by any one family. That it seems to him that the spirit of the agreement between Sir F.B. Head and the Indians will be observed by securing to the Indians on the Island a limited quantity of land for their houses, or disposable as their own property, taking care to provide such portions as will furnish them with firewood.

He has the honor therefore to recommend, 1st. That the Manitoulin Island be laid out in townships, and such portions of it as may be found fit for settlement be surveyed into farm lots, with suitable reserves for Town Plots, &c., and with the view that the same with the circumjacent Islands be erected into a County.

2nd. That each Indian family be allowed to the extent of about 25 acres of land, to be laid out in the vicinity of, or as convenient as possible to their present holdings, and in such a manner as to secure them a supply of firewood; or, if this latter object cannot thus be effected, then, that a sufficient quantity of wooded land be also reserved for their use.

3rd. That a suitable person be selected to visit the Island and explain to the Indians the intentions of the Government as above indicated.[19]

The governor general approved in council the memorandum's plan on 10 September. Vankoughnet assumed the treaty could be accomplished expeditiously. He sent an experienced treaty negotiator and a journalist, as commissioners, to achieve the surrender and a surveyor to examine the land.

William Bartlett, the Toronto-based superintendent of Indian Affairs for the Central Superintendency, who was about to deliver the annual annuity payments to Manitoulin, was told to collaborate with Ironside to present Vankoughnet's plan to the residents. Bartlett was a long-time government employee who had just concluded a treaty with the Colpoy's Bay Indians. Both Bartlett and Ironside had previously persuaded Indians who had earlier been settled on reserved land created by treaties to cede additional land.[20]

Bartlett was to be accompanied by journalist Charles Lindsey and surveyor William Hawkins. Lindsey's participation was a political decision. He was the editor of *The Leader*, the Toronto newspaper that brought Manitoulin Island's status as an underutilized refuge to the public's attention in the fall of 1859. Lindsey, as mentioned previously, was also a former business partner of William McDougall, but the two men at this time were political opponents. Bartlett was instructed to

proceed to Manitowaning, Manitoulin Island, with the view of making known to the Indians through Captain Ironside the Superintendent of Indian Affairs, the wishes of the Government as specified in the accompanying Order in Council.

It is the desire of the Government to deal liberally with the Indians, and to allow them Twenty-five acres of land to each family in the immediate neighbourhood of the village or settlement, and you will endeavour to explain that altho the Island was set apart in 1836 as a place of abode for Indians generally yet that so few have since then availed themselves of the privilege that it is absurd to keep it longer a wilderness.[21]

Bartlett was told to act quickly, provide additional forest land for firewood if necessary and "ascertain who and where are now the Chiefs of the Tribes of Indians who made the arrangement with Sir Francis Head." He was provided with a copy of the 1836 treaty "for your own special guidance." It was hoped "that the grant to each Head of a family of 25 acres as his own property will more than compensate them for any imaginary interest they may have in the island."[22]

The news of a potential surrender of Manitoulin Island broke in a few newspapers in early October. "The Manitoulin Islands are, it is said, about to be purchased from the Indians," the *Perth Courier* reported. "They are large and fertile islands, and the land will be readily sold to settlers."[23]

William Bartlett, Charles Lindsey and William Hawkins travelled to Manitoulin in October 1861 to convene a council of island residents. As the parties gathered, the commissioners learned that the Indians "were indisposed to listen to terms for the surrender of the island." Moreover, "for two years past they have been expecting that some proposition would be made to them for this purpose, and during the last winter councils were held to determine the question in advance," and the young men had tried to persuade the chiefs "to refuse to listen to any terms for a surrender of any portion of the island." Though the objective of the commissioner's council had not yet been announced, "the Indians had become possessed of the idea, that it related to the settlement of the Island by the white population, and they had resolved almost unanimously to oppose any proposal to that effect."[24]

About 130 Indians, including four of the fifteen signatories to the 1836 treaty, assembled in Manitowaning on Saturday, 5 October 1861.[25] Reverend Peter Jacobs, Manitowaning's Anglican missionary, translated the commissioner's speeches from a written copy provided for the purpose. Charles de Lamorandière,[26] a trader from nearby Killarney, translated the replies of the Indians for the commissioners. Captain Ironside, Dr. David Layton and surveyor William Hawkins were also present. William Bartlett opened the council with a speech, and then entertained responses from several chiefs.

Spragge, who was more familiar with the expedition's details, interrupted McDougall to continue the account. Spragge explained that Bartlett's entire approach had been wrong. He said the government's negotiators had immediately raised the ire of the Indians when Bartlett declared that, since the 9,300 Indians under the governor's protection at that time had not settled on the island as expected, the government's intention of settling the island with Indians had not been carried out. Bartlett then said the quantity of land deemed sufficient in 1836 for nearly 10,000 people was too great to be cultivated by the limited number who actually settled upon it. As a result, he offered a title or deed for 25 acres to every family and to young men of 18 when they reached the age of 21. The remainder of the land would be sold to non-Native settlers, who would provide markets and supplies. Bartlett concluded by announcing that the surveyor was going to explore the island so that the wishes of the government could be carried out with as little delay as possible.[27]

The spokesperson for the Indians firmly rejected Bartlett's proposal. The Indians maintained that the land had been given to them by the Great Spirit, and they intended to retain it for their children. Spragge noted that the only chief in favour of a surrender was the spokesperson's elderly father, who was a renowned war chief and former interpreter for the Indian Department. The Indians refused to permit a survey, though the meeting concluded amicably. All the chiefs and Indians came forward and shook the commissioners' hands in a friendly manner.

Bartlett, Lindsey and Hawkins left Manitoulin Island without obtaining a surrender or a survey. They reported to Vankoughnet that the Indians were "possessed of the idea that their title to the island is perfect and was not impaired by the conditional surrender they made to Sir Francis Bond Head in 1836." The commissioners concluded:

> The Indians were not in a mood to have listened to any terms when we visited them, there is no reason to fear that they will long continue to hold out if more favorable conditions be offered to them. This is the opinion of Captain Ironsides, and it coincides with the impression derived from all we heard and learned on the subject. It is nothing new to fail with the Indians in a first attempt. From what has been done the Indians have become convinced that it is the intention of the Government to settle the island, and it will hereafter be with them a question of receiving the most favorable terms they can obtain.[28]

Charles Lindsey investigated the island's history and proposed a revised surrender to Vankoughnet in which he recommended allowing 150 acres per family of four, with 50 or 25 acres for additional children, as well as giving the Indians a portion of the proceeds of land sales. He informed Ironside that the "propositions have not been formally accepted but Mr. Vankoughnet is willing that they should be talked about on the Island."[29]

Ironside, undaunted by the rejection of the initial surrender offer, called a council of Chief Okemah beness' Whitefish River band and on 22 October 1861 obtained another surrender of their land. This document replaced an 1859 surrender that had been rejected by his superiors for technical errors.[30] The chief and many of his band members were living at Manitowaning, though several of them still returned to their traditional land on the North Shore to fish, hunt and farm.

Surrender negotiations were suspended for the winter. Vankoughnet headed to Britain to discuss railways. Manitoulin was isolated by ice and snow. The American Civil War distracted Canadians.[31]

Viscount Charles Stanley Monck replaced Sir Edmund Walker Head as governor general in November 1861. Head had occupied that office since 1854, and was very familiar with the Indian Department: his former secretary was Richard Pennefather, later the civil secretary and head of the Indian Department, a position directly responsible to the governor general. Monck was a skilled diplomat but unfamiliar with Indian Affairs, so was dependent on the Department of Crown Lands for advice.

The Department of Crown Lands announced increased restrictions on timber sales in November 1861. This was immediately viewed on Manitoulin Island as punishment for the land surrender refusal. The declaration that "authority" from the department was required to cut or buy timber on Indians Reserves— otherwise penalties, including loss of timber, fines or imprisonment, could be imposed—was objectionable to most Manitoulin residents. All local superintendents, including Ironside, were directed to convene councils of the tribes under their jurisdictions to obtain permission to grant licences for cutting timber on their reserves and to explain that the interest on the proceeds of the timber sales would be distributed among the Indians.[32]

Ironside convened a council, but whether he requested permission to grant licences or simply announced the regulations is unclear. He reported that the Wikwemikong residents continued to sell wood from their wharf, despite his warning in July that they could not sell wood directly to steamboats. In January 1862 the department issued a clarification. If timber was obtained from clearing land for crops, superintendents could give written permission to sell the wood, but they should collect and hold the proceeds until they saw that the land was actually cultivated.[33]

The new timber regulations prompted the Indians on Manitoulin Island to hold another council, on 24 February 1862. Ironside reported that they had decided to

> prevent any Surveyors coming to the island in the spring from carrying on their operations and that they were determined to follow out the advice given them by their Priest Rev Chonii last fall namely to take possession of the Surveyors Chains & move them aside and if resistance was made and the Surveyors in defence presented fire arms and one Indian should be injured they even state to continue removing the chains & resist, if two Indians should be killed they were then to kill all the Surveyors and party after which all those Chiefs who had been favorable to give up the island to the Government were to be treated in like manner.[34]

Ironside requested guidance and continued to confiscate the wood of those who he felt did not comply with the regulations. The Indians protested.

In spring 1862, the commissioner of Crown Lands was twice replaced and the branch of Crown Lands that dealt with Indian Affairs was reconstructed. George Sherwood succeeded Philip Vankoughnet as commissioner in March 1862. Vankoughnet's resignation had been rumoured for more than a year, so the only surprise was that Sherwood, a man known for his lack of action, would replace Vankoughnet, a man known for his relentless action.[35] Sherwood, who had served almost invisibly as receiver general, maintained his predecessor's plans for the department. Concurrently, Spragge's position as the permanent head, or deputy superintendent general, of Indian Affairs was created.

Within days of his appointment, Spragge learned from Ironside that some Manitoulin Indians felt amiable to ceding their land:

> Three of the oldest & most respectable of the Chiefs of the Island who, in a private conversation I had with them, intimated to me their willingness that the Government should have its own way as to the disposal of the Island—that they felt sure its settlement by the whites would be of much service to the Indians provided some more land were allowed them than what had been mentioned. That they were afraid to express their opinions openly in the matter as it would expose them to persecution or perhaps to something worse.
>
> I have spoken to other Indians in reference to the same thing & their replies were almost invariably to the same effect. A few again have said they would assist &

protect the Surveyors if necessary. I think, however, they could not be depended upon if any ~~the least~~ resistance were offered. Knowing pretty well the state of matters here I believe that were a force of some kind to accompany the Surveyors to the Island to show thereby that the Government is in earnest, there would be little or no difficulty in carrying out the views of the Authorities. Delay on the other hand would be prejudicial.

I may mention, too, that an old Chief whose word can be relied on told me he was present on one occasion at a meeting of the Indians of Weqwemikong where he heard the Revd. Pere Chone tell the people that they must stop the survey of the Island.

The Indians of Manitowaning and the Little Current are altogether favourable to the survey & settlement of the Manatoulin.[36]

At the same time, Judge John Prince of Sault Ste. Marie reported that a large meeting had taken place in Wikwemikong to denounce the reported government scheme to force the Indians to surrender their interests in the island and to resist any interruption in their cutting down and selling of timber and firewood.[37]

The George-Étienne Cartier–John A. Macdonald government was defeated on a militia bill in May 1862. The Reform party's John Sandfield Macdonald and Louis-Victor Sicotte were sworn in as co-premiers. William McDougall was appointed commissioner of Crown Lands and superintendent general of Indian Affairs. Spragge brought the Manitoulin land surrender issue to McDougall's attention on 27 June 1862, in his "Report Regarding Manitoulin Island."

To give journalist Samuel Day a better idea of his capability, Spragge quoted from his report: "It being manifest that it is a matter of great importance to acquire for general settlement the Manitoulin Islands in Lake Huron with the exception of such limited portions as the Indians residing thereon are desirous to retain," and "an unavailing endeavour having been made by Messrs Bartlett and Lindsay in the autumn of the year 1861," "it appears advisable to recommend the conditions upon which overtures to the Indians might be renewed with a reasonable hope of success."

Spragge suggested that the 1861 negotiators were unsuccessful because no compensation had been offered to the Indians, and the premise that the 1836 treaty had created a title to the Crown was incorrect. He then recommended that future negotiations replicate the arrangements already made with other tribes, whereby any land not required or desired by the Indians was surveyed at their expense and sold for their benefit, or acquired by the provincial government for a guaranteed annuity.

He explained: "If the land were to be sold for the benefit of the Indians they would doubtless be prepared to yield up a large quantity of land and of a more saleable description, aware as they would be that the periodical payments arising from interest on moneys realized would be beneficially affected thereby. But if the inducement to yield up the lands be an annuity, they with the acuteness they possess would in all probability stand out for reservations for their future use which would comprise as much of the most valuable land as under the most extreme circumstances they possibly could require."

Spragge noted that Manitoulin had 1,290 residents in eleven settlements on only 2,100 of the island's 750,000 acres of land. He had reported that "It would be important to induce a concentration of these various bands, in a very limited number of localities. Both with a view to their further social, moral, and intellectual, as well as Religious improvement—and that they may to as small an extent as possible stand in the way of the lands being turned to the best possible account for settlement."

He recommended offering 200 acres to families with sons, and 100 acres to families without sons, all in 600-acre blocks in four different locations, while implementing the system used for many bands in which department-approved chiefs received salaries from the band's funds.[38]

Then he confided that the same day he tabled his report, 27 June, one of the Manitoulin chiefs had written to the governor general reminding him of past pledges and insisting the island had not been and would never be given up.

McDougall supported Spragge's plan, and upon receipt of some details launched the process for acquiring the island.[39] Spragge notified Ironside of the government's intention to reopen negotiations:

> The Government feeling the importance of such portions of Great Manitoulin Island are not actually required for the use of the Indians being turned to a beneficial account and propose in the course of the present Season to reopen negotiations on the subject. And it is anticipated that the propositions which will be offered will be of that liberal character that the Indians will have no hesitation about cheerfully accepting them. And in order to prepare their minds to appreciate justly the advantages which must to a certainty result from a termination being put to the present unproductive condition of so large a portion of the Island it is desirable that you should have it in your power to intimate to the Indians that reservations for their use of a very sufficient extent will be permitted.
>
> And that they will find when the propositions are brought forward that among other benefits proposed will be one under which they would receive through the Government periodical payments of money in the same manner as other Tribes and Bands of Indians, with which to increase their comfort and promote their welfare. You please to communicate to me freely your views and impressions upon this important subject. And also name the individuals and means through which in your judgement the objects in view may be most successfully promoted.
>
> The Gentleman who on this occasion will act for the Government will probably proceed to Lake Huron at the same time as the annual payments are made to the Indians of Lakes Huron & Superior.[40]

Ironside responded with a cautious but optimistic reply on 14 August 1862. Evidently, he was hesitant to approach the Indians in council. He preferred to speak to them individually. He maintained that the majority was in favour of a treaty, but afraid to speak publicly. Ironside had been in contact with Charles Lindsey, who had outlined a more generous offer that Ironside had subsequently described to the Indians.

> I have been obliged to have recourse to addressing myself to the Indians individually on the subject, as opportunities presented themselves to me. And that in the majority of cases, they expressed their willingness to accept the offer, adding however, "I would be afraid to say openly what I have now told you, because it would expose me to persecution from certain parties in the Island."

> I may now mention in response to this matter that when first the report of the intentions of the Government to settle a portion of the Manitoulin with whites, reached the Island, a certain party here represented to the Indians that unless they were very careful they would lose their property. Consequently a Paper was drawn up and to which nearly all the Indians of the Island were induced to subscribe their names, to the effect that they, by mutual agreement, were determined, on no account whatever to part with any portion of their lands. Moreover threats were held out to all who might hereafter in any way hinder this arrangement. Hence the cause of the fear before alluded to.
>
> Under the circumstances, then, the plan I have adopted to intimate to the people of the Island the intention of the Government is the best. If had I assembled them in Council in the present state of matters it would have only done injury to the cause.
>
> Were it not for the interference of the Half breeds on the Island and its neighbourhood backed by other influences in operation here the Indians, I am sure, would be more manageable and open to persuasion.

Ironside recommended that Lindsey return with more generous terms. He also advised that the "Indians require to be convinced that the Government means well towards them by making such a liberal offer, and that if rejected their *compliance will be enforced.*"[41]

Spragge responded immediately. He observed that Ironside had misunderstood the instructions. He was supposed to list "the principal men among the Indians—persons whom it would be important to induce to second the influence they would be capable of exercising over their people," not to suggest a person to carry out the mission. He instructed Ironside to meet and conciliate the individuals and to transmit suggestions for conducting successful negotiations, immediately.[42]

Two days later, Spragge responded again:

> In replying rather hurriedly on Saturday to your letter of the 14th Inst. I overlooked an idea thrown out by you upon which it would be unwise in me to withhold a remark.
>
> It is to this effect. "The Indians require to be convinced" that should the Government make a liberal offer (one to which you allude as suggested by Mr. Charles Lindsey) "if rejected their compliance will be enforced."
>
> Neither the Imperial nor the Colonial Government have at any time employed intimidation by threatening coercion under any form when endeavouring to induce the Indians to make cessions of land for sale and settlement.
>
> And I consider it to be my duty to point out to you the extreme imprudence & impropriety of intimating to any of the Indians the possibility that recourse could be had to coercion. It would be wrong in principle, it would be impolitic and the validity of any instrument obtained from them under such circumstances would be indubitably very questionable.
>
> You will have the goodness therefore in your intercourse with the people to refrain from expressing yourself in terms that would carry with them the idea that the Government would attempt to enforce upon them any terms for a cession of their interest in the Manitoulin Islands.[43]

Day finally interrupted the monologue. He asked if the superintendents were apprehensive about the recent Indian Revolt on the Minnesota River. The

Dakota, who surrendered most of their Minnesota territory to the government of the United States in 1851, had attacked settlers in August 1862 after delayed annuity payments caused starvation among their people. Spragge paused, smiled, and replied that Day sounded like his wife. Then he declared that a revolt would never occur here.

McDougall resumed the story. He had had a particularly busy summer, he said. Just seven weeks earlier, the department had announced new timber regulations. Notices explained that "cutting timber or staves or wood for any purpose upon Indian lands, except by licence," had "been rendered unlawful," and warned that, as of 7 August 1862, "Indians or others, offending against the said statues will be prosecuted with vigor."[44] This was a much harsher stance than the previous timber enforcement, specifically warning that even the Indians would be prosecuted. Once again, the Indians of Wikwemikong, Michigiwatinong and Sheshegwaning protested. Ironside confiscated the wood of those he felt were not complying with the regulations. McDougall recalled that the residents of Manitoulin wrote several petitions to the governor in the summer of 1862, but noted their complaints would be resolved by a surrender.

Based on Ironside's information, Spragge had written an "Additional Report relative to opening the Manitoulin Islands for Settlement," indicating "that the reluctance of those people to a surrender and survey of the lands thereon for settlement has diminished to such a degree that were a liberal proposition made to them in Council assembled by the Government they would accede to it." He recommended reopening negotiations as soon as possible. He suggested that the treaty negotiations required a payment that would be repaid by the sale of land, as well as a feast, provisions, a supply of pipes and tobacco.[45]

McDougall and Spragge, determined to obtain a surrender of Manitoulin, decided that, as the highest-ranking persons in the Indian Department, they would make "a more liberal proposition" to the Indians. A memorandum from William McDougall, chief superintendent of Indian Affairs, "relative to negotiations for surrender" of the Great Manitoulin, was approved in the Legislative Council on 12 September 1862.

McDougall offered to read the memorandum aloud, in order that Day might be completely up to date on the expedition:

The Great Manitoulin Island in Lake Huron contains about 3/4 of a million acres, half of which at least is believed to be of good quality and fit for settlement.

As nearly all the cultivatable land of the Peninsula along the Eastern Shore of Lake Huron has now been taken up by settlers there can be no doubt that if this Island were resumed by the Crown and the good land surveyed and offered for sale on favorable terms it would soon be occupied by an enterprising and industrious population. Its only inhabitants at present are Indians and half breeds (including two or three Missionaries and Officials) who obtain a precarious subsistence from the cultivation of a few patches of soil and from the fish which they take in the neighbourhood.

Their number is about 1290 and they cultivate about 2000 acres. These Indians claim title to the whole Island by virtue of a Treaty or Contract made with them 9th of August 1836 by the then Governor of this Province Sir Francis Bond Head. It appears that previous to that arrangement this Island was in the possession of a few

Indians of the Ottawa and Chippewas Tribes, while portions of the Peninsula and Country Eastwardly of Georgian Bay were occupied by scattered Bands of these and other Tribes. Sir Francis Head obtained a surrender to the Crown of the Indian Title to the Island with a view to its being held for the use and benefit of all these scattered Bands (as well as the Indians then upon the Island) who it was agreed should remove from the Mainland. Twenty-six years have since elapsed and but few of the Indians occupying the Peninsula or Main-land have repaired to the Manitoulin. The agreement so far has not been effectuated. On the 24th Sept 1861 WR Bartlett Esquire Visiting Superintendent & Commissioner Indian Office and Charles Lindsey Esq're of Toronto were instructed by the then Commissioner of Crown Lands Mr. P.M. Van Koughnet to proceed to Manitowaning and make known to the Indians the wishes of the Government with respect to the Island, they were authorized to offer 25 acres of land to each family of Indians with a sufficient quantity of waste land for firewood, and this it was hoped, would more than compensate them for any imaginary interest they may have in the Island. A surveyor accompanied the above named gentlemen to make a preliminary exploration of the Island with a view to subdivision into lots. From the Report of Messrs Bartlett & Lindsey Oct. 12th 1861, it appears that their mission was unsuccessful. In the language of their Report "when the statements in which the wishes of the Government were expressed had been read and interpreted the Indians without a word of consultation among themselves at once declared their refusal to acquiesce in the conditions proposed."

The Indians they assert are possessed of the idea that their title to the Island is perfect and was not impaired by the conditions of surrender they made to Sir F B Head in 1836. But although the Indians would not even discuss the proposition of Messrs Bartlett & Lindsey and threatened violence to the Surveyor if he attempted to enter upon his duties these Gentlemen express the opinion that the same difficulty would not in future be experienced if a more liberal proposition were made.

Very shortly after the undersigned entered upon the duties of his office this subject engaged his attention. The great importance of reclaiming and opening for settlement without longer delay so valuable a tract of land (in the direct line of communication between the Great Cities and marts of the Province, and the mineral regions of Lakes Huron & Superior, and the yet undeveloped but fertile territory of the North West) could not be denied. The undersigned accordingly instructed the Deputy Superintendent of Indian Affairs to communicate with Captain Ironside the Government Agent & Visiting Superintendent and Commissioner residing on the Island with the view of ascertaining the present disposition of the Indians in regard to this matter. The reply is favorable to a reopening of the negotiation. The undersigned has also conversed with Mr. Bartlett, and Mr. Assickenack (a son of the old War Chief of Manitoulin a very intelligent young man now a clerk in the Office of Mr. Bartlett at Toronto) both of whom express the opinion that if a larger portion of land were reserved for the Indians and their right to a share at least of the proceeds of the land to be sold acknowledged, a surrender of their right or pretended right might be obtained. It appears that the Indians distrust or at all events do not much respect the authority of Subordinates and specially appointed agents of the Government the undersigned therefore is of opinion that the Chief Superintendent of Indian Aff's in this Province ought in person to reopen the negotiation. The following measures ought in the opinion of the undersigned to be taken and the following terms be proposed. 1st A sufficient quantity of provisions, pipes, tobacco &c to supply the wants of the Indians who may assemble to meet the Chief Superintendent in Council ought to be provided. 2nd A sufficient sum of money to advance say one dollar per head as a payment on account of the proposed surrender ought also to be provided a sum of $1500 (£350) will suffice for both objects and can be taken in the meantime from the Indian Management Fund. 3rd The right of the Indians to a beneficial interest in the whole Island should be at once frankly admitted and the negotiations proceed on that basis. 4th One hundred acres at least should be reserved for each head of a family and 50 acres if desired in respect of each child. 5th That portion of the Island surrendered should be surveyed and sold on terms of actual settlement at such price per acre as may be fixed by the Government and the proceeds after deducting the expenses of survey and the cost of constructing such leading roads as may be deemed necessary should constitute a fund the interest of which should be payable to the Indians as in other cases.[46]

Spragge admitted he had been so confident their plan would be approved that he wrote to Ironside on 11 September, the day before official sanction, to inform him that he and the chief superintendent of Indian Affairs would meet the Indians of Manitoulin Island in council at Manitowaning in two or three weeks to reopen negotiations for the surrender, survey and settlement of portions of the island not required for the use of the Indians. He instructed Ironside to notify the residents to be ready "to assemble when called upon to do so."[47]

A press release was prepared at this time. *The Quebec Mercury* reported "The Commissioner of Crown Lands will leave Toronto tomorrow, on his trip to Manitoulin Island. He will meet the Indians on Friday, to negotiate for the surrender of their title to the occupancy of the island."[48] In an article entitled "Opening Up New Settlements, Manitoulin Island," the London (England) newspaper *Canadian News, New Brunswick Herald, and British Columbian Intelligencer* reported:

> The acquisition of the Manitoulin Island, in Lake Huron, for the purposes of settlement has been considered desirable by successive administrations. Containing not less than three-quarters of a million of acres, half of which, at least, is believed to be of good quality and adapted to cultivation, the island really presents the most eligible field for settlement now available in the vicinity of the older portions of the western peninsula .... The Great Manitoulin will offer inducements to settlers that may nowhere be obtained on the mainland of Upper Canada.[49]

Day acknowledged that the acquisition of almost three-quarters of a million acres of land was an incredible achievement, and perhaps some of his countrymen would be inspired to emigrate.

McDougall suggested they retire for the night. He reminded Day that he could ask questions in the morning after he read the papers that awaited him in his cabin.

The next morning, conversation over a leisurely breakfast turned to the geographical features of the country. The steamboat stopped briefly at Killarney (Shebawahning), but Day was unimpressed by the simple plank houses, Jesuit chapel and post office. He was, however, struck by the deep crimson foliage of the La Cloche (or Bell) mountains. Though to Day the area appeared wild, primitive and uninviting, McDougall commented that it was "Not so bad a place to live in after all," where "one at least would have plenty of fish."[50]

The Treaty and the Government

At noon on Friday, 3 October 1862, William McDougall and his companions disembarked at Manitowaning, on Manitoulin Island. Captain George Ironside, Dr. David Layton, Reverend Peter Jacobs and four chiefs wearing silver medals around their necks welcomed the visitors. Ironside introduced the travellers to his colleagues.

Dr. David Stark Layton was presented as a Scottish emigrant who had been the government-appointed surgeon at Manitowaning since 1849. The father of four admitted he struggled with isolation, limited resources, incurable diseases and competition from local medicine men. He insisted that he restricted himself to the practice of medicine and rarely became involved in government issues, though he acknowledged that a surrender and settlement of the island would end his family's isolation.

Reverend Peter Jacobs was introduced as the son of the noted author, spokesperson and Methodist missionary Peter Jacobs, Sr. Jacobs smiled warily as Ironside pointed out the young reverend's Ojibwe heritage, education by the Bishop of Rupert's Land, ordination in Toronto just six years earlier and popularity among the people of Manitowaning. Then Ironside confided that Jacobs was a newlywed.

The visitors were then taken to their lodgings in Captain Ironside's house. Though the finest building in the settlement, the modest one and one-half storey frame building's only notable feature was the large Union Jack flag that flew from an adjacent flagstaff.

Ironside had instructed the Indian people to assemble in Manitowaning. In addition to the several hundred island residents, three more government employees arrived: Joseph Wilson, William Gibbard and A. McNabb.

Joseph Wilson was also a Scottish emigrant. He had been the Crown Lands agent at Sault Ste. Marie since 1845 and had witnessed the Robinson Huron treaty of 1850. "Joe" was described as a customs collector, fishery overseer, crown land agent, magistrate and general government factotum, as well as a Highland Scot.[51]

William Gibbard was an English-born civil engineer and land surveyor who in 1859 had been appointed inspector of the fisheries of lakes Huron and Superior. Gibbard, who considered himself an authority on Indians, warmly welcomed the superintendents. He was a vocal supporter of surrender. McDougall reminded Gibbard to remain vigilant and prevent the distribution of liquor during the negotiations.

Mr. A. McNabb was identified only as being from Owen Sound, an associate of Mr. Gibbard's.[52]

Day and the other guests explored the settlement with Reverend Jacobs and Dr. Layton while McDougall, Spragge and Ironside reviewed the local situation.

Ironside had recently assembled a list of chiefs who were willing to surrender and of those who were reluctant to do so. He believed that seven chiefs and two leading men were amenable but reluctant to admit it openly, while six dissentients still needed to be conciliated. He admitted that, "in consequence of the apparent determined resolution of the dissentients to hold out, I am not at all sanguine as to the success of the contemplated negotiations." "The names of the most prominent dissentients, in this matter," he said, "and whom it will [be] necessary to conciliate are Chiefs Toma, E,dowish,cosh, Tai,bos,egai, Paim,a,quo,naish,kung, and also several of the leading common men among whom are Wah,cai,kez,hik and Mai,to,sah,gee. The names of the willing ones are Chiefs Teh,kum,mah, Mo,co,tai,she,gun, Tah,gai,we,ne,ne [Atagiwinini], Ass,ig,i,nack, Mai,she,quong,gai, Okemah,beness, & She,we,tah,gun, also Edawe Kesis and Ahbedossowey, the two latter being leading men or warriors."[53]

Ironside's idea of who the chiefs were was based largely on loyalty and obedience to the department. In reality, chiefs were elected for their leadership qualities as well as their hereditary claims to the office. Ironside still referred to Tehkummah and Mocotaishegun as chiefs, even though Tomah, Wakekijik and Augustin Ominikamigo had replaced them in an election in 1861.

Despite the inaccuracy concerning official titles, this was a valuable list, and with it Ironside had provided McDougall and Spragge with their key to success. In brief, the Manitowaning, Wewebijiwang (Little Current) and some Wikwemikong chiefs were willing to cede, while others from Sheshegwaning, Michigiwatinong and Wikwemikong needed to be conciliated.

On Saturday, 4 October 1862, a council to discuss the surrender of Manitoulin was convened in Manitowaning. Between two and three hundred Indians and twelve non-Natives met in the government warehouse. Considering that Manitoulin's population in 1861 was about 1,450, of whom only 282 were men over 21 years of age, the attendance was remarkable.[54]

The non-Native participants were Superintendent William McDougall, Deputy Superintendent William Spragge, David Reesor, John H. McDougall and Samuel P. Day, who had travelled together from Toronto; Captain George Ironside and his 24-year-old son Alexander McGregor Ironside, Dr. David Layton, William Gibbard, Joseph Wilson and A. McNabb; and Father Jean-Pierre Choné, who was the only cleric who attended the council.

Francis Assiginack and Reverend Peter Jacobs, both Ojibwe, attended as translators and witnesses.

As Spragge later acknowledged: "Previous to the Indians being assembled in Council under the Presidency of the Superintendent General, it became apparent that influence had been at work, which rendered it improbable that a surrender of the entire Island, would be obtained; although there was good reason to believe that the band occupying the western section of the Island would be prepared to accept the term offered." "Nevertheless," he continued, "the Superintendent General for the purpose of enabling all the bands to avail themselves of the propositions, decided to invite the entire body of Indians present to become parties to a Treaty, upon the conditions described."[55]

The council was held on the upper floor of the decaying plank warehouse on the shore of Manitowaning Bay. It was a bitterly cold October day. The rickety edifice swayed as a storm howled outside and the waves of the bay lapped its sides. The 20-year-old, 60- by 30-foot frame building was pressed to its capacity to hold the several hundred people who were so anxious to participate; even the stairway was overflowing.

McDougall and his colleagues sat on the only bench, behind a pine table. Two piles of tobacco cakes and clay pipes separated the government party from the Indians, who stood or sat on the floor. The guests enjoyed "the proffered presents, and puffed away until the apartment was dark" from smoke. Many of the participants were dressed for the occasion. Some wore blanket capes, headdresses, leggings and moccasins embellished with ribbons and beadwork. Many wore medals illustrating their allegiance and service to the Crown. Day noted "one fierce looking fellow had rouged his cheeks and eyebrows, and had a head dress of feathers that extended down his back, together with rings of brass round his neck," and had a large knife in his belt.[56]

William McDougall, on the advice of his interpreter, eventually rose and approached the chiefs to shake their hands. First, through the interpreter, he introduced himself as the head of the Indian Department, acting on behalf of the government and the Crown. He warned his audience that many people coveted the island and the government intended to take action. He then admitted the government's first surrender offer had not been generous enough. He assured the Indians that they were the owners of the island, but suggested that if they transferred their ownership they would receive deeds, protection and a secure future. He proposed "that the Indians should consent to such portions of the Island being opened for sale and settlement, as would not be required, after liberally providing for each family, that the proceeds of such sales after deducting expenses of survey and management, would be placed at interest for the exclusive benefit of the Indians, then resident on the Island, that upon such consent being given, the Government, although the question had been raised that these Indians had not an exclusive right to the Island, would recognize their right to an interest on the whole Island, and deal with them accordingly; that for the benefit of each head of a family, and families consisting of orphan children of two and upwards, a Farm lot of 100 acres should be set apart; and for each young man of lawful age 50 acres. The selection to be left to the Indians themselves, excluding only lands upon which mill sites exist, and situations required for landing places."[57] "The Indians met the proposition with a storm of indignation," Day recorded, "the chiefs of the Wequimakong tribe being most strongly opposed to a relinquishment of their reserves." Day continued:

> Several chiefs or persons deputed by chiefs, delivered lengthy speeches, wherein they set forth in very poetical language and logical order, the grounds of their opposition. After every speaker had concluded, he shook hands, first with the commissioner and then with all those round the table. During the sitting of the council great excitement was manifested, and, horrible yells, and even the war whoop was given.

Among the leaders assembled in the swaying warehouse, "Only poor old Assickinack was favourable to the proposed arrangement," noted Day. "He expressed his confidence in the Queen and the Government, and said the Indians were infinitely better off since they had come under the protection of the white man; for his part, he was satisfied with the proposition made to him, and he advised his brothers to accept it. The poor old warrior's address created wild commotion," Day reported, and "the painted Indian placed his hand on his war-knife. But the chief's two sons stood ready to protect him. A Pagan Indian immediately stood up at the desire of his fellows and attacked the old man in very abusive speech, and, fearing lest he should come to grief, one of the officials removed him from the Council." Day then turned to the collected wishes of the chiefs:

> The chiefs opposed the project with great vehemence. "As for you, brother," said one, addressing the Superintendent General, "God has given you money; as for us Indians, we have been living without it. God has given us the land to cultivate for our own use, on which we get what we want. I cannot rob my children of what belongs to them. The propositions made by the Government to us long since, have never been realized, and the poorer we are. We are not able to receive your propositions now. I wish, as poor as I am, that I would be left alone. I want only to keep the strip of land I now hold for my children, and I wish you to pity me in my state. My wish is to keep the land just as it is." Finally the Council was adjourned for a couple of hours, in order to give the chiefs an opportunity of consulting together.[58]

Upon reassembling, most of the Indian chiefs were firm in their opposition to the intentions of the Government.[59] According to Spragge, "Two of the dissentients addressed their fellow Indians in exceedingly inflammatory language, denouncing by gesture and speech, those who were favourable to the improvement of the Island by white settlers, and the introduction of improved Agriculture, civilization and open trade, through their instrumentality. The Superintendent General, in order to counteract the effect of the menaces which were used, assured those who were disposed for renewed negotiations of the protection of the Government, and warned the turbulently inclined, of the consequence of violence on their part."[60]

In Day's opinion, "The possibility of entering into any negotiations seemed hopeless, and Mr. McDougall further adjourned the assembly until the following Monday, at the same time, informing the Waquimakong Indians and others who made the most formidable opposition to the projected treaty, that they may return home, as their presence was not again required."[61] Or, as McDougall saw it, he sensed that "the chief opposition came from Indians living eastward of Heywood Sound." McDougall "determined to modify the propositions of the Government so as to meet in some degree the objections from that quarter." He therefore "adjourned the Council until the following Monday" and "informed the Indians that those who were disposed to continue the negotiations would remain while those who had resolved to reject every proposition of the Government might go home."[62]

McDougall told Charles de Lamorandière, the interpreter for the Wikwemikong people, that he was astonished by the unanimous refusal of his first proposition, since he had been informed that the majority were favourable to a transaction.[63]

Many Wikwemikong residents went home, but with the intention of returning on Monday. Between Saturday evening and Monday morning, several chiefs were persuaded to cede. According to Samuel Day, "At length the leading chiefs were got together, the propositions in the proposed treaty and the intentions of the Government more lucidly explained, the result of which was, that, before the final Council was held, three chiefs had signified their adhesion—an object in part effected by the immediate pecuniary advantages offered to them and each Indian of their respective bands."[64] Other witnesses, however, alleged that promises, threats and even liquor were used to persuade the chiefs.

The council was reopened on Monday with a new line of negotiation. A proposal was put to the people occupying the western part of the island "to become parties to an agreement, based upon the terms provided." "The bands occupying the Western section of the Island without hesitation consented by their chiefs and principal men to the conditions offered."[65]

McDougall asked the Wikwemikong people, who occupied the eastern part of the island, if they wanted to accept his proposal and share in the payment. Jako Atagiwinini, the son of aged Chief J.B. Atagiwinini, firmly refused the offer on behalf of the chiefs at Wikwemikong. Day recorded one translation of the speech: "Friends have listened attentively, and are not going to change their minds. We know, brother, that you are a great man, have great authority, and we look upon you favourably. Think of no evil thing that you have heard or seen; let it not be in your heart. Don't think it hard if we do not say all you would wish. We pray you, brother, to keep our land firmly for us. I wish to see my land and to look at it from time to time carefully. The Queen did a great deal for us, and placed agents amongst us to whom we could address ourselves if we wanted to say anything. We are always ready to listen to the words of the Great Father, and to those sent to speak to us; and we wish the Governor-General would make the land secure which he is going to give us."[66]

Seventeen chiefs or leading men whose bands lived west of the Wikwemikong Peninsula accepted the offer and requested specific reserve lands. Tehkummah, a former Wikwemikong chief who had been deposed from office for supporting surrender, also agreed to accept McDougall's offer. McDougall thanked the ceding chiefs and informed the Wikwemikong people that they were free to cede in future. Jako Atagiwinini responded by asking McDougall to remove the restrictions on firewood. McDougall responded that he had to ask the governor whether that could be done.

Samuel Day later recalled that the Monday assembly "went off pleasantly as marriage bells, contrary to what had been anticipated." It "was largely attended even by the recalcitrant Indians of Wikwimekong, was protracted till a late hour; and everything was arranged for the signing of the treaty on the following morning."[67]

On Tuesday, 7 October 1862, the ceding chiefs and men assembled in the superintendent's office. The vellum document, "The Deed of Cession," was laid on the table, read, interpreted and signed. Then "a few hundred pounds were divided among the chiefs for themselves and their bands, varying in sums, from one to two dollars, which amounts were not given as a gratuity, but as advances upon the anticipated emolument to be derived from the sale of the lands in the island."[68]

Though the document was dated 6 October 1862, it was actually signed on 7 October. After the treaty was signed, "the Superintendent-General informed those present that his father, when a child, was adopted by the Chief of the Snake Tribe Indians, duly initiated into their order, and called Whasaneese (Catfish); and that was one reason why he took such an interest in Indian affairs. The Indians, upon hearing the story interpreted, exclaimed with excitement and wonder, Whasaneese! Whasaneese!—a cognomen by which the Commissioner of Crown Lands will in future be distinguished," Samuel Day later recalled.[69]

William McDougall left Manitoulin triumphantly with his treaty the next day. He was obviously anxious to return, or as Day put it, to "get away from that desolate region," as "the thought of being on the island was intolerable." They left at 5 a.m. on Wednesday, 8 October, in William Gibbard's 20-foot open boat, despite squally weather, strong winds and high seas. Day accompanied McDougall and Gibbard, but Spragge and Reesor decided to wait for the steamboat. Day's six-day return voyage included four days in rough seas, a stark contrast to the comfortable 30-hour westward journey. McDougall stopped in Toronto to announce his victory to the press, and then continued on to Quebec.

McDougall was confident the governor general and council would approve his treaty. On 31 October, before he had even written his report or submitted the treaty document for approval, he ordered an exploratory survey of Manitoulin Island. Provincial land surveyor John Stoughton Dennis was sent to Manitoulin with a team of surveyors to explore the island.

In order to conclude the treaty, McDougall had modified the surrender proposal that had been approved by the Legislative Council in September. The actual agreement excluded the Wikwemikong Peninsula, the part of the island east of the Manitoulin Gulf and Heywood Sound. McDougall submitted the modified document to the governor general for approval on 3 November, with a summary of the treaty negotiations:

> The undersigned has the honor to state for the information of His Excellency the Governor General in Council, that under the Authority of the Order in Council of the twelfth day of September, 1862, he proceeded early in the month of October last to visit the Great Manitoulin Island, accompanied by William Sprague, Esquire, Deputy Superintendent of Indian Affairs and Mr. F. Assickinack of the Indian Office in Toronto, as interpreter. The resident agent Capt. Ironside under instruction from the Department had caused the Indians residing on the Island to be notified of the intended visit of the undersigned and of its object, and had summoned them to attend at Manitowaning on the fourth ulto.
>
> The chiefs and Principal men with the exception of one or two detained by illness and nearly all the males above the age of eighteen years were present at the Council.
>
> The undersigned stated the object of his visit explained the wishes of the Government in regard to the settlement of the Island and proposed the terms in respect to the Indians specified in the Order in Council authorizing the negotiation. The Indians had selected one of their Chiefs to reply to the overtures of the Government, and without taking time to consider these overtures he proceeded to announce the determination of the Indians to reject them unconditionally. The undersigned made some further explanations and directed an adjournment of the Council for an hour during which time the Indians were requested to consider the

propositions he had made with care and deliberation.

On reassembling there was an evident disposition among the Bands living westward of the place of meeting to listen favourably to the propositions of the Government but the majority were still unwilling to treat and by intimidation and threats of violence prevented any open expression of opinion except by the old war chief Assikinack who declared his full assent to the wishes of the Government. Ascertaining the chief opposition came from Indians living eastward of Heywood Sound, the undersigned determined to modify the propositions of the Government so as to meet in some degree the objections from that quarter. He accordingly adjourned the Council until the following Monday, the first day of meeting being Saturday—informing the Indians that those who were disposed to continue the negotiations would remain while those who had resolved to reject every proposition of the Government might go home. He also informed them that no threats or intimidation would be allowed and that anyone who should attempt violence would be surely punished. Nearly all the Indians remained or returned on Monday and being apprised of the nature of the proposition the undersigned intended to submit namely: to exclude that part of the Island eastward of the Manitoulin Gulf and Heywood Sound from the proposed agreement they came to the adjourned meeting in a more friendly mood and expressed their willingness to surrender for sale and settlement all that part of the Island westwardly of the Gulf and Sound.

The undersigned submits herewith the deed or instrument which embodies the agreement made and concluded between the respective parties. It was executed by the undersigned and the Deputy Supt. of Indian Affairs on behalf of the Government and by nineteen of the Chiefs and principal men on behalf of the Indians.

In consequence of the notification of the terms of the agreement authorized by the Order in Council as above mentioned and the addition of other terms deemed necessary to prevent future difficulty and which will be found in the Instrument the undersigned caused a provision to be inserted that it was not to take effect until approved by the Governor General in Council. The undersigned therefore now begs to submit the same for such approval.

Wm McDougall. Nov. 3 1862.[70]

On 14 November 1862, the "Articles of Agreement and Convention made and concluded at Manitouawning, on the Great Manitoulin Island," on 6 October 1862 between the Government as represented by the Chief Superintendent and Deputy Superintendent of Indian Affairs and nineteen of the Chiefs and Principal Men on behalf of the Indians was approved by the governor general in council.[71] Two months later, McDougall released a map of Manitoulin based on John Dennis' land survey.[72] The map, obviously a tool to promote land sales, indicated proposed roads, good land, hardwood, burned land, swamp, thicket and seven tiny "Indian clearings."

Chapter 2
Odawa Minising and Ogimaa Itawashkash

Sasso Itawashkash
Mimanda keijiwebisiian ininina biian kawitakijig nandawabandan kidabinodjiim obimadisiwin awadi wendji mogiset kisis inabiian kigawabama kisis tchibimiskwabikagodjing missa ajinawag amiskokwa naieian nage achpimeing dach kibiagodjing awi kisis nitawasikoso missa keijinagwadinig kidabinodjiim obimadisiwin.[73]

Here is the place that will be yours. When you look around you under the vaulted heaven looking for the support of your children, when your gaze turns towards the rising sun you shall see that sun rising red similar to the colour of the coat that I wear, when it rises higher that same sun shall be very bright with light, there is the image of the life of your children. After that sun has been up a little longer you'll see in different places the flowers bloom. There is the image of the life of your children.[74]

Ogimaa Sasso Itawashkash, known as *le chef* Samson Itawachkach of Chichigwaning by the island's Catholic priests and as Chief Sassow Edowishcosh of Sheshegwaning by the island's government agents, stood and remembered. He recalled the words of a great English chief as he stood on the shore and stared across the turbulent autumn waves toward the rising sun. Despite his apparent focus he was not thinking about the sun or the water but rather about the land, and about the *Anishinaabeg*.[75]

Itawashkash (?-1882?) was the son of renowned war chief and orator Jean-Baptiste Assiginack. Both men had been born where the land divides lakes Huron and Michigan. Their history was shared by many of Manitoulin Island's Odawa. Their family had been a trading partner and ally of the French and then of the British. The family's warriors had fought to preserve their lands, but their territory south of the Great Lakes was assigned to the United States after the wars. Then foreign settlers and treaties pushed the Odawa onto ever smaller parcels of land. For as long as he could recall—and his memory was almost as renowned as his speech—he had fought to save his land. He was one of a long line of *ogimaag* (chiefs) who had tried to do so.

In March 1836 he, as a third class chief entitled to an annuity, and the other chiefs living in what the government agent called the Michigan territory, placed their names on the Washington Treaty ceding much of their land in exchange for secure land reserves. They soon learned that the government added a removal clause that could cancel their reserves in five years, moving them west of the Mississippi as many bands before them had been.

In August 1836, at the annual British present ceremony for allies, Itawashkash, his father and fourteen other Odawa and Ojibwe chiefs responded to the Great

Chief Francis Bond Head's offer to withdraw their respective claims and make the Manitoulin islands "the Property (under your Great Father's Control) of all Indians who he shall allow to reside on them." The sixteen *ogimaag* signed Head's proposal that was now called his treaty on 9 August 1836. "Itawachkach" and his father had signed their names in the English manner, but the others had put their clan symbols or a mark beside the English agent's writing of their names.

Itawashkash and many others settled on Manitoulin, or as they knew it, *Odawa Minising*, the Island of the Odawa.[76] They considered Manitoulin to be the land of their forefathers, the land *Kitche Manitou*, the Great Spirit, had given them. By signing Head's proposal they had simply agreed to return to the home of their fathers and share it with other *Anishinaabeg* who also wished to live there.

Most of the immigrants settled at Manitowaning or Wikwemikong, though Sheshegwaning, Naimonakekong, Wewebijiwang and Sheguiandah were established settlements long before the treaty. Itawashkash settled on Manitoulin's east coast at Wikwemikong. A French-Canadian Catholic priest, *Nosse* (or Père) Proulx, joined the community in 1838. Itawashkash and many of Wikwemikong's residents were accustomed to priests and welcomed them into their villages.

Wikwemikong grew quickly from a 70-person settlement in 1835 to a village of more than 500 residents in 1844. This rapid growth prompted some of the residents to move to more isolated island locations. Itawashkash moved to Sheshegwaning in 1844. His friends Sakiwinebi and Taibosegai moved to Mindemooyasebe and Mitchigiwatinong respectively, with their families and bands. Though the government agent in Manitowaning claimed they were trying to escape the priests, many of them maintained the Roman Catholic religion. Taibosegai said they had moved because of the depletion of the sugarbush and inadequate quantities of hay for cattle in winter.[77]

Itawashkash was determined to maintain religion and literacy for his people. When the new *nosse*, Père Choné, visited Sheshegwaning in 1845, he was met by almost one hundred *Anishinaabeg* who gathered to see and hear him. Itawashkash liked to recount how astonished the *nosse* had been when Itawashkash asked him to repair their worn books and to bring them more. Another *nosse* was so surprised at their literacy that he made a drawing of *Ogimaa* Wahcowsai reading a book.

Itawashkash himself had had his image captured by a visitor at the annual present ceremony in 1845. Artist Paul Kane had preserved a likeness of him with lead pencil and paper, as a young chief with a feather in his dark, tousled hair.

By 1850 Itawashkash was the head of a 114-person village. To support the *nosse* and the people, Itawashkash had encouraged his followers to build a church, a *petite église*. All were pleased with their efforts. Père Hanipaux, who had replaced Père Proulx five years earlier, could not contain his enthusiasm and admiration when he first saw the church in the autumn of 1850. The finest building in the village, it was also the largest, measuring 35 by 24 feet, and 15 feet just to the eaves. Thin wooden planks clad the outside, and the inside had beautiful, well-cut wooden boards. He asked the workmen to build him an altar on columns, side altars and a communion table, plus benches for the singers. Together, the *nosse* and the *Anishinaabeg* decorated the walls with holy pictures. The women filled the building with great bursts of red, yellow and white flowers. The people also built a small house for the *nosse* and finished it with the things they knew the priests favoured. They made a chimney, a plank bed, a table and even a footrest. Père Hanipaux was so content that he remained in the village for six weeks and celebrated the feasts of Christmas, Epiphany and the New Year.[78]

Life had sometimes been difficult. In some years, game was scarce; in other years, fishing was unsuccessful. Even maple sap was not always plentiful. The *nosse* did not come as often as Itawashkash would have liked. Occasionally, a new *nosse* would come and stay for a large part of the winter season in order to master the Ojibwe language. But then the *nosse* would depart and the people were left on their own. Only the traders were predictable: they arrived regularly and left with sugar, fish and sometimes pelts.

By 1860, when the first rumours of change began to circulate, Sheshegwaning rivalled Michigiwatinong as second largest settlement on the island. Its exact population depended on whose numbers you believed. The priests counted more than 131 residents in Sheshegwaning but the government agent counted only 105, and it was his number that appeared in the records of the Indian Department.

Itawashkash was pleased that the number of his people was rising again. He and his wife Sophie (Madjiganikwe) had been blessed with sons, daughters and even grandchildren. Their son John (Wabanosse) could read and write, and showed promise as a thinker and speaker. John was also determined to resist surrender and retain the land for his children, now that he was a father himself.

Even the government agent, Wabiwiokwan (The White Hat), Captain George Ironside, in Manitowaning admitted that nearly fifteen hundred *Anishinaabeg* now lived on the island of the Odawa, more than half of them children and youths.[79] And these were the agent's numbers; many people were reluctant to participate in anything that might be a treaty, so they disappeared from view when the agent was counting. Since he rarely left Manitowaning, Wabiwiokwan's count only included people on his lists of annuitants or recipients of charity.

Sheshegwaning was growing in prosperity as well as population. In addition to fishing and maple sugar production, the people grew corn, potatoes, oats, turnips, peas, beans and squash. They raised horses, cows, pigs and fowl. Many of the men were skilled carpenters and could build a boat or a building if one was needed. Almost every family owned a boat for fishing. Though Itawashkash and his neighbours still thought of the land in terms of trapping or hunting territories, divisions based on the distance a man could walk in half a day, hunting and trapping were less relevant notions now on the island. *Anishinaabeg* travelled off the island to the North Shore of the mainland to hunt for game.

Some of the people were literate and could read and write in the languages of the agents and the *nosse*. Like most of his fellow *ogimaag*, Itawashkash had insisted that at least one of his children must learn to read and write.[80] His son

Joseph (Nishkadjiwin) tried to instruct the children during the winter that Père Frémiot was with them, the winter of 1854. But Joseph complained that the children did not attend regularly.

Itawashkash believed reading and writing were the most important skills the people could learn from the foreigners. The only thing that Itawashkash wanted from the agent was education for all the young people. He wanted them instructed as were the young in Wikwemikong and Manitowaning. Education would help them recognize a fair trade, correspond with other bands and write to the governor themselves and not have to depend on a priest or the agent to put their words down correctly. But the agent ignored his request for a teacher.

Once again Itawashkash had been summoned to Manitowaning, the village of the government, to discuss his land. How many times had he explained that *Kitche Manitou* had given the island to his forefathers, and the people intended to keep it for their children and their children's children forever? And how many times had the agent or foreign visitors acknowledged his words, shaken him by the hand, departed—and then returned to try again? He used to think they didn't understand the language, but now he suspected they just didn't listen.

He knew the *Anishinaabeg* were unanimously opposed to any further surrenders. Well, almost unanimously. Sadly, his own father had gradually fallen from a powerful, independent thinker to an ancient government pawn who had been bought by coins, blankets and medals. Jean-Baptiste Assiginack had once been a learned and renowned warrior, orator and leader, a member of a family of great chiefs in Michigan. He was a signatory to the 1836 Manitowaning treaty and had moved to the island as interpreter for the government. In his ninth decade he was still a persuasive speaker.[81] But now Itawashkash accused him of having lost all sense of independence. His father had apparently switched his allegiance to the government agent, with whom he had argued for many years, and now believed in a surrender of the island. He had even persuaded his younger sons to obey the agent and to surrender if requested.

Itawashkash's three younger brothers followed their father's lead. Francis, the brightest student, had been sent away to school at the government's expense and now worked in the Indian Department. Isaac had a wife and young family. He was a traditional healer in Manitowaning. Itawashkash had heard that he was promoting a surrender for the agent. Benjamin was visiting the daughter of Louis Tehkummah, a former Wikwemikong chief who also was known to favour surrender. The Assiginack family shared a log house in Manitowaning and a lodge and garden plot four miles west of the village.

And so it was that on Thursday, 2 October 1862, to count in the English manner, Itawashkash had awakened early, prepared his mind on the shore and headed toward the rising sun with the few members of his band who could be spared on short notice for the second year in a row to abandon their fall fishing and harvest to attend the agents.

Rumours and Resolutions

As Itawashkash travelled, he recalled the past and tried to understand why the government agents thought they could take the island. He had a lot of time to think, with more than 50 English miles of land and water to cross. And he had to travel swiftly. This was not a time of year to stop and visit. He should be at work.

Rumours that *Odawa Minising* was going to be surveyed and sold had spread across the island last year. The *Anishinaabeg* understood land loss. Their fathers had lost their territory south of the Great Lakes after the American Revolution; most of their Michigan territory to treaties; Drummond and Mackinac islands to British-American boundary agreements; and most of their land on the north shores of lakes Superior and Huron under the Robinson treaties of 1850.

Manitoulin Island was their only undivided land. But the change in the governance and leadership of the Indian Department brought rumours of further changes for the department and the *Anishinaabeg*.

Despite believing Manitoulin had been reserved for them by the governor on behalf of the King, and the recent assurance of protection from the commissioners on behalf of the government, island residents were nervous because their superintendent was promoting and obtaining land surrenders.

Anishinaabeg on the mainland's North Shore were persuaded in 1859 to surrender reserved land that had been set aside by Robinson's 1850 treaty. Manitoulin's agent, Wabiwiokwan, Captain George Ironside, was credited with securing these surrenders.[82] He even approached three Manitoulin *ogimaag* about surrendering their North Shore property. One of them, Okemah beness, actually signed a surrender paper for Whitefish River, but now said that it was not accepted.[83]

That same year a new government agent had appeared. He claimed the government had appointed him to lease their fisheries, and the people must now ask permission and pay for the right to fish in their own waters. His name was William Gibbard, but the people named him Eshkamejwanoke (The Gatherer Of Fish Guts). When Itawashkash refused to let him land and inspect the *Anishinaabeg*'s territory, he threatened to shoot any Indian who laid hands upon him or his men. He had called Itawashkash a troublesome American chief of an American village. But it was Eshkamejwanoke's accusation that *Ogimaa* Itawashkash was controlled by the priests that the *ogimaa* considered the ultimate insult. The new agent threatened to tell the governor that the *Anishinaabeg* wasted their resources and that Manitoulin should be settled by White men immediately. His attitude and actions, combined with the local agent's activities, provoked the *Anishinaabeg* to act.

A council was convened in Michigiwatinong in February 1861. The time and place were well chosen. February was a quiet month of ice fishing or cutting and transporting cordwood to sell during the shipping season. Equally to the point, Michigiwatinong was centrally located, yet away from the local agent's prying eyes.

The people gathered, expressed their opinions and agreed to hold onto Manitoulin. Then they wrote a letter declaring their intention to refuse any propositions to surrender their island. The letter was endorsed by more than 200 men and then taken to Wikwemikong, where it was presented to the *ogimaag*. Head *ogimaa* Michel Cainooshimague accepted the council's proposition and signed the document, but chiefs Tehkummah and Mocotaishegun claimed that their loyalty to the Crown required them to consult the agent before accepting the council's decision. They were deposed from office for their reluctance.[84]

Itawashkash had heard later that Tehkummah, who had refused to attend the council had told the government agent that it was convened principally by the Wikwemikong people, and it was ordered that, should the government make any propositions to the Indians about a surrender, they should not accept them on any consideration but oppose them with all their might.[85]

No sooner had the council ended and the Anishinaabeg returned to their homes, the rumours appeared to the *Anishinaabeg* to have been confirmed. Their council's fear of land loss was reinforced by the agent's demand that they participate in a census. Though the agent said it was a demand from the Queen and the governor, most of the *Anishinaabeg* were uneasy. Why did the man urging surrender want to record on a piece of paper for the governor their names, their children's names, their ages and even the amount of their harvest? No one wanted to put his name on anything that might in fact be a treaty. Further fuelling suspicion, the agent's paper was printed in English only, and the people knew from past experience that English words did not always respect *Anishinaabeg* words.

Despite threats of the loss of treaty annuities if they did not cooperate, the *Anishinaabeg* resisted. Itawashkash learned from his brother, who worked for another agent, that Wabiwiokwan (Ironside) had recorded fewer than 300 names on the census forms.[86] The official lists included Manitowaning and some residents of Wewebijiwang and Wikwemikong. But most of the people of Achitwaigunning, Mitchigiwatinong, Mindemooyasebe, Naimonakekong, Sheguiandah, Sheshegwaning, Sheshegwanasing, Wewebijiwang, Wikwemikong and Wikwemikongsing refused to be counted, so the agent simply listed them by name and guessed at their numbers.

Ogimaa Paimoquonaishkung of Michigiwatinong explained the response of his people to the census: "Even now he [Ironside] frequently has recourse to threats in order to obtain the signatures of the Indians, when they refuse to give them. We think he is going to deceive us once more and this is our reason for withholding our names from him."[87]

The census and the surrender rumours prompted the *Anishinaabeg* to act. In May 1861 they wrote two petitions in which they recalled past promises and described the objectionable activities of their agent, George Ironside. Unable to believe that the Queen and governor would intentionally break their promises to them regarding Manitoulin, they assumed that Ironside was acting on his own when he advocated surrender, enumerated residents or threatened to withhold annuity payments. They intended to present their complaints at a grand council near Detroit later that summer, but the American War prevented that action. Père Choné offered to translate their complaints and send them to Quebec City.

Itawashkash knew every word of the first protest. It recalled the governor's past promises of protection and rejected the present agent.

Wikwemikong 1861 May 23
Father
I now stand up to repeat the promises you made to our forefathers when for the first

time you put your foot upon this Island of ours, you said, "behold the sun, you see when he rises he is red. My coat is red because I imitate the color of the sun."

You said to our forefathers "if at any time you should feel aggrieved I myself will look after your grievances, my arms are powerful and my heart is big and it is white. You have a place in my heart and you shall be under the protection of my hand, and no one shall be allowed to oppress you."

Now it is well known that Superintendent never takes any trouble to impart to us useful information. Whenever he has anything to do he does it (without consulting the Indians) and we are generally informed what has been done after it is settled.

Perhaps he represents what he does himself as coming from the Indians.

He never listens to any representation from us. Sometimes he does not even allow us to enter his house but comes out to meet us outside. We, who are chiefs, are refused admittance.

Now, we, the inhabitants of this Island, have unanimously agreed, Odahwahs and Ojibwas not to recognize him any longer as our Superintendent.

We request very strongly that it should be done according to our wishes viz—he should not remain here.[88]

The second petition expressed the complaints of the *Anishinaabeg* by *Ogimaa* Paimoquonaishkung:

Mitchigiwatinong. May 23 1861

I am going to state what we know about our Superintendent. Some time ago he questioned me. He mentioned the Governor General and the Queen. He said to me the Queen asks you to surrender your land. If you let it go, you and your children shall never be in need. I complied with his request because I love the Queen and the Governor General; but some time after I made the surrender I began to think that my children would be reduced to poverty.

I have already seen that his promises have come to nothing. Now I make my thoughts known together with the thoughts of those living on the Island.

The subject which occupies my thoughts at present is the land which I surrendered two years ago, at that time he made me to understand that my annuity would increase, but the time is now long past when, after obtaining my land by fair promises, he said the increase would commence.

I state clearly the manner in which our Superintendent treats us. Now last summer—he only gave me six shillings, this does not look like an increase. I do not blame the Governor General, but my suspicions rest upon our Superintendent.

Two years ago he asked me to give up what land I had reserved formerly. I did what he said, because he made use of the Governor Generals name—he told me that my income would be derived from two sources, and that I would see the payment of my money, before the fall of that year, up to this time I have not seen it.

Now I have refused to listen to him, because I think what he wants me to do, comes from himself, not from the Governor General. I take back the land which I have surrendered. I do not mean the surrender in the main land which I made to the Crown.

At present we do not feel disposed to follow his advice, we think he only wants to deceive us, and because he has so often deceived us we do not want to do any thing with him any longer.

Sometime since we were anxious to have a saw mill. He promised to assist us, but in this matter also he deceived me in many ways. I received no annuity for three years on account of this saw mill affair—he only wants to make us poor, he takes no interest in our welfare, we think his object is to keep us in poverty.

There is another complaint we wish to make—When we go to his place, he sits by the window watching us, and if we make an attempt to go in, he comes out to meet us in the open air, he makes us stop at the door outside the house, and if at any time, we succeed in going into the house to speak to him, he goes away, leaving us alone, before we have time to say a word.

This conduct of his makes us think he is not discharging his duties according to the wishes of the Governor General. He takes no trouble to promote our welfare

At the time of making the first distribution which took place at Manitowaning, the person who made the payment was in a great hurry to go, as soon as he finished he went on board the steam boat because he was hurried by the Captain of the steamer. After the boat had left, I went towards the house of our Superintendent and when I got as far as the door I found that he was engaged in counting money. I did not go in, but stood at the door, listening to his counting. I stood there for a long time. When he had finished counting the money, he got up, opened the door, and said to me "are you just come?" I saw by his face he was in a state of confusion, he asked me the question because I stood there long listening whilst he was counting the money. The money he had was what remained after the payments were made. Whether he has ever given any portion of that money to any Indians I know not.

This is the way he treats us, and this is our reason for suspecting him.

The first payment was made partly in goods; our Superintendent selected the best articles—put them in a root cellar and had them removed to his house—you see the way he is robbing us.

There is a government regulation which says "Watch in our villages lest any one should whiskey"—if it be a white man take away the liquor from him and bring it to me and when you have brought it you will be paid for your trouble. We have seized liquor according to directions, but have never received so much as a copper in remuneration.

We have stated what we know about our Superintendent. We don't want to acknowledge him any longer as such. We remove him, we don't want him.

One time when I went to receive my money I missed nearly the half of it. He told me he would give the rest as soon as the payments were completed, after finishing the distribution I applied to him for it, but he did not give it to me. I am under the impression that he is robbing me.

When a party of Indians went to the "Little Current" to settle there permanently he made an attempt to drive them away, he got a party from Wikwemikong to act for him as soldiers.

When he gave permission to have a house (store) put up at the "Little Current" he said that it was the wish of the Governor General, that the matter had been settled between the Governor and the great merchant (Hudsons Bay Co) and that a house and a wharf would be built there.

It is not permitted for any Indian to sell his cord of wood (at the "Little Current") in order to supply his ordinary wants—but it is sold for him by a white man who takes a portion of its value. We were made to understand that Indians would be permitted to cut wood and from each cord there would be a deduction of two shillings, which would go to the Government until the amount was fully refunded which had been paid to the Hudson Bay Company for the house and wharf; that after this the Indians there were to have to sell their wood, in the mean time no one would be allowed to buy it from them.

When the wood was sold fifty cents were deducted from each of those Indians who cut it.

He went to lease a certain fishery to a yankee in the name of the Indians, he told them that the lessee would give a large amount of money for it, and that it would be given to the Indians; but he has not as yet given one copper to the Indians on account of the rent.

With regard to the leasing of fisheries in general we beg to say that he would not permit us to make any remonstrances against the leasing of our fisheries; he acted entirely as he pleased. He reprimanded the Indians sharply for daring to oppose to the leasing of their fisheries.

Even now he frequently has recourse to threats in order to obtain the signatures of the Indians, when they refuse to give them. We think he is going to deceive us once more and this is our reason for withholding our names from him.

He has from time to time captured American traders—a portion (of the fines paid by them) he said, would go to the Indians and the rest to the Governor, he has never given any thing to the Indians on this account. Whether the Governor has received his share we know not.

Some time ago the inhabitants of Wikwemikong were desirous of building a saw mill on some chosen stream, on the Manitoulin Island, but our Superintendent would not permit the work to be done (on the Island) but he pointed out to us the main land which is surrendered to the Crown as a proper place where to build one.

Also we wanted to have a Grist mill and we told our Superintendent that we wished to ask for some assistance in order to obtain the necessary iron machinery— he directed us to put up the frame in the first place and that when that part of the building was finished, he said he would write to the Governor laying before him our wishes. We accordingly put up a good and substantial building, poor as we are, we worked hard and we paid the man who superintended the work out of our own pocket. All our labor has been lost. We have often urged him to inform the Governor of what we had done but he would not move in the matter.

Sometimes he says that the cost of the Iron would be $1500 and he does nothing more than this.

We have sometimes requested him to send a letter from us to the Governor but he would not comply with our wishes on any account.

At last we have placed this document in the hands our Reverend father, the missionary, to be transmitted by him, in which will be found our words in writing.[89]

The names of 184 men of Wikwemikong, Sheshegwaning, Sheguiandah, Michigiwatinong, Mindemooyasebe and Wikwemikongsing were attached to the documents. The *nosse*, Père Choné, translated the petitions into French and sent them to Quebec City. Itawashkash knew that they had been received—though not acknowledged or answered—by the Indian Department because his brother Francis working in the department had translated them.

The *Anishinaabeg* also wrote to Nahneebahwequa at Owen Sound and asked her to send her people's complaints to the Queen. Nahneebahwequa, or Catherine Sutton, the daughter of Bunch Sunego of Credit River, was famous for her struggle for the rights of her family and of the Newash people. She had even spoken to the Queen.[90] She wrote a letter to the editor of the *Christian Guardian* on behalf of the Manitoulin Indians. In her letter she acknowledged the papers interest in the Indians and declared:

> Although I have been robbed of my birthright during the last nine years—in connection with my family—yet I would never have troubled you had it not been for the late shameful transactions at Manitoulin. I think the inhabitants of Canada ought

to have their eyes opened on the subject, and the power of the press and the voice of the public should be raised against such wholesale robbery and treachery, otherwise there will be no end to it as long as the Indians are in possession of a single acre of arable land.[91]

The anti-surrender momentum that had been building since February peaked in mid-June. The question of ceding the island was discussed in council in Michigiwatinong. A unanimous resolution was passed to resist any pressure to surrender made by the government. The Wikwemikong residents then held an election that determined the destiny of the Wikwemikong Peninsula.

Louis Wakekijik and Augustin (or Ogiste) Ominikamigo replaced the two *ogimaag* who favoured surrender, Tehkummah and Mocotaishegun. Both Wakekijik and Ominikamigo were the sons of deceased Wikwemikong *ogimaag*, Vincent Paimosegai (Bemassige or Essiban) and Antoine Makons. Tomah (or Thomas) Kinojameg replaced his recently deceased father, *Ogimaa* Michel Cainooshimague.

Itawashkash knew that Tehkummah had complained to Ironside that their *nosse*, Choné, had said that the *Anishinaabeg* must be watchful as the government wanted to deprive them of the island, just as they had deprived others who now lived in poverty. The priest's words caused the people of Wikwemikong to rule that their chiefs should not speak to the agent without six *Anishinaabe* witnesses.[92]

Itawashkash had often thought during previous year that it was good to be far away from the agent and his control. He heard that the agent had been approaching the *ogimaag*, one by one, to persuade them to surrender their land. He also knew that the people lived in fear that *arpenteurs*, or land surveyors, would come soon and measure their land for sale.

In September, the *Anishinaabeg* followed up on their unanswered May petition with a brief note in Ojibwe, translated and sent to Quebec City by *Nosse* Choné. Seven *ogimaag* of Wikwemikong, Sheshegwaning and Michigiwatinong signed the note:

Wikwemikong 3 September 1861.
Governor,
We are writing to you today for the second time. We wrote to you on the 31st [23rd] of May 1861, to inform you about how we are treated by our Superintendent on our island, and your response has not yet arrived. We think about it a lot. We await a response to our letter. If someone doesn't take our maltreatment into consideration, we will make it known, and it will be known everywhere.
We have entrusted our Father the Black Robe to interpret our words.[93]

Their letters were not answered. They soon discovered that their fears were justified: at the beginning of October 1861, Itawashkash and the other island *ogimaag* and their men were summoned to Manitowaning by Wabiwiokwan, Captain Ironside.

They knew that the agent wanted their island, and when their petitions were not answered they suspected that the Queen and governor wanted it also. Their only consolation was that they were prepared. They had agreed to resist together, forever. They were determined to retain their island. They would not listen to any terms for the surrender of the island, or any part of it.[94]

Despite their confidence in their decision, *ogimaag* and men from all parts of the island felt obliged to descend on Manitowaning in a display of force for the visitors. About 130 *Anishinaabeg*, including four of the fifteen signatories of the 1836 treaty, assembled in Manitowaning on Saturday, 5 October 1861.[95]

Two agents who claimed to be appointed by the government, William Bartlett and Charles Lindsey, were introduced. They brought with them an *arpenteur,* a land surveyor. This action alone confirmed for the *Anishinaabeg* the rumour of survey and settlement, and spoke of the government's assumption of success.

Reverend Peter Jacobs, the missionary for the Church of England, translated the agent's speeches from a written paper. Charles de Lamorandière, a trader from Shebawahning, translated the replies of the *Anishinaabeg*. Wabiwiokwan (Ironside) and the doctor were also present.

Itawashkash sat close to the visiting agents. He wanted to see and hear them well. He knew his response did not depend on their words, but still he wanted to understand their thoughts.

William Bartlett spoke, he said, for the governor because the Queen had given the management of the Indians to the governor and parliament of Canada. Then he said the governor had asked the commissioner, who had asked him to come to speak to them and declare the wishes of the governor.[96]

Itawashkash wondered then (and still wondered long after) where this governor was who wanted their land. Why didn't he come to speak to them? It was the governor himself who had come 25 years before to assure the *Anishinaabeg* of possession of their island when they signed the paper of 1836. Perhaps this was not a true offer, just a test of loyalty or understanding.

But then this agent said some remarkable words. He said that the governor had expected *all* those under his protection—more than 9,000 Indians—would come to settle on the island, but since "the people had not availed themselves of the opportunity of collecting as settlers," the intention of the government in settling the island with Indians had not been carried out.

He said the governor, their Great Father, wished to secure them the same title as the White men, that every family would get 25 acres and a deed, and in addition that young men of 18 years would receive 25 acres when they became 21. The rest of the island would be granted to the White children of the governor. The lands would be the property of each, just as boats, houses and cattle were, and so they would be free to dispose of it, just as the White man could. He said the White settlers would bring prosperity, skills and markets. He then said the governor himself had sent the surveyor so that there would be no delay in carrying out his wishes.

What a generous offer! Only twenty-five acres for an entire family, and then nothing if they sold it like the White men did. Itawashkash responded to the agent's offer:

> You my English Chiefs, listen to what I say to you this day, I am employed by my superior Chiefs and by my warriors also, to say to you that this land on which we are now, has been the land of our forefathers, on which the Great Spirit has put them,

they kept it till now for us, and it is our duty to keep it for our children and grand children. Would you not think that it would be a great sin to rob our children and grand children of their inheritance?

The treaty of 1836 which you allude to today was not concluded the way you read it now, it was understood by our Chiefs then that this Island was to be exclusively for the Indians.

Itawashkash's father Jean-Baptiste Assiginack also spoke. Unlike his son, he recounted his people's allegiance as warriors and said that he would continue to be guided by the wishes of the Queen's government.

The council was suspended so the offer could be discussed. When the council resumed, Itawashkash spoke again:

We have not changed. There is very little good land upon the Island. I have travelled through it, and have hunted through every part of it. There are many rocky places, also many marshes and lakes. There is only enough land for the Indians. You must not have any hard feelings against me for saying this, as I am stating what my young men have decided.

Then Maishegonggai spoke for the Odjibweg:

I cannot speak otherwise than my friend Ottawa did, I do not want to repeat his words, I look also for the future of my children, I do not want to rob them of their land, therefore I approve in full the speech of my friend Ottawa.

Wahcowsai spoke for the Potawatomi:

I was present at the treaty of 1836, heard with my own ears its discussion; it was said by our Great Father then (Sir F.B. Head) that this Island was to be the exclusive property of the Indians, and [he] had given up his claim in our favour. I am very surprised, I am astonished today to hear that the promise of so great a Chief, so high in position was not to be kept. I am only a poor low miserable Indian. I would be ashamed to break my words to my own children.

Gahbow of Wikwemikong said:

That they had frequently been told that the land would not be taken from them. That a great lawyer [Judge Prince of Sault Ste. Marie] had lately been here, who also told them their Island would not be taken from them unless they rebelled, and that now, ten days after that, the Government sends up persons to take their land away from them.

Then the agent, Bartlett, suspended the meeting. On Monday, the same people reassembled. Itawashkash spoke first:

You my English Chiefs. Since Saturday we reflected, we have meditated also on the past as well as the future, and we always come to this determination, that we cannot deprive our children of their land, so we advise you to go home, and take back with you your Surveyor, Land measurer, we will not allow him to measure our land.

The second agent, Lindsey, replied that it was the government's right to explore the island, that the Government would send troops if necessary to protect his employees. Itawashkash consulted the others and responded that the *ogimaag* did not like the presence of the surveyors and wanted them to leave.

Lindsey persisted. He said that the Indians were misinformed as to their rights on the island: they had surrendered their rights, and the island, in 1836. He maintained that, since Indians had not settled the island, others must settle it.

Itawashkash replied: "I am empowered by my chiefs to get up the same as I did before. Those chiefs that employ me to speak now have the idea that they are going to be wronged, and that the authority is not from the right source."

The first agent produced his instructions and had them translated by de Lamorandière. An *Anishinaabe* rose and spoke without identifying himself:

> Listen to me. I call you friends, because the whites and Indians are friends. I wish you to understand what I say. If I understood English, I would not employ another man to speak for me. I hope you will not do anything to cause me to be angry against you. This island, of which I speak, I consider my body; I don't want one of my legs or arms to be taken from me. I am surprised to hear you say the island belongs to white men, for I have not seen any white men on the island before, and I am not very young. I know there is an Evil Spirit, of which I am afraid as well as of the Great Spirit above. As I said before, I am surprised to hear you say the island belongs to you. My father said the English only borrowed the land on St Joseph's Island to live upon. I don't want to go against the Government and laws; at the same time I wish them to listen to me. You are afraid of you superiors, and must do as you are told. I am the same.

Bartlett replied that he was glad to hear the friendly words of the "young man," who immediately responded that Bartlett had misunderstood him: he wanted Bartlett to take the surveyor away.

The council ended. Everyone came forward and shook hands in a friendly manner. The agents and their surveyor left the island without obtaining a surrender or a survey. But their final words haunted Itawashkash and the others: they declared they would return in the spring, and Ironside said that the government would take the island, voluntarily or by force.[97]

The *Anishinaabeg* returned to their homes to complete their fishing and harvest. Itawashkash reflected as he travelled home. Even though he had expected an attempt at surrender, some of the agent's statements had astonished him. The claim that they had not fulfilled the 1836 treaty because 9,000 of them had not settled on Manitoulin was not correct. He and three other *ogimaag* had been present in 1836, and were very familiar with the rules and promises. The *Anishinaabeg* were allies of the Queen and governor but the agent had behaved as if they were subjects. His claims only strengthened Itawashkash's resolve and increased the *Anishinaabeg*'s distrust.

Ogimaa Paimoquonaishkung had also been surprised to hear Bartlett say the English were the masters of the island of the Odawa: "These words filled us with astonishment. No, we have never given up our island, not any one of our little islands. We are strongly attached to our little islands. We shall keep them for our children, to derive their subsistence from them."[98]

Two weeks later, everyone learned that once again their agent had not heard their words. He had called a council of Okemah beness' Whitefish River band and obtained another surrender of their North Shore land.[99] Though most of the band lived at Manitowaning, many of them still returned to their traditional North Shore land to fish, hunt and farm.

Yes, the *Anishinaabeg* were determined to retain Manitoulin. Now if only they could make the agents listen and understand. Just as winter set in, new rules for wood sales were posted. The words "authority from the department was required to cut or buy timber on Indian Reserves or penalties including loss of timber, fines or imprisonment could be imposed" were objectionable to most island residents. The people believed the new rules were punishment for their refusal to surrender the island.

Itawashkash knew that everyone was frustrated with the local agent's control of their wood. Not only did he keep some of the money they earned from every stick they cut, hauled and sold to steamboats, but now he forbad those at Wikwemikong to sell wood on the wharf they had built specifically for that purpose. He insisted that wood had to be delivered to him or his son, in Manitowaning or Wewebijiwang, where it was sold and a fee deducted. The fee was supposed to benefit the *Anishinaabeg*—but they had not seen any benefit.

As the number of steamboats around Manitoulin grew, so grew the demand for fuel wood. It was now the most lucrative of their resources, and moreover was not dependent on traders or the weather, as were fish, maple sugar and produce.

The new wood rules reminded the people that they must retain control of their land. Another council was called in February. Head men from all over the island gathered in Wikwemikong. The speeches continued late into the night. The people agreed unanimously to maintain their rights on the island and to prevent surveys.

Four months later, in June 1862, a council was convened in Michgiwatinong. The *Anishinaabeg* strengthened their union against cession. Once again they resorted to their only known ally, the governor, in the belief that he and the Queen were unaware of how their agents were treating the *Anishinaabeg*. They wrote to remind him of former pledges and allegiances. They asked him to preserve their island and to restore their timber and fishing rights. Paimoquonaishkung of Michigiwatinong recalled past promises made to his people and declared that they had never ceded their island or the little islands, and intended to keep them for their children. Itawashkash and 32 *ogimaag* and head men from all parts of *Odawa Minising*, including Sheshegwaning, Mindemooyasebe, Wikwemikong and Michigiwatinong, signed the petition. Itawashkash was not the only one who could recite the words:

Mitchigiwadinong, June 27th 1862
I know how you have spoken to my forefathers when you bid them go to war I wish to chase any one who comes near your lake—Your children shall possess their lands yonder. Did you say this to my forefathers at the place where the water runs into the sea?
Here is the place that will be yours. When you look around you under the vaulted

heaven looking for the support of your children, when your gaze turns towards the rising sun you shall see that sun rising red similar to the color of the coat that I wear, when it rises higher that same sun shall be very bright with light, there is the image of the life of your children. After that sun has been up a little longer you'll see in different places the flowers bloom. There is the image of the life of your children.

That is what you said, you whom we call English.

You said again, "Here I plant a tree in the centre of your little Island and I sweep the place about this tree. I laid down a mat" these are the words you have said to my forefathers. My children I place there a fire to warm you. This fire will never go out so that your children may always keep themselves warm. Moreover I pile wood for your use as fuel. I again say your fire will never go out. The Great Being hears me I say so my children.

Moreover again I place a poker, here is where I leave it, my children, poke your fire if you see that it wants to go out—ought the fire of my children ever to go out? Such will my thoughts ever be—this is what you said to my forefathers—you whom we call the English. Come on my children the Great Being is witness of what I say to you. When the world shall return to darkness it is then only that these things will end.

You afterwards promised some thing mother.

This vessel I give you, it shall never be empty my children I tie a rope to this vessel which has become yours. My children you are twelve bands in number who hear my words, you will come in the same number to draw up your vessel. If any day my children you see something wanting I shall say my children are in want of some thing. I'll go aboard the vessel I'll try to get what is wanted and I'll ship it.

And when I shall have brought it you will then draw up your vessel. This is what you have said you whom we call English.

We are still of the same number us whom we call Indian, that is to say twelve bands. It is still our number we who are living miserably here and that tree which you have spoken of does not shade us any more. It is not we who deprived it of its leaves this tree, our mind would not be so stupid as to do such a thing, it is those to whom you have given charge over our persons, those are the persons whom we blame for having deprived the tree of its leaves.

Again it is not we who have extinguished the fire at which we were warming ourselves, our mind would not be so stupid as to put out the fire at which we were warming ourselves. It is those to whom you have given the charge of it those only are the cause that our fire went out.

Again this vessel that you have promised us that you have said shall never be empty us that we call Indians, we have not destroyed that vessel, we have not emptied it, those who were in charge of our business those alone destroyed the vessel, now therefore we say to you fill the vessel tie a rope to it but a strong one and when you have filled it, we will draw up the vessel.

Here my children I make a mountain, I make it high. I place there this bird he is beautiful and white. All you Indians which are around, you will fix your looks upon him, when ever you want to tell me something, it is to him that you will confide your words and he will make them known to me. More over my children, I make a road which will convey you here, on this height that I have erected for you. I also I [*sic*] shall keep a very pretty bird and when I shall have any thing to tell you it is to him that I will speak in order that he may make known the means of supporting life to the other bird, and all the other birds about shall come to him. Those who will contradict this do not listen to them [T]his is what you have said to our chiefs which are gone. And this Ottawa, behold he was yesterday on the mountain to which our attention is now directed, now I say that we are miserable here living in anxiety here where our forefathers lived; they were the masters of this Island since a very long time and are still at present. Twenty-six years have elapsed since the Governor came here to assure us the possession of our Island, that we Indians should be the absolute masters of it and that no whites should disturb us.

There is another thing which brings revenge to our minds, it is a good word that we have heard from the mouth of the Queen's son when we went before him "I shall keep you in memory; you also keep me in mind, I give you a place in my affection." This is a word that we keep in our mind. Last fall we heard with surprise him who came here, saying that he was sent by the Queen. We English, we are the masters of this Island of Ottawas; your chiefs have ceded it said he. This word surprised us wonderfully. No we have never ceded our Island nor the little ones. We keep them for our children, to gain their livelihood on. Now again they want to trouble us, while we reflect upon in our minds the fine promises which have been made to us. But we wont [sic] take that matter into our consideration, we reject the whole proposition. This is what we have to say

I Bemigonechkang [Paimoquonaishkung] never put my name to any document, however now I put my name to this one. I also have been robbed of my fisheries which are in our reserve. Here follow the signatures: Ogimag Ottawaminissing [Chiefs of *Odawa Minising*]: Itawachkach, Chawanigwanebi, Bemossadang, Wakaosse, Naganiwina, Seianikwebato, Webean, Ketakewabi, Niganadjiwan, Bebassige [Debassige], Bemigonechkang, Ebins, Newategijig, Bebonaang, Anatin, Atwassigijig, Bikwakwade, Sosens, Wakegijig, Jako Atagewinini, Ockabewissens, Wabigekek, Michinini, William Kinechameg, Moise ozawie, Sagiwinebi, Owanegima, Gigiebinessi, Makate Ottawa, Ganassawe, Makosid, Kitchigekek, Madjik.[100]

Itawashkash also knew that the people of Michigiwatinong and Wikwemikong had written another protest letter a month later. They complained about timber regulations, fishing leases, the superintendent, the doctor and government interference:

Mitchikiwatinong and Wikwemikong the 21st July 1862.
The Indians having assembled discoursed amongst themselves as to the manner in which they are treated here in the Island of Ottawas, and also they recalled to their minds how their forefathers used to make use of language of such a good character that it was calculated to maintain fraternity and union—the next thing that they treated about was their own welfare that they should have every thing that was requisite for them.

1. They desire to sell wood to the steam boats and to make the wharf profitable to them which they built last summer. They also remarked that as soon as they had built the wharf, public notice was given to the whites not to buy any wood from the Indians, fire wood or wood for building purposes. Now then our chiefs request of His Excellency (to whom they make these representations) to give liberty to those who are willing to buy from the Indians their fire wood some of which is deposited for sale at <u>Point aux Cranes</u> (North East of the Island)

2. They strongly recommend to His Excellency's consideration the conduct of Wabiniokwan (Mr. Ironside) at Port Sarnia, at the arrival of the Prince of Wales, medals were given to chiefs some of whom were not fit to hold that office, this is what Mr. Ironside did.

3. They want to make new chiefs, this has been going on for some time since last winter, they made proposals to two men, but nothing resulted from them, the subject

of these proposals was this: you must agree to give up the Island when ever we ask you for it. The man who has been employed to effect this is Isaac Assiginak. We cannot help making this reflection: To come to the point at once, are we to make new chiefs to deprive us of our land? And this is not the first time that this has been attempted. As for us we wish to choose our own chiefs in accordance with Indian custom we have had as chiefs for a long time those descendant from our ancestors, and these are those whom we wish to have over us.

4. The Medical Man does not do his duty here, when we go for him, he does not always come but only some times but very seldom. It is only when we bring a horse for him, and not all the Indians have a horse.

5. The fishing locations are own property in as much as they are our Islands. They told us that the Indians would receive payment, but we have not received any. We demand payment forthwith for we dont [sic] know what that promise will amount to. Now that the lease of the location is over, we require that they be not leased any more. This is what we have to say.[101]

The *Anishinaabeg* of Wikwemikong followed *Nosse* Choné's advice and formed a council to make and carry out new regulations. The people assembled several times. They named councillors and drew up regulations. Although the council was not yet permanently constituted, Itawashkash heard that some of the elders were already exercising some surveillance in the summer of 1862.[102]

The agent continued to approach *ogimaag* about ceding their land, offering 100 acres of land for each family and a bonus of money. People were refusing, but the agent was telling them that everyone else was in favour of a treaty.

While the agent pushed for surrender, the *Anishinaabeg* were distracted by more wood rules. New advertisements appeared, stating that "cutting timber or staves or wood for any purpose upon Indian lands, except by licence" had "been rendered unlawful," and warning that "Indians or others, offending against the said statues will be prosecuted with vigor" as of 7 August 1862.[103] This was a much harsher stance than previous timber rules, warning that even the *Anishinaabeg* would be prosecuted.

This was too much. Itawashkash and the *ogimaag* and men of Michigiwatinong, Sheshegwaning and Wikwemikong protested:

Protest of the Indians of Manitoulin Island against the Notice from Quebec, Indian Department, of 7 August 1862. Translation. Wikwemikong 25 [29] August 1862.
On the 26th of August a notice from Quebec was posted here secretly that announced a law of Canada.

It said that the Indians can no longer cut their own wood, that they can no longer make planks or barrels, or anything else!! This is how they watch over us Indians—we may not cut wood anywhere! Why do they treat us so, we, the residents of the island of the Ottawas, known masters or proprietors of this island. It's reprehensible!

That should not have happened. It is very disgraceful. And another shameful thing is that they put up the notice in secret, on Sunday and during mass.

There is a lack of understanding.

Shouldn't someone act in broad daylight if one wants to establish a rule? To act in darkness is not good, it's disgraceful.

Great Chief, I ask you: what do you think if someone is forbidden to touch something that belongs to him? What do you think if someone forbids its use? What if someone breaks your bed into pieces? What do you think of someone who acts thus?

Think about this question.
For my part, I do not view it favourably when someone forbids me the use of my own property.
You want to treat me like a beast. If someone takes an animal and ensures that it can no longer go anywhere, it shall perish with hunger.
And if it gets cold, very cold, it shall perish on the spot. That is how you want to treat me. It must not be so.
Do not forbid the steamboats to buy my wood at my wharf at Skull Point, so I may sell the wood to obtain farming implements and clothing for myself. That is all. Thomas Mokomanish, Wakegishik, Jako Atagewinini, Omikamigo, Okakogan, Kitchiosawesi, Debasig, bemigoneshkang, Enbins, Newategishik, Itawashkash, Shawanigwanebi, Bemosadang, Wakaose, Semikebato, Naganiwina.[104]

It seemed to Itawashkash that the very existence of the *Anishinaabeg* of Manitoulin Island was threatened. Treaties had been signed, and more treaties were being pressed upon them. While some *ogimaag* considered ceding more mainland North Shore lands, most were adamant that Manitoulin Island should be retained for their descendants. The regulation of the fishing and timber industries upset traditional employment and income. Some traders used liquor and high prices to keep the *Anishinaabeg* in debt. Advice and pressure confused the issue. The government agent pushed for a land surrender; the Roman Catholic priests discouraged surrender and encouraged the *Anishinaabeg* to organize and protest; the Protestant minister supported the superintendent's position on surrender.

Everyone knew which *ogimaag* had yielded to the agent's persuasion. Some appeared to have given in to presents and promises, though Itawashkash also knew that his father and others who had served the Queen and King in their wars had given their word of loyalty. To them, a man's word was all-important. This was their reason for capitulation, not the presents or promises. He also knew the young men of the island did not understand this, and this was causing rifts in families.

The government agent's promises were tempting, and his threats were growing. Promises of farms, markets, employment and, especially, instruction for the young were hard to resist. So was the threat that if they did not cede their land to the government, others who were less honest men would come and take the lands piece by piece.

Itawashkash knew the agent had an odd idea of who was a chief. It was based on loyalty and obedience to the Indian Department. The *Anishinaabeg*, on the other hand, elected *ogimaag* whose qualifications included leadership qualities as well as a hereditary claim to the office. He knew Tomah, Taibosegai, Paimoquonaishkung and Wakekijik remained opposed to any further surrenders, but a few others were less committed, and were therefore more easily swayed by promises and threats.[105]

Itawashkash continued to reflect as he travelled toward the place where the sun rises.

The Treaty and the *Ogimaag* of *Odawa Minising*
When Itawashkash arrived in Manitowaning at dusk on Friday, 3 October 1862, the shore was overcrowded with boats and men. He was pleased to see so many people gathered to meet the new agents. He went immediately to his father's house to pay his respects and to greet his brothers. Though they did not always agree, they were family.

Ascending the hill, he spotted his younger brother. Francis Assiginack stood out in any crowd. His tall, lean form was easily recognized, and a sharp white collar emphasized his jet-black hair and dark, piercing eyes. Though he was well into his third decade, he still looked like the youth who had once raced on foot against a mounted British officer and won.[106] As a child, he easily mastered not only the skills of a warrior but also the languages of the agents and the priests. He read, wrote and translated better than anyone. His father and the agent had decided that he should be sent away to continue his education. And just as Itawashkash had feared, he had not returned. Francis now worked for the Indian Department and was clearly here to assist the agents. Three years earlier he had acted as witness and interpreter for the North Shore treaties. Francis had always wanted to study medicine, but the agents had denied him further training once he proved useful to them. If he had realized his dream, thought Itawashkash, he might have returned to his people.

Francis looked almost relieved to see him. He quickly explained that he was here to act as interpreter for the two most important men in the Indian Department. Francis apologized for his inability to sit and visit, but he had to work. Itawashkash respected his commitment but regretted his allegiance to the enemy.

Itawashkash continued on to his father's house. It was a gathering place for Catholic residents and visitors, but was unusually quiet on this day. Itawashkash was shocked to see how his father had aged. He was dressed in his finery, just as he had been exactly one year earlier, but he appeared shrunken, tired, even old. His fine blue cloth coat decorated with golden buttons and epaulettes, his crimson sash, his boots and his fancy plumed hat could not hide the fact that his polished medals weighed down the emaciated old man. They greeted each other politely but did not discuss the reason they were gathered. They shared news of family and their communities. They both knew that tomorrow they would battle with words.

Itawashkash returned to the shore to greet his fellow *ogimaag*.[107] He approached his Michigiwatinong neighbours Paimoquonaishkung, Taibosegai, Naiwotaikezhik and Abence. They shared Itawashkash's desire for independence from Wikwemikong, for education for their young people and for maintaining their allegiance to the Roman Catholic religion.

Paimoquonaishkung was the senior *ogimaa* at Michigiwatinong.[108] He had signed both the 1836 Manitowaning treaty and the 1850 Robinson treaty. Though he lived on the island, he had reserved tract number 1 at Maganetawang River on the mainland for his band in 1850. The land reservations on the North Shore were valuable, since Manitoulin Island lacked game. This was why many men travelled to the mainland to hunt to feed their families. Paimoquonaishkung had been an outspoken critic of the local agent for many years. His words had been written down and sent to the governor, but had not produced any results.

Louis Taibosegai[109] was the son of *Ogimaa* Niibaakhom and the grandson of the renowned warrior and *ogimaa* Oga, the Pickerel, of Drummond Island. Taibosegai settled at Michigiwatinong in 1847 with 31 band members, emigrants from Drummond Island via Coldwater, Beausoleil Island and, most recently, Wikwemikong. They were emigrants due to government actions rather than personal choice.

Abence (or Ebins)[110] was descended from Drummond Island *ogimaa* and orator Ashagashinh (or Shageshi). Abence formerly lived on the North Shore, but had been living at Michigiwatinong for many years.

Naiwotaikezhik[111] stood with the *ogimaag*. Though still a young man, he was known to be steady and industrious.

Itawashkash strode over to greet the *ogimaag* of Wikwemikong: Tomah Kinojameg, Louis Wakekijik and Ominikamigo; and leading men Francis Metosage and Jako Atagiwinini. Though the former three had been *ogimaag* for less than two years, they were all senior men with hereditary and proven leadership claims to the office. They were not pawns of the agent or the priests but independent thinkers.

Tomah Kinojameg (or Mokomanish)[112] had been elected *ogimaa* of Wikwemikong in June 1861 in the place of his recently deceased father, *Ogimaa* Michel Cainooshimague (Michel Kinojameg). Tomah was a vocal opponent of surrender and had played a role in deposing the pro-surrender *ogimaag* the previous year. Like Itawashkash, Tomah's grandfather, also known as *Ogimaa* Mokomanish (or Frederic Bebametabi), was listed as a chief entitled to an annuity on the March 1836 Michigan Peninsula treaty and was a signatory on the 1836 Manitowaning treaty.

Louis Wakekijik[113] was the son of *Ogimaa* Vincent Paimosegai (Bemassige or Essiban), who was listed as a second class chief entitled to an annuity on the March 1836 Michigan Peninsula treaty and also a signatory of the 1836 Manitowaning treaty. Wakekijik had been elected *ogimaa* in June 1861 to replace Mocotaishegun and Tehkummah, who favoured surrender.

Augustin Ominikamigo (or Nessegigabow),[114] the son of *Ogimaa* Antoine Makons (or Little Bear), had also been elected *ogimaa* in June 1861 when the two pro-surrender *ogimaag* were deposed.

Francis Metosage[115] was the son of *Ogimaa* Vincent Paimosegai and the brother of *Ogimaa* Louis Wakekijik. Francis was a literate resident of Wikwemikong who acted as secretary to the Wikwemikong *ogimaag* in the 1860s.

Jako Atagiwinini[116] was the son of aged *Ogimaa* J.B. Atagiwinini (or Tahgaiwenne), who had emigrated from Drummond Island to Coldwater and then to Manitoulin Island. The senior Atagiwinini signed Robinson's North Shore treaty of 1850, but had reserved land between Nipissing and Whitefish lakes for his band. Jako Atagiwinini and his father were examples of the attitudes of different generations in a family towards surrender. The older *ogimaag* and men, those who had fought for Britain, believed they must continue to prove their loyalty by respecting the Queen's wish for a surrender of their land. The younger men believed the Queen's or her agent's interference in their fish and wood trade proved how badly the *Anishinaabeg* would be treated if they gave up ownership of their land. Itawashkash was not surprised that elderly J.B. Atagiwinini was nowhere to be seen. The old man was blind and frail. Itawashkash also knew that J.B. Atagiwinini, like his own father, was vulnerable to the agent's demands of loyalty.

Itawashkash saw Louis Tehkummah and Mocotaishegun, the *ogimaag* who had been deposed the previous year, standing alone near the agent's house. He knew they continued to support the agent. Tehkummah (or Tekamosimo)[117] had moved to Wikwemikong from L'Arbre Croche, Michigan. Itawashkash recalled that Tehkummah was the youngest Odawa *ogimaa* in Wikwemikong when he had left the settlement almost 20 years earlier. Mocotaishegun[118] had also emigrated from Michigan to Wikwemikong.

Itawashkash saw, but did not approach, the Wewebijiwang (or Petit Courant) men camped at the far end of the shore: George Obettossoway, Kushkewahbic and Shewetagun.

George Obettossoway[119] was the grandson of *Ogimaa* George Abram Obettossoway, who had died the previous winter. The Obettossoways and three or four other families had moved from Manitowaning to Wewebijiwang (Petit Courant) in 1854 to supply wood to steamboats, and all were reported to be doing very well for themselves. George had married an Irish-American woman who had worked for the Church of England missionary in Manitowaning. George had embraced many of the English agent's and missionary's traditions. He wore what appeared to be one of their jackets, and a round hat. George Obettossoway could have been a perfect model for what the agent praised as "enfranchisement." Itawashkash and the senior Obettossoway had shared a common desire for education for the young. The old *ogimaa* had repeatedly asked the English church people to send them a teacher, but he had no more success than Itawashkash had been with his requests for teachers from the Catholic *nosse*.

The other Wewebijiwang men camped with George Obettossoway were Kushkewahbic (or Columbus),[120] who by 1857 was an Odawa *ogimaa* of the 47-member Petit Courant band, and Joseph Shewetagun (or Salter),[121] an Ojibwe *ogimaa* and resident of Petit Courant who was receiving annuity payments for 125 band members in 1862.

The Manitowaning residents were standing together greeting friends and relatives up in the village. Itawashkash saw *Ogimaa* John Maishegonggai, *Ogimaa* Okemah beness, Charles Keghikgoobeness and Baibomsai.

John Maishegonggai (Mejakwange)[122] was an Ojibwe *ogimaa* born at Sheguiandah, Manitoulin Island, who moved to Manitowaning after the 1836 treaty. He had signed the 1850 Robinson Huron treaty, reserving tract number 13 at Ogawaminang (or French River) on the north shore of Lake Huron for his band. Itawashkash had heard that he had recently rejoined the Church of England.

Okemah beness[123] had become *ogimaa* of Asinmatwai (Ringing Stone or Bell Rock) at Whitefish River in 1858, after *Ogimaa* James Wahbegakake (White

Hawk) had died in Manitowaning. Wahbegakake had signed the 1850 Robinson Huron treaty, reserving tract number 4 around Shebawahning for his band. Okemah beness signed surrenders with Superintendent Ironside in 1859 and 1861, ceding some of his band's land at Whitefish River, though the former surrender was rejected as unofficial and the latter was considered invalid, since its provisions were not carried out by the government.

Baibomsai[124] was a member of *Ogimaa* Okemah beness' Whitefish River band who lived in Manitowaning. He was a descendant of the grand *ogimaa*, Shauwanausoway (One With His Face To The West or From The South), who signed the 1836 Manitowaning treaty. The artist Paul Kane made a drawing of Shauwanausoway when he visited Manitowaning at the time of the annual presents in 1845, the same event where he had captured Itawashkash's likeness on paper.

Charles Keghikgoobeness[125] was also descended from the famed medicine man and *ogimaa* Shauwanausoway. Kezhikgoobeness was a member of *Ogimaa* Okemah beness' Whitefish River band, living at Manitowaning.

Itawashkash did not see Church of England minister Peter Jacobs,[126] who some called an *Anishinaabe* of Manitowaning, but who Itawashkash considered another pawn of the government. Jacobs, like Itawashkash's brother Francis, was the son of a well-known *Anishinaabe* spokesperson and had been educated at a boarding school—and considered by the agents to be "civilized."

Itawashkash was surprised to see *Ogimaa* Pahtahdagwishkung[127] of Naimonakekong. He had lived on the land between Michigiwatinong and Sheshegwaning since long before the treaties. He was fiercely independent and rejected government or missionary interference of any kind.

Also from the western part of Manitoulin Island was Wahcowsai,[128] a Potawatomi whose band lived about six miles south of Sheshegwaning, at the big hill. Like Itawashkash, he had attended the 1836 Manitowaning treaty.

Itawashkash was happy to see his old friend Sakiwinebi,[129] who lived with his band at Mindemooyasebe (or Sand Bay) on the island's south shore. Sakiwinebi was dressed for the occasion. He was painted and wore a robe of hawk's feathers. He continued to refuse religion and government interference.

Before heading back up into the village, Itawashkash acknowledged aged *Ogimaa* Waibenessieme[130] from Achitwaigunning on the west side of South Bay. Though he was a devout member of the English church, most of his band members avoided religion.

Itawashkash was pleased with the attendance. Almost everyone he expected to see was there. This was the second year in a row that the agents had demanded their presence during the important autumn fishing season. The council meeting looked promising. Now, feeling as if he had just accomplished a successful roll call, he climbed the slope from the shore to the village, thinking he would like to look at the new government agents before retiring for the evening.

Itawashkash did not sleep well. He awoke early to a bleak and windy dawn. There were no bright, warm rays of autumn sun. The red maple leaves rustled and fell silently onto the land. Though men filled the tiny village and shore, it was surprisingly quiet. There was no joy in this reunion of the people. Men nodded greetings but passed each other in silence. Itawashkash walked alone through the throng of *Anishinaabeg* to the rickety government warehouse, where he climbed the stairs and sat down on the floor with his fellow *ogimaag*. Within minutes of the *ogimaag* entering, several hundred men filled the space in the room behind them and overflowed down the stairs onto the ground below.

Once again, Itawashkash was the spokesperson for the people of *Odawa Minising*. As was his way, he remained silent, watching and listening until it was his turn to speak.

The first thing he noticed was that the agents did not appear surprised or frightened by this show of strength. He knew then that they had been well advised, and that this day might not end as surely and swiftly as he hoped.

Itawashkash focused on the council. He intended to listen to the agent's English words, as well as the translation. At least the translator spoke his language well; who better than your own brother to interpret the speeches? Sometimes he had to depend on the Reverend Jacobs or Charles de Lamorandière, both fair men but less skilled in the island words.

He concentrated on the proceedings and depended on others to recount the day. He had to listen to their words and watch the language of their bodies. (Later, when he heard the account of the negotiations as repeated and recorded by the people of Wikwemikong, it all came back to him only too clearly. That is, the written words were clear, but the actual event was as a dream, a bad dream in which he had lost control.)

The two great English men sat and waited. The *ogimaag* also sat and waited. Itawashkash saw his brother Francis rise and speak to the agents. Only then did Commissioner of Crown Lands William McDougall understand and act. He rose and came to give his hand to the *ogimaag*. Then McDougall spoke:[131]

> My comrades, my Indian friends, the time has come to explain to you why I have come here to your island. The Great Chief has given me the job of taking care of you. I am the head of the Indian department and it is in this capacity that I come to ask you for your little island. I have not entrusted anyone with my commission. I come myself to bring you this decision. I have thought about settling what may be advantageous for you. I do not want to treat you in a way that may hurt you. I have hurried despite the multiplicity of my jobs; as I have not only you to occupy myself with where I come from. But the thought of coming to see you has prevailed.
>
> There are a great number of people from all around who look at your island. And they do not look at one single place to settle themselves but on a great number of places. If you do not accept what I propose to you today, all your efforts will not be enough to repel the farmers; nor even mine, nor those of the Great Chief; and you shall find yourself put aside without any benefit. If on the contrary you give me your land today, you shall congratulate yourself on the benefit that it shall bring to you. This is why I thought I must come quickly to work for your well-being. If you do not accept the offer that I bring you today, perhaps others shall come and shall treat you in a way that may not be good for you. Perhaps I shall not be a long time in the first position. Some of those of whom I speak have plans, without grounds, it is true, to take your land from you. This is how they think: The Great Chief, F.B. Head, decided that all the Indians of the area should come to settle here. That has not taken place. Consequently, if one really wanted to consider these things one should say: You are not owners of the island, as the condition laid out has not been fulfilled.

You alone are not in sufficient numbers to occupy it. You unnecessarily encumber this fine land. There are a great number from below the flowing water who want to cultivate this land. They also want to go farther west to find land to cultivate.

As for those who came last autumn. Certainly, they came by commission. Someone here said that they came without a commission. Assuredly, they were sent. But also certainly, they promised you too little. Assuredly, one cannot live with so little. They said to you that you are not owners of the island. Today I do not say that to you. Assuredly, you are owners of the island.

If you make me a cession of it now, I shall treat you perfectly well. It will be a way, a reason, for me to watch over you. I shall give you an authentic title, called a *Deed*, which will assure you your ownership. You shall choose good land and it is there that you shall live from now on. When the survey is done, they will give you 12 months to make your choice. You may not choose where there is a river as that would obstruct the building of a flourmill or a sawmill; nor in the bays that could serve as harbours for vessels. You shall not be there. You must make your choice somewhere in the centre of the island. Your choice made—it is only then that they shall sell. The Great Chief does not want to have the money from the sale. It shall be for you. What remains after paying the surveyors shall be put in the bank and the interest shall always be paid to you.

If you accept the proposals that I make you today, you shall be perfectly happy. The Whites shall come here in great numbers bringing with them all sorts of things. There will be farmers and merchants. Everything will be very cheap. You shall no longer have trouble with anything. You shall not be obliged to go find someone to exchange your products. You shall receive fair payment for them. It shall no longer happen, like in the past that you may be deceived. From now on you shall be treated well in all things. You shall have all with ease; they shall bring everything here. There will be flour mills, sawmills and forges here near you. You shall not go far for your farming tools. You shall be, in short, surrounded with all the care of the Great Chief.

It is also very advantageous for the Great Chief to have this island, as it is principally here that he will derive what is necessary to make a road for fire wagons on the mainland as far as the top of the flowing water.

This is the land they shall give you each: a family, 100 acres; a young man over 21 years, 50 acres; a young male orphan of 21 years, 100 acres. And the payment that people give to the Great Chief (taxes), you shall not give it; and your children shall be well instructed.

I have learned that you came with weapons. And I also, I have come with the force of the Great Chief. Anyone who wants to use violence against those who speak shall be treated severely. Everyone must be free to speak; all must express their thoughts.

I invite anyone to speak who wants to. Or perhaps you want to think and deliberate first on the proposals that I made you.

Itawashkash responded that the people wanted time to consider. McDougall agreed to this, but Pekoneiassong insisted that he should make their thoughts known to him immediately. He urged Itawashkash to tell McDougall that they wanted to hold this thing that they came to ask for; to hold it firm, insist that there was nothing new to consider.

McDougall went out and the *Anishinaabeg* reflected on his words. Once again they said together: "We have not thought for an instant to give up our land that they came to ask us for as we do not own any other land anywhere else. It is all that remains ours."

Then they recalled what they had been promised. Only adult men would receive 100 little measures, "acres," by family. And the young people of 21 years, 50 little measures. The orphaned young men of 21 years, also 100 little measures. That was all. But there were also a great number of children: little boys, little girls from 1 year to 20 years, and those who are born today and who shall be born after, to consider. They mulled all those things and thought they must not harm their existing children or those who shall be born. The people agreed: "If we give up our land, they would not have any property."

When the English chief returned, Itawashkash spoke:

> My brother, I will make known our thoughts to you, having first reflected on the words that you addressed to us. It is not the first time that we considered these things. No, we think of them always. This is my thought: I hold onto my land, I do not cede it. What I said last autumn when they came to make me this request is still my thought and my word today. Always, I too, I want to keep my land for my children, the little land that I still possess. It is here that the Great Spirit has given me to live and I do not want to give it up. For you, it is over there on the other side of the great water that has been given to you to live. And it is over there, that the measurement that you name is probably held, not here. It is necessary to deal with you quickly, as we have a great deal of work to do, collecting what we have grown. None of us that you see here were at rest. You delay us. You must hurry to finish. These are the thoughts of my chiefs present here for whom I speak.

McDougall responded that he had come to hear their thoughts, but it was pointless to resist. The Great Chief wanted their land. Others would come and talk to them, not in council together but individually. Those who accepted would have their word taken, then their land. Other people who lived beyond the flowing water spoke just as the people of Manitoulin had—that the Great Being had given them their land, but they had ceded their land. "You will not be able to stop them in spite of all your efforts to dismiss them. I shall not be able to either, nor the Great Chief himself. They will come here to put up their camps despite you."

He said the people from Wikwemikong could return to their work. He would not speak to them further. If some of them liked what he said and accepted his proposal, he would speak to them after Sunday passed.

Itawashkash's 94-year-old father Jean-Baptiste Assiginack spoke to the English chief: "I give you my hand, my father. I clasp yours with all my strength and I embrace the queen."

Then Assiginack spoke to the *Anishinaabeg*: "My little brothers, my co-Otawas. I am the first born of all of us on the island of the Otawas. In fact I am the first born of all the chiefs and warriors. You have no reason to say: my ancestor lived here. You have originated in various places. Only the ancestor of the Otawa lived here. For me, my Otawa ancestor has been over there where the sun sets. It is from there that I came. Over there at Madjitashki, as they say. I lived and then I came here. That is why I think I am owner here, and I yield all that I possess."

Assiginack's words excited the people. Itawashkash noticed that his brothers moved in to protect the aged speaker. Wikwemikong's Jako Atagiwinini arose while Assiginack was speaking, though the agent tried to stop him. They traded words. Jako said that the chiefs wanted him to speak. Assiginack asked him to identify himself and Jako replied that he was Jako the son of Atagiwinini. But Assiginack replied that his word was rubbish, without value. Jako countered that Assiginak was too old to speak, that he was not capable of dealing with the matters being discussed.

Then Jako addressed McDougall. He acknowledged that he was delighted to see him, as he wanted to see and hear the head man and to have the head man hear him, an *Anishinaabe* who people called an Indian. "My brother, now my chiefs express their thoughts to you: Is it really now that the good fortune of the Indians begins. Now that you come to ask him for all his land?" Jako said that the people who ceded the main land had not received what they had been promised. They were promised four *piastres*, the price of the pants he wore. But his pants came from the maple sugar from the island's trees not from a land payment. Jako remarked that he was a chief of the mainland that his father ceded to the Great Woman Chief, and if his father had been able, it would have been him speaking to McDougall. He said that he was not ashamed to display his poverty. He was astonished that the Great Woman Chief, whose riches were reputed to overflow in her own land, needed their land. Those who had ceded already were poor. "This is what my chiefs say to you through me: we do not give up this land that you come to ask us for. I am still astonished by what you said: that the little number should perhaps have the right to make this cession! Such a thing never happens. It is the greater number; the majority who decide what must be done. And now you say: There are perhaps some here who like what I say and who accept it. No, as for me, I shall not reject a gift that you want to make me of your property; but I, my property, I shall never listen to you that you want me to give you."

Jako advised McDougall that he was surprised the agents said his land was excellent. He described it as full of rocks, with many lakes and swamps. He said that there was not enough good land for ten of McDougall's farmers. He stated that he was unable to make anything grow on rocks, and that he would not waste the Great Chief's money by saying the land was good.

Sakiwinebi then spoke briefly. He declared that Assiginack, who had spoken so proudly, was descended from a man who had been captured where the sun sets, that he was an Akiwewigiwamê. He dismissed Assiginack as a slave who did not speak truthfully in saying that he, Assiginack, alone was Odawa.

Some of the *Anishinaabeg* agreed. But Francis Assiginack declared that it was shameful to speak thus to their elder, who was already so near to death. Sakiwinebi replied that the elder Assiginack should not have spoken as he did either, that he had almost caused a riot. Francis insisted the matter would be decided by the *Anishinaabeg* together, and not by Assiginack alone.

The day's meeting ended late on Saturday. On Sunday some went to Wikwemikong for prayers, Taibosegai and Wahcowsai among them. Itawashkash remained in Manitowaning with his family. There were many men from all parts of the Island of the Odawas biding time until the following day in order that they might speak. They felt they knew how to hold onto their land that the outsiders were demanding.

Itawashkash struggled to remember the events of Sunday night. Miskomanatons had *l'eau de feu*, firewater, and he gave it to others to drink. Itawashkash was invited by his brother to share in the drink and the talk; he resisted, but eventually joined in. They talked of ceding the land, but he refused to consider it. He drank, and lost consciousness. During that time of talk and drink he gave his word; he said: I cede. He could not take back his word.[132]

When it was light, the others reminded him of his words. They went to see *Ogimaa* John Maishegonggai (Mejakwange) and he related the promises made them: that they should be first chiefs, respected by all the Whites, honoured and in a state of perfect wellbeing, forever.

McDougall called on them individually and promised that he would treat them well. Then they gave their word to him. Itawashkash and three others had given their word before the others returned from Wikwemikong.

When the others returned they reminded Itawashkash of the resolutions made and confirmed together to preserve the island for present and future children in order to live there always, together, in union and in peace. Itawashkash could not explain his decision. He had yielded.

He knew the island belonged to the people. He recalled their three titles to ownership: the land that our ancestors have always lived on, from the beginning until now; the land that was given to our fathers, including several still living, after their service in the wars; and the land of the Island of the Odawas that was given to the *Anishinaabe* only, by the Great Chief F.B. Head in council at Manitowaning.

When the returning *Anishinaabe* learned of the action, *Ogimaa* Wakekijik asked the men of Wikwemikong if they still wanted to hold onto the land they possessed in common, and if they did, to raise their arms and respond. They all raised their arms and responded together. Wakekijik asked again and they responded again, louder. He asked a third time and they responded even louder: "With all our strength we hold it, we do not give it up."

Wakekijik then acknowledged that some were known to think differently, that Tekoman (Tehkummah) wanted to give up the island for some time, but had not spoken. He asked those who thought like Tekoman to join him where he stood. A single person went to join him. At this point Wakekijik said: "Those who hold onto their land come where I am." And the rest went to his side.

When McDougall returned it was past mid-day. He said he was surprised to see so many from Wikwemikong and that he would speak to them again, but his words would be the same as before. He hoped they had reflected and would accept his proposal. He said that he brought money that he had borrowed from the Great Chief to give them if they agreed. When the land was sold the money would be paid back to the Great Chief. He said he heard that they had come armed before, but he learned from the interpreter the nature of their actions.

Jako Atagiwinini rose once again to speak for the Wikwemikong chiefs. He spoke well for one who was still just the son of a chief. "My brother! Our elders have spoken of a perfectly beautiful bird. It is with its feathers, that I want to dust your ears, so that you really hear all that I say to you." He said that he was happy to see McDougall, and happy that McDougall could see his brothers who lived on the island. He reminded all that the Great Spirit who made all things had permitted this occasion. He acknowledged that McDougall appeared fine, handsome and White, with a pure white heart. He said they were content that their brothers had surrendered their good land, but "for us, absolutely, we do not want to surrender our land." He said if all the promises were kept, they might consider his proposals in the future. He said he spoke for all his Wikwemikong chiefs.

The ceding chiefs then spoke in turn in favour of the proposal. *Ogimaa* John Maishegonggai said he accepted the proposal and ceded what he and those with him of the Anglican prayers possessed: from the middle of Manitowaning Bay to the entrance to Atchitawaiganing Bay. He asked the government to be good to his children if they were in poverty somewhere. He said he had been promised happiness before when asked for his land, but he had not received what had been promised and hoped that now they would see happiness. Then he spoke to the Odawas. He asked that they not bear a grudge against them for what they had done, as "they came to ask us; it is not us who went over there to surrender our land." He promised to remain good brothers and hoped that they would also.

Itawashkash spoke after Maishegonggai, saying the proposal appeared good, that he accepted it, and that he ceded all he possessed. He claimed for his band the land at the great strait, which McDougall agreed he could have if there was land there to give. He asked that their brothers of Wikwemikong be left in possession of their land.

Taibosegai followed next. He acknowledged the presence of the Great Being and accepted the proposal. He claimed the land where he was, but McDougall said such a claim would obstruct settlement and Taibosegai must move. Then Taibosegai asked that his elder brother, the Wikwemikong Odawa, be left in possession of their land.

Tekoman (or Tehkummah) surprised no one when he said he accepted the proposal. For a long time he had endorsed it because, he said, his chief, Wabiwiokwan (Ironside), had made it known to him. He asked for a strong paper that he might be complete owner of the land that McDougall gave him. But McDougall said that the land at Wikwemikong was not surrendered and he should come to this side of the island for a title.

Paimoquonaishkung spoke next. He reminded the English chief that he had ceded the mainland long ago and had not seen the promises kept, that he had not been paid well, and that he had ceded again and not ever been paid. He had been told that the Great Woman Chief and the Great Chief also had wanted his land, so he ceded. They promised him the payment would triple, and now again he heard that they would pay well. But then he too accepted the proposal. He also asked that their brothers the Odawas be left in possession of their land and hoped they would remain good friends.

Wahcowsai also accepted the proposal and claimed his reserve where he was settled in the island's interior. He acknowledged that the promised happiness might not arrive soon. Then he also asked that their brothers of Wikwemikong be left in possession of all that they had now. He declared: "He is truly Otawa; he is the first owner of this land."

Waibenessieme spoke last, and claimed his reserve in his field where the rocks were interrupted.

McDougall spoke again. He assured those from Wikwemikong that they would remain owners of their land from the middle of Manitowaning Bay as far as that of Atchitawaiganing at the entrance to the lake, and they would also have a valid title. But as they had too much land for their number, he asked that they would take in those who had no land. He reminded them that they might cede in future if they saw those who surrendered were comfortable. Then he declared that the residents of Wikwemikong would not be given any of the money paid for the island, that none of those who received the payment for the island would remain in the reserve, as those there would have only land.

He thanked the chiefs who accepted the propositions and assured them that he would keep his promises and provide a title of their mutual agreement. He said the mainland that had been surrendered might not have provided the profit expected. And while he could not tell them how much they would be paid, the next day at 10 o'clock the agent would give them a dollar or two or three when they put their names on the paper.

Jako Atagiwinini rose one last time and said that his chiefs wanted him to speak. He thanked McDougall for his words and said they understood now that they were the owners of their land and they would receive their brothers if they were wandering in poverty. They did not envy the payment the others would receive, he said, but that they wanted the obstacle, the rule, removed that prevented them from earning income by selling firewood.

The great English chief said that he did not have the power to lift the obstacle, but he would ask the governor to repeal the law that forbad them from selling their wood and perhaps it might be lifted. The council ended with the shaking of hands.

On Tuesday, 7 October 1862, Itawashkash and his fellow ceding *ogimaag* assembled in the government agent's office. The papers were laid on the table, read and interpreted.[133]

Then the names and dodem marks of J.B. Assiginack, Maishegonggai, Okemah beness, Benjamin Assiginack, Waibenessieme, Shewetagun, George Obettossoway, Paimoquonaishkung, Abence, Taibosegai, Atowishcosh [Itawashkash], Naiwataikezhik, Wahcowsai, Kushkewahbic, Baibomsai, Keghikgoobeness and Pahtahdagwishkung were inscribed on the paper. Tehkummah signed "as one of the chiefs of the Wequaimekong band," "in testimony of his general approval and his assent as an individual to all the terms of the above agreement." Paimsahdang witnessed his signature.

The English chief William McDougall and his deputy William Spragge signed their names. Their agent George Ironside, the agent's son, the doctor, the English minister, Eshkamejwanoke the fishery inspector, three of the English chief's friends and Itawashkash's brother, Francis, also put their names to the paper.

After signing, a few hundred dollars were divided among the chiefs for themselves and their bands. The money varied from one to two dollars, the government's understanding being that these were the "amounts that though not given as a gratuity, were promised advances upon the anticipated profits to be derived from the sale of the lands in the island."[134]

Of the eighteen signatories, six were from Manitowaning, four from Michigiwatinong, three from Wewebijiwang, and one each from Sheshegwaning, Big Hill, South Bay West, Naimonakekong and Wikwemikong. Three had signed the 1836 Manitowaning treaty and two had signed the 1850 Robinson Huron treaty. Ten of the fourteen chiefs the local agent had invited to meet the Prince of Wales in Sarnia in 1860 were signatories. Three signatories were members of the Assiginack family.

The superintendents achieved their desired treaty. Itawashkash knew that he, Taibosegai, Paimoquonaishkung, Tomah, Wakekijik and Metosage had been managed at the negotiations. The first three were persuaded or intimidated over the course of the weekend, and the latter three silenced by removing their territory from the discussion. After Itawashkash yielded, the others fell like trees succumbing to fire. In addition to the threats, Itawashkash knew promises had been made. Baibomsai and Maishegonggai were promised land at Sheguiandah, and George Obettossaway was assured that he alone could remain at Petit Courant. Itawashkash's own father Jean-Baptiste Assiginack, feeble in body and mind, had signed to honour his pledge of loyalty to the Crown. Itawashkash was unable to explain his own part in the surrender, except to say that he and others had been afraid of losing all and gaining nothing.

After the money was disbursed, the *Anishinaabeg* returned to their homes, or at least the then-current site of their homes, since many of them would soon be relocated as a result of the treaty.

When Itawashkash later reflected on the extraordinary events of 1861 and 1862, perhaps he would recall *Ogimaa* John Maishegonggai's thoughts: "the future will tell what Indians will be better off, you who refuse to make a treaty, or we who consented to make it."[135]

Chapter 3
L'île Manitouline and Père Jean-Pierre Choné

Jean-Pierre Choné
On Friday, 3 October 1862, the steamboat *Ploughboy* arrived in Manitowaning Bay at midday. This was unusual. Steamboats usually avoided the shallow bay and stopped instead at Petit Courant and Shebawahning on their route between Collingwood and Sault Ste. Marie. People around the bay took notice, and when some very elegant gentlemen disembarked and were escorted immediately to the *surintendant*'s own house, news of their arrival spread across the island like a forest fire.

Seven miles away in Wikwemikong, Père Jean-Pierre Choné was disturbed by loud voices outside his window. He had sequestered himself in his tiny room to catch up on correspondence, but he rose to investigate. He soon learned that the *Ploughboy* had arrived with men who were reputed to be government agents. Within minutes a large crowd of Natives[136] had assembled beside the priest's house.

Normally, island residents eagerly awaited the arrival of the steamboat. It brought supplies, visitors and news. But the visitors who arrived that Friday were the dreaded governor's men who the local government agent, *surintendant* George Ironside, had warned would come. These were clearly men coming to obtain a surrender of the island.

Choné felt he had to intervene and calm the people down. "*L'île vous appartient*," he said to the crowd outside. The island belongs to you. "The treaty of 1836 assures you of possession," he added firmly. He had used the same expression successfully once before. It seemed to pacify the crowd. He returned inside to compose his thoughts in private.[137]

He had known for a year, and had suspected for several years, that the government wanted to take *l'île Manitouline* from the Native people. The previous autumn two agents who claimed to represent the governor tried to obtain a cession of the island, but the Native people had firmly refused to cede. Since then, the local government agent had approached the Natives individually and urged each to surrender his land. Recently, the agent had told them to assemble in Manitowaning in early October to hear a more generous offer from the governor.

Choné shook his head in dismay. Just thinking about the visitors was *exaspérant*, infuriating. Surely the governor had received their complaints about the agent's actions and about the new laws concerning wood and fish. Surely, he would have heard how firmly the Native people had refused the agent's demand last year. Choné's only consolation was his knowledge that the Native people were well prepared for this attempt at cession. They had met together several times, and were nearly unanimous in their desire *de tenir à leur terre*—to hold onto their land.

Of course a few of them, mostly the old and pliable, had listened to the agent's promises, threats and reminders of their pledges of loyalty to the Crown. Choné could name the "yes" men on one hand—Assiginack, Tehkummah, Mocotaishegun and probably old Mejakwange [Maishegonggai]. They were *too* loyal; they just did not understand that kings and governors changed as did the meaning of their words; that promises might be broken; that the written not the spoken word was what the English remembered. Unfortunately, these things could not be explained well without casting a shadow on everything foreign.

He returned to his work. He had several letters to complete before the steamboat returned on its eastward run. That same evening he received two letters. The first was from *Vicar-Général* Charles-Félix Cazeau, the Roman Catholic bishop's emissary to the government. He and Choné were regular correspondents, as all the Jesuit's and Native's complaints were sent through him, to be conveyed to the governor. Choné eagerly opened the letter. He expected to find a follow-up to the letter he had written last August to the chief *surintendant* of Indian Affairs. That letter had been deliberately *franche et vigoureuse*—frank and forceful—in order to ensure a reaction. He had sharply denounced the government's treaties, promises and regulations.

He read and then reread the vicar-general's letter. His heart sank. Clearly it was a letter rooted in government promises, lies and deception. It informed him that the government envoys acknowledged that the Natives had been neglected up until then; that the complaints that he had written to the government were justified; that, consequently, he should have no trouble arranging the affairs of the Natives with the commissioners; and that he must do all that was in his power to bring about the objective of their mission. The second letter invited him to Manitowaning the next day.[138]

As he read the letters he was filled with a feeling of dread. This was not a real acknowledgement that the people had been wronged, but a *ruse* to put his superiors at rest while the island was taken from the Native people. They and the Jesuit priests had been expecting a second attempt, but now, for the second year in a row, the people must interrupt their fall fishing and their harvest to attend the agent in Manitowaning. If the people could not fish they could not eat or earn money, and then perhaps a cession would be necessary. Should they refuse to attend? Truly, only he had been ordered by the vicar-general to attend—but then who would refuse?

He wished he could consult his colleagues, but only the recently appointed Père Blettner was present. Père Kohler had replaced Choné as superior of the mission in June, but Kohler and Père Hanipaux were travelling on mission work. Choné alone had to decide what to do.

Jean-Pierre Choné (1808-1878) had lived and worked among the Native people for 18 years. Born in France, he had become a priest, taught, joined the Jesuits and then immigrated to Canada at the age of 35 in 1843. One year later he received a much desired posting to Wikwemikong to assist Père Jean-

Baptiste Proulx, who had founded the mission six years earlier. Choné was the first member of the Society of Jesus—the Jesuits—in the region since the late eighteenth century.[139] Choné was known by the Native people as Kamaskawittagosit, The Man With A Strong Voice, though he and all his fellow priests were generally called *nosse* (father).

Choné was an eager student of the Native's language and culture. He relished the isolation and challenge of the vast new mission. He had worked at the *Mission de Sainte-Croix* (Holy Cross Mission) in Wikwemikong until 1848, when he was sent to establish a mission on western Lake Superior.

At the western mission he saw how Native bands and families had been divided by the international boundary, pre-treaty rumours, negotiations and treaties. He witnessed first-hand how government-spread rumours of generous land payments could be metamorphosed into meagre cash and land allocations. With his own eyes he saw at the preliminary treaty negotiations in 1849 how Fort William's Chief Peau de Chat's reasonable request for land, money in perpetuity, and a teacher, doctor, blacksmith, carpenter, farmer and superintendent was dismissed by the government agent, who claimed that the Americans were paying Native people for only 25 years then moving them west. A year later, in September 1850, Choné reported that, despite the band's winter deliberations and written decisions, the treaty, "a true monument of deception or of error on one part also of a lack of foresight on the other was concluded and signed, in the middle of darkness by the blind natives, in such a way among other things it enacts through its contents, that the native might not even have one single place where he could throw his line to fish. He finds himself in a pen in the middle of the forest on some measure of land that they have reserved for him." Worse, in 1859 the land set aside in the 1850 treaty was surrendered in return for annuities and considerably smaller land reservations, "leaving them only just what they must to contain them at present."[140]

Based on his experiences, Choné concluded that treaties did not benefit the Native people. When he returned to Wikwemikong in 1860 to serve as superior he encouraged the Native people to resist any further cessions of their land.

A second Jesuit priest had joined Choné in August 1845. Père Joseph-Urbain Hanipaux,[141] known locally as Nissasuakouat (Three Pronged Fork), was sent to *l'île Manitouline* to replace the mission's 37-year-old founder, Père Proulx. Hanipaux was also French born. He was one of eight Jesuits who came to Canada in 1842, when the Society's priests were finally permitted to return after having been subjected to a vigorous suppression by the British since 1763. After three years in the hamlet of Laprairie, Quebec, Hanipaux was sent to Wikwemikong, where he struggled to learn the Native's language. He obtained a little printing press and printed hymns and prayers for the Native people. He carried a trumpet to announce his arrival and to call the people to service. Choné admired Hanipaux as a man who was never unoccupied, who enjoyed listening to confessions and taking care of the sick as much as repairing and decorating the church and chapels. Hanipaux adhered to an even more meagre life than his colleagues. He followed a strict diet and took "his repose like a native: a mat, a buffalo skin, and a wool blanket" instead of his allotted bed with a mattress.

Père Hanipaux had been the superior at *Sainte-Croix*, Wikwemikong from 1853 to August 1860.

The superior at the Holy Cross Mission in October 1862 was Père Auguste Kohler, known as Songiteeskang (He Who Makes The Heart Strong). Kohler was born in 1821 in the Upper Rhine Valley in France.[142] He joined the Jesuits in 1842, and five years later the newly ordained 26-year-old priest was posted to Wikwemikong. After nine months immersion there he was sent to work among the Native people of the north shores of lakes Huron and Superior. Kohler travelled extensively; his medical skills made him particularly useful and popular. His colleagues described him as extremely pious and religious, yet a man with a sense of humour who enjoyed adventures. Kohler and Hanipaux spent most of 1862 travelling or visiting missions.

In addition to the priests, Wikwemikong was home to four Jesuit brothers in 1862. They carried out the physical work of the mission, as farmers, cooks, carpenters and teachers. The most notable—indispensable, actually—was Joseph Jennesseaux,[143] the schoolmaster. Born in France, he had trained as a carpenter before joining the Jesuits. Like Hanipaux, he came to Canada in 1842. He worked at the Walpole Island mission until 1850, when he was posted to Wikwemikong and put in charge of the schools. His limited English skills meant Wikwemikong students were schooled only in Ojibwe and French until the government intervened and threatened to withdraw funding unless English was taught.

So, though the mission was technically the home of four priests and four brothers in October 1862, Choné was in essence alone to deal with the government agents who arrived that day in October.

Choné loved the *Mission de Sainte-Croix*, Wikwemikong. It was a marvel, an achievement of the people, who now numbered more than 650. Whenever he was troubled he would walk through the village. The regularly laid out houses rose up the hill like rows in an amphitheatre, and all overlooked the magnificent bay. Normally at this time of year the bay would be peppered with small mackinaw-style fishing boats, but today they were all pulled onto the shore. The highlight of the village was the massive stone church, *l'église de pierre*. It was a demonstration and reminder to all of what the people could achieve. Granted, it was an achievement realized with much encouragement, and even some prodding. The church had been the special project of another superior a decade earlier, the widely travelled and ever-industrious Père Nicolas Point.

Père Point joined the Jesuits as a young man in France and worked in missions in Kentucky, Louisiana and the Rocky Mountains.[144] He was posted to Wikwemikong in 1848, where he designed and supervised the construction of the mission's massive stone church. The Native people themselves built the 40- by 100-foot structure with 60-foot-long cross-shaped arms between 1849 and 1852. Point also documented Wikwemikong life in sketches and written accounts. Regrettably, despite his acknowledged achievements in construction and education, he was unpopular with many for his cost-cutting measures. He cancelled non-essential expenses and insisted that everyone work to support the mission. He discouraged fishing and sugaring, and instead encouraged farming. Complaints about his economical methods for the mission eventually passed out of common memory; *l'église de pierre*, though, was a lasting legacy.

Point had built the church, but Choné liked to think he had filled its space with music and Hanipaux its walls with decoration. Choné believed in the power of music. He had translated many hymns into the Native language while working among the people of Lake Superior. Many of these translations had been printed in small booklets for the Native people.

Père Choné shook his head in astonishment at the current troubles. They were truly of much greater concern than financial cuts, regulations and work. Over the previous decade, new difficulties had arisen to threaten not only the mission but also the Natives *en général*. Treaties, traders, fishermen, steamboats and liquor dealers had all multiplied. The threats increased, but the assistance did not. To complicate things further, the local government agent, *surintendant* Ironside, grew older and less able or interested every day. Choné knew that Ironside worked to have the island surrendered, just as he had done with the Natives on the mainland's North Shore. Choné heard stories that the agent had approached people all over the island to urge them to sign a treaty.

Tears came to his eyes if he thought too long about *l'île Manitouline*'s people. While struggling to learn their language he had spent many hours learning their theology, laws and sanctions. Less than 20 years earlier, when he had arrived, the Native people were still untarnished by the foreigners and retained their old laws. These laws forbad *le vol et le mensonge*—theft and lies—while prescribing generosity, goodness, hospitality, respect, obedience to parents and the obligation of parents to instruct their children. *Certainement*, change was not always good or welcome.

Threat and Action
As Choné prepared to walk through the forest and cross the bay to Manitowaning he recalled the past promises and actions of the government and its agents. When he had returned to Wikwemikong two years earlier, the people had told him of their complaints and fears. He had replied that they must *se connaître et s'unir*—meet together and unite—though he had not really expected them to take any action.

He had tried to explain the situation to his colleagues and superiors. "*La convoitise, dit-on, ouvre de grands yeux sur l'île que nous habitons*"—Envy, they say, casts its large eyes over the island on which we live. He continued: "It is proclaimed that Whites will form a settlement on it, that it is excellent lands being wasted, occupied as it is by a handful of lazy Natives who only cultivate a little corn, potatoes, sugar and fire wood, etc."[145] But he had received no response to his remarks.

He had been pleasantly surprised when the Native people, without informing him, "summoned all the men and the young people; they signed an expression of union against all attempts on the part of the Whites. That done, they called three chiefs. The chiefs came forward, and it was proposed to them to unite with their brother chiefs. One of the three accepted the proposition. The other two pleaded that first they must consult the agent and rely on his decision."

"Then one of the band, who had put things in motion, rose: 'Two chiefs refuse to unite with us! Oh well! Those among you who believe them unworthy of leading us, raise your hand like me!' Right away a forest of arms pronounced the dethronement of the two uncooperative chiefs." About nine o'clock in the evening, continued Choné, a deputation came into the house, presented him "with the *formule d'union* signed by more than 200 persons," and asked him to bless it.[146]

He had considered the Natives' actions important enough to have them recorded in the mission's journal on 4 February 1861: "All the men of the village gathered together in a house to come to agreement in case the Government asked for their island. Those of the other villages of the island are already united. Those of Mitchikiwatinong made a document which all the others must sign. They put their names there after agreeing together, called their chiefs to find out if they wanted to unite with them [*"faire cause commune"*]—two refused."[147]

Head chief Michel Cainooshimague accepted the council's proposition and signed the document, but Tehkummah and Mocotaishegun refused to sign. They insisted they must consult the government agent before accepting the council's decision. They were deposed from office for their reluctance.[148]

Several days later, the deposed chiefs came to Choné and told him about the affair. As he was busy conducting catechism for a first communion, Choné simply said that he believed they had been wrong not to join with their brother chiefs and asked them to return in three days when he had more information. But they did not return, except to make their confessions.

The agent in Manitowaning had increased *les bruits*, the rumours, of a cession in the spring when he insisted on taking an official census. He sent a form, printed only in English without any explanation, to the chiefs of Wikwemikong. This caused displeasure and mistrust amongst the people. Père Kohler tried to explain the form, but the people remained suspicious and questioned Père Choné. He urged them to comply, because the Bishop of Montreal had asked all people to participate in the census. Despite Choné's assurance, the people refused to provide their names or details to the agent when he came in the spring. The agent, equally stubborn, insisted on their participation and accused Choné himself of encouraging them to refuse.[149]

In May 1861, the chiefs wrote a letter of complaint about their agent, which they intended to send to a tribe near Detroit. "You act like children," Choné admonished them "What's the use of sending your complaints against your agent to another tribe? If I were in your shoes, I would make a copy of this letter, make the complaints that you yourselves wish to make, and send it to the Governor." When the chiefs replied that they had no one to translate the letter and send it, Choné offered his services, and the complaints were "written, signed, translated and sent."

A few weeks later, in June 1861, Choné reported that "a deputation from all the villages met in the geographically most central village of the island. There, they confirmed their union. Those who had not yet arrived hurried to sign their names, and our people of Wikwemikong returned home with three new chiefs."

Though he had been away when they had gathered, he was aware of the meeting. He acknowledged, almost proudly, that the Native people knew that he preferred "*qu'ils agissent seuls*"—that they act on their own.

When the Native people returned he recorded what he learned of the event in the mission's journal: "The natives returned from Mitchikiwatinong where there were deputations from the whole island. They confirmed their union there and created 3 chiefs—the son of the late Kinoshameg replacing his father, [and] Wakekijik and Ominakamigo replacing the two who were deposed last winter."[150]

The new chiefs returned to Wikwemikong and held a feast. Choné attended and shook hands with the new chiefs, who he considered "*les héros de la fête*"—the heroes of the feast. He invited everyone to the church that evening. Men and women filled the church, where he spoke at length and emphasized the necessity of having a council of justice responsible for making resolutions and looking after their implementation.

That summer, the Native people reacted to the government agent's insistence that they could sell their wood only through him, so he could collect a fee for the governor. In response, they built a wharf just north of Wikwemikong to sell firewood directly to the steamboats. Choné had encouraged them in this project. But their hard work was thwarted, as he reported:

"The administration or its agent forbids the natives to sell even a piece of wood. It obliges them therefore to burn the wood right in the field they are clearing. No, I am mistaken. The administration makes the native do the work, and the agent gives his son the task of selling the wood to steamboats, buying from the worker at a discounted price of 2 francs 50 per cord; the workers must still transport their wood in their little boats and put it on the wharf. It must not be forgotten that all this is being done on the island and with wood from the island.

"The native can sell pieces of cedar, fence poles, wood for carpenters, coopers, etc., fire-wood, only to the administration so that by its wise rules, it can provide for the renewal of the forests."[151]

Choné recalled how anxious the people had been that year. A rumour spread that *arpenteurs*, surveyors, would come in the middle of summer to go over the island. When a boat arrived in the bay and a group of men visited the village and the church, one of the visitors was recognized as an *arpenteur*. The Native people had no doubt: "surveyors have arrived, we are dispossessed!" The alarm spread from village to village, and even to Manitowaning across the bay. Choné offered to accompany a small delegation to question the visitors at their camp on the shore. He was forced to enquire in English, but was able to determine that they were simply on a pleasure trip. Thus, Choné noted, the Native people "*avaient laissé un gros poids dans la tente*," left their great worries in the tent.

But the people were right to be afraid of being expelled. Everyone knew the agent had already requested a cession from the chiefs of various bands of the island. Some chiefs had openly affirmed it, some withheld the information, while others appeared to be in league with the agent who neither wanted to listen to or to receive anyone except the favoured chiefs.

The Native people wrote to the governor in September 1861 to remind him that he had not responded to their letters of complaint sent the previous May. Choné translated the new letter into French and sent it to Quebec City. Seven chiefs of Wikwemikong, Sheshegwaning and Michigiwatinong signed it.[152] Their letters remained unanswered, and they soon discovered their fears were justified.

In October the Native people were summoned to Manitowaning. Choné recalled the momentous event with equal parts pride and apprehension. He described it all in detail to his superiors in order that they might understand the danger that threatened the mission:

> At the beginning of last October, a Commissioner accompanied by an employee of the Indian Department, along with a surveyor, arrived in the village of Manitowaning where the Agent resides. The native people were summoned from all over the island. Our people came to consult me before leaving for this meeting:
> To all the questions, I told them, answer: "We cannot." Do not let yourself be led into a discussion; above all be careful to avoid answering the speech that will be addressed you. You will confuse yourselves, and they will take your uncertainty for consent. The island belongs to you, the Treaty of 1836 assures you of possession.
> It was a Saturday; they did not return until Sunday morning. They limited themselves to a simple refusal; and well they did. I have had in my hands the series of arguments and questions, the things that were presented in a manner so intoxicating that one could have easily let oneself be duped. Everything depends on this truncated clause in the Treaty of 1836:
> "The island has been ceded to the natives on the supposition that 9,000 souls would settle there."
> That has not happened, so the island remains the property of the Government, who owes the natives only what is necessary to live: 25 acres of land for each family, without other compensation.
> Our men were to return the following Monday, having received instructions to reflect on the propositions that were made. But on Monday, the atmosphere was more conciliatory; the firm stance among the natives had given the Government messengers a reason to reflect. I will speak more truthfully: The Commissioner had attempted trickery, and wanted thereby to obtain what he could not take by force. He then asked for only permission to survey the island. The refusal was definite.
> "But" added the Commissioner, "the Government could employ force to protect its workers." A confused sound of voices followed that threat. When calm was restored, one of our men said energetically: "The Government has soldiers, it can send them to kill us all, and when we are stretched out on the earth, it will have fun with our property. We have no powder or guns, and if we had them, we would not have used them."
> The Commissioner saw that it was too late and that the voice of intimidation would not succeed any better then cunning or authority. He tried to give some explanations, but they could not erase what the people had found odious in his first words. The meeting lasted until 4 in the evening, when the envoys of the Government and the surveyors who had orders to remain on the island, decided to leave. Their departure was announced by two canon shots. The detonations were heard in all the fields where people were harvesting corn and it caused alarm everywhere. People thought that the gun-fire came from a victorious enemy, the defeat or misfortune of the natives.
> The envoys, however, did not consider themselves beaten; they declared they would return in the spring. The agent said in precise terms that the Government would take the island willy nilly.[153]

A few weeks later, Choné and his colleagues read about the surrender attempt in the newspapers. Even the popular Toronto *Globe* was not as positive about surrender as Choné had feared. Though usually anti-French and anti-Catholic, it was also anti-Conservative government. The author criticized Charles Lindsey's appointment as a commissioner and described his threat to send soldiers to dispossess the Indians as foolish and wrong. He quoted some of the chief's responses that, he acknowledged, had been provided to him by the Native people themselves. Unfortunately, the author favoured extending settlement towards the North-West. He insisted that Indian titles to lands should not stand in the way of the progress of the country, but admitted the people should not be compelled to surrender their claims without full compensation, and that the offer of 25 acres each was very inadequate.

The last boats of the season to *l'île Manitouline* brought copies of other journals. Some writers simply copied *The Globe*'s statements. The Methodist's *Christian Guardian* and the Catholic's *Canadian Freeman* spoke out against the government's action. The *Freeman* printed: "We learn from the *Globe* of the 18th, that, the Government has appointed Mr. Lindsey of the *Leader* a Commissioner, in connection with the Superintendent of Indian Affairs, Mr. Bartlett, to treat with the Indians of the Manitoulin Islands for the surrender of all lands over and above what will be required to furnish twenty-five acres to each head of a family. If this be true we are inclined to the opinion that the Government is about to violate the treaty ratified between Sir F.B. Head and the Indian Chiefs at Manitoulin, in 1836." After describing the treaty, the writer commented: "We trust that no injustice will be done the poor Indians. Surely there is enough of the public domain locked up and in the hands of speculators already, without seeking to encroach upon the last and limited settlement of the red man. The Indians have protested against the proceeding in their own simple but dignified manner. It is to be hoped that this protest, will meet with consideration at the hands of the Government."[134]

Choné was frustrated to learn in November that the government had made new regulations for wood sales. He noted in the mission journal that Whites were forbidden to "buy wood from the natives without authorization from the Indian Department." He wrote a letter of complaint to several Quebec newspapers and encouraged the natives to write to the superintendent general of Indian Affairs.[155]

He heard that many people had complained. The government made a small concession a few months later: firewood cut on one's own farm could be sold through the agent, but the seller would not be paid until he was shown to have complied with the regulations.[156] Truly, concluded Choné, the agent and his superiors obstructed every little step the people took towards financial independence.

Père Auguste Kohler replaced Choné as superior in June 1862. The mission was doubled in size and staff. It now extended from Lake Nipissing past Sault Ste. Marie. Though the number of priests increased from two to four, two would need to be travelling almost continuously.

When the Native people wrote petitions to the governor in June and July 1862,

Choné decided to add a letter of explanation. Not only had the Natives been confirmed by the governor as the proprietors of *l'île Manitouline* in 1836, he pointed out, but the land was moreover a sacred reward made to servants of the government in recognition of services rendered. He included a copy of a letter from the commander of Fort Michilimackinac, who so valued the loyal service of Odawa Chief Mokomanish that he had presented the chief with a silver-mounted sword in 1815. Choné concluded his letter by asking for removal of the prohibitions on wood sales.[157]

Meanwhile, the *surintendant*, Ironside, continued to approach the Natives about ceding their land. The mission diary entry for 15 August 1862 noted that the agent "invited the chiefs, one after the other," and "said to them that he had very advantageous things to tell them; that it was understood that the propositions made to them last year were insufficient; that soon someone would come again and ask for their island, but with better conditions: 100 acres and $100 per family annually; that he had spoken to the other island chiefs and they had accepted; [and] that they also had to accept." The chiefs' response, as recorded in the diary, was brief and clear: "We said that the island belongs to us and that we will not cede it."

Choné's experience with the effects surrenders had on the North Shore inhabitants led him to believe there was no benefit for the Natives. He felt obligated to deal harshly with those Natives who looked as though they might surrender to the agent's will. One evening he declared to Tehkummah that he would not attend the dying sick of any Indians who favoured giving up their land.[158] Harsh words, but he was determined to make them consider their actions and choices carefully.

While Ironside promoted surrender, Choné and the Natives were distracted by new timber regulations. Unprecedented advertisements proclaimed that "cutting timber or staves or wood for any purpose upon Indian lands, except by licence" had "been rendered unlawful," and warned that "Indians or others, offending against the said statues will be prosecuted with vigor" as of 7 August 1862.[159]

The people of Wikwemikong, Michigiwatinong and Sheshegwaning wrote a petition rejecting the rules. Choné wrote passionately and at length to the chief *surintendant* of Indian Affairs:

> Sir, It is truly astonishing how relentlessly people rush over the poor remains of the Indians, who confident in the words of the representative of S.M.B. [the Crown], have abandoned their lands, reserving only this miserable Manitoulin Island to settle on, and live tranquilly in their work, in the practice of Religion, far from contact with the whites. Nevertheless, people question the ownership of the lands. The facts speak for themselves. The Government has made treaties with the Natives and these treaties stipulate on the one hand a cession and on the other a payment. In whatever manner one interprets them, the treaties proclaim a right, an ownership.
>
> To him, who does not own a thing, one should not demand the cession of that thing; one should not agree to pay him for that thing. Yet it has been done, and one wants to do again it with the natives. Their right of ownership is acknowledged. They have been and are still owners.
>
> Despite that, people want to force them to cede what remains to them today. And how is this done?

They said to them (in October 1861): We are the masters of the island; so cede it to the Government, with such a condition. What an anomaly! Do we sell a thing of which we are owners with such a condition!

Upon refusal: At least allow us to survey.

They have not obtained anything. But are not beaten.

There is an agent to watch the well being of the Natives on the island. They say this agent went to great expense: He called the principal Natives one after the other, and by authority, promises or threats, he pressed them to consent to the invaders.

But that was not enough. You do not want it—They shall wear you down, right or wrong. It doesn't matter. They shall make friends with you; they shall force you to give up your property by threats of poverty and death.

The means will be found.

The Natives or their agent sold their wood to the steamboats. They cut it themselves, transported it in their little boats, put it on the wharf, and received only two thirds of the payment.

They thought that they themselves could make the profit that their agent was making. They built a wharf.

The wharf was not even finished and the Indian Dept. office prohibited whites to buy any wood cut on their land from Natives.

This is how they watch over well-being—not the well-being of the Natives!

In spite of this prohibition, against which the Natives have previously complained, without anyone deigning to answer them, they have cut and carried the wood to their wharf. Someone immediately judged the first prohibition insufficient. It only affected the buyers of wood. It was enough. But no.

It's odious: This handful of poor Natives that the Government itself has attracted here. They do not want to kill them with their own hands: go force them there or admit that they are not the owners, that they do not even have the right to cut a piece of wood without the permission of their masters.

Read the notice of the 7th August 1862: "Cutting timber, staves or wood for any other purpose upon Indian lands, has been rendered unlawful by etc." But it is a precaution against invasions by the whites.

Read farther on: "any persons whether Indians or others" (the Indians in 1st line, for what person is unaware the regulations are against them and against them alone) "offending against the said statues will be prosecuted with rigour."

But the last line offers them one last hope: they can ask permission and the local Superintendent can grant it.

Yes. It is said to them: Die of hunger and cold or put chains on your feet and hands; admit you are slaves.

See the wisdom of the regulations: The wood rots on the land. The Native will rot drawing some benefit. Your wood shall rot and your limbs shiver while someone watches. I do not permit you to even take a log, for any use whatever.

One does not treat slaves in this way.

With respect

Sir, Your humble and obedient servant. Missionary to the natives of the island. Choné[160]

Choné also wrote to *The Canadian Freeman* newspaper and included the new wood regulations. It published an article titled "Unjust Proceedings of the Indian Department Towards the Indians of Manetoulin":

There has been a great deal of talk concerning the cruelties of the Spaniards towards the Indians at Southern and Central America. They have been vindicated even by Protestant writers. Moreover, the facts are these, speaking louder than all the clamors of some ignorant scribblers. There are up to our days, not hundreds and thousands, but millions, of Indians living in the old Spanish possessions, more or less mixed with the blood of their conquerors. But where are all those numerous nations formerly living in British America? What will become of the few remnants of them? Have they been reduced to such a state of degradation by our civilization as to dwindle necessarily away in the course of a few years by exhaustion? The registers of the dead and living in Manetoulin evidently show quite the contrary. They prove better than all reasoning, that, if the Indians are left quiet, sufficiently remote from the contact of the white population, in a climate not made for the wolves and bears only, they will continue to live, and to increase nearly as much as our white people. But that they are not allowed.

The property of these islands has been secured to them by the most solemn treaties. They have been, up to this time, always their sole possessors. They never made any cession of them to anybody; yet, last summer, there appeared amongst them an agent of the Government, calling himself master of their island, and, by a most strange contradiction, requesting them to abandon the property of them to the Government, telling them at the same time that if they would not do this willingly they would be forced to do so. The Indians repelled with indignation all that tyrannical nonsense. They sent an energetic defence of their rights to His Excellency Viscount Monck, Governor General of British North America. In the meantime, the resident agent called in succession on the various chiefs, in order to induce them, by premises and menaces, to an act of cession. No longer ago than last Sunday the following notice was placarded through the island:

NOTICE. INDIAN DEPARTMENT. Quebec, 7th Aug., 1862.
The public are hereby notified that cutting timber or staves or wood for any other purposes upon Indian lands, except under licence by competent authority, has, by the 23rd chapter of the Consolidated Statutes of Canada (which by order in Council has been made applicable to Indian Lands), and by other acts of the Legislature of this Province, been rendered unlawful. Any persons, whether Indians or others, offending against the said statutes, will be prosecuted with vigor.

Licenses to cut timber can only be obtained from the Local Superintendent of Indian Affairs. Signed, Wm. McDougall, Chief Supt. Indian Affairs.

Is that the way of dealing of a great nation with a few weak allies, in a matter in which their very existence is at stake? Does the Government or its agents not know, that the treaty made in 1850 with the Indians of the northern shore does not concern these islands? They are, and remain, according to the treaty of 1836, their absolute property as long as they do not alienate them, which they are not willing to do.

*Some time previous to this notice the agent of the Indians of the northern shore sold the woods of the Indians of Manetoulin, paying them $1 per cord, without giving them any account of half a dollar more he received. The Indians thought they could just as well sell their wood themselves, and take $1.50 per cord instead of $1. Inde irce [Latin: Hence this resentment.] an order is issued from the Indian Department, forbidding the whites to buy any wood of those Indians. They on their part protested against such an unjust measure, and continued to sell their wood as before. All this was now followed by the above order.[161]

Choné was frustrated. Every aspect of the lives of the people of *l'île*

Manitouline was threatened. Treaties had been signed and more treaties were being pressed upon them. Though some chiefs considered ceding more of the North Shore mainland, most were adamant that *l'île Manitouline* should be retained for their descendants. The regulation of the fishing and timber industries hindered traditional employment and income. In addition, unscrupulous traders used liquor and excessive prices to keep the Natives in debt.

The Treaty and the Jesuits
On Saturday, 4 October 1862, Père Choné travelled to Manitowaning to attend the grand council. Not surprisingly, he stood out in the crowd: he was the only priest and non-Native Catholic present; he was already well known to the superintendents, due to his involvement in Native issues; and, as journalist Samuel Day remarked, his blue cloak, with a red cotton kerchief around his neck, made him look "anything but ecclesiastical." "Certainly his presence was not considered desirable," added Day, "as his bitter hostility to the intentions of the government had transpired."[162]

"I went to the place indicated," Choné later explained to his colleagues. "The superintendent general of the Indian Department, received me cordially; but the Commissioner of Crown lands, Macdougall, gave me a gloomy look. That reception did not astonish me, as I had recently placed a well-justified complaint for the natives that I had drawn up and which began with these words: 'It is truly astonishing how relentlessly people rush over the poor remains of Indians!'"

Choné and interpreter Charles de Lamorandière met privately with McDougall. McDougall revealed that he wanted the natives to give up the larger part of the island, retaining for "each head of family 100 acres for himself and 50 for each child" for which "they would receive between $1 and 2 shill[ings] as rent on the sale of that portion which they would give up." McDougall asked the priest "to use his influence to induce the Indians to accede to these proposals." I "not only refused to be the tool of such a disturbing measure," Choné reported, "but also refuted all the reasons that the h[onorable] g[entleman] brought forth to support them."[163]

"Soon after my arrival," continued Choné, "the meeting was opened. First there were some explanations, then I said to the envoys that my presence was pointless, that I had by no means come to take part in the debates, but only to respond to the honour of the invitation; that as for my convictions, they knew them from my letters, that they were unchanged; that in all matters, I was only the head of the natives and these last words committed me reluctantly into the discussion. They asked me if I counselled the natives; because since I was here, they were no longer negotiating. I responded: 'I do not attend their councils, but I give advice to those who ask me: as minister of religion, I think I am obliged to work for their temporal well being, because it is very useful in the peaceable practice of their religious duty.'

"After this response," said Choné, "Mr. MacDougall explained the objective of his mission. Here is a résumé of his speech that I shall recount at length later: 'We come in the interest of the Indians. The offers that were made them last year were unacceptable; the concessions that we bring them today are more generous: 100 acres to each head of family, and to orphans, 50 to each child over 21 years. The rest of the island will be sold, and the revenue will be paid to you annually.'

"Why," Choné asked McDougall, "should the natives abandon their properties for at the very most 25 *sous* per head each year?" "But they are not the owners of the island," answered McDougall, "the Government interprets the Treaty of 1836: the surrender is conditional." "You are mistaken, Sirs," Choné countered, "we have meditated over all the words of the treaty; the reserve is absolute, and the government has no right to interpret it otherwise. The natives have always been regarded as owners and treated as such; the government has made an alliance with them; they have surrendered one part of their lands, and reserved the lesser part. The facts are there to attest to the accuracy of these statements."

McDougall said "The Government needs the island to promote the colonization of the west." "Sirs, the island is useless, absolutely useless," replied Choné—to which McDougall responded: "It does not matter; the government and the public want it." "The government, I agree," said Choné, "the public, no. The public does not know the island, and the government no better." "The natives have not used it," noted McDougall. "Each uses his property as he intends," replied Choné. "Besides, why are you amazed that the natives are not more advanced in farming, considering that they have only been here for 26 years? Were 26 years enough in England to make people farmers? What aid have these people received from the government? None. And again today when they want to sell wood from their land to steamboats, you prevent them with two successive by-laws; moreover, in the recent by-law, they don't even have the right without government permission to cut a tree for heat."

"Oh no!" disagreed McDougall. "According to the terms, anyone who cuts a tree without previous authorization is liable to punishment; if that had not been meant, then there is an oversight or blunder by the author. Sirs, I ask you: are the natives your slaves, your subjects or your allies? They should not be either slaves or subjects; they are allies. Well then! You must treat them as such; you must judge their acts as those of friends."

"Other questions and responses of the same type took place," Choné advised his colleagues, "but I leave it there and send you the complete report, written by the people themselves, of all the events that occurred at Manitowaning in this sad circumstance. My translation will be as faithful as possible; the force of expression and the turn of phrase leaves something to be desired. This account must be sent to the governor of Canada."

To his Excellency the Governor General, residing at Quebec
"You who art Great Chief and high in dignity, who occupies the place of the Great Being to exercise your power over all the men in the limits of the land called Canada, this is the thought of the Great-Being about you: As his heart is good, beautiful and pure, his thought concerning you is that your heart be compassionate and generous, that you guard with care those under your charge and your authority, in order that no one makes awkward regulations and also that no one suffers unreasonable harm in the application of your laws.

"To you then, Great Chief, whose quality is that of sovereign justice, we address our words: We place before you this written appeal, so that you may know and consider carefully what has taken place at Manitowaning, namely, all the evil elements contained in this contract of sale. No righteous man, once he knew the facts, could say: Here is a true contract! And that is why we bring these facts to you, so that you may judge them yourself. For us, we have seen the progress of things and cannot say: This is a valid treaty! On the contrary, it is simple deception! If the promoters had intended to make a valid deed, they should not have accepted the words of those who said: I surrender (the land). For no one, by himself, be he even a chief, can cede a thing that we all possess in common. If we had all consented, then a true treaty would have been concluded, but it was not so.

"Those who gave their assent, consented as private individuals; they had not sought the advice of their tribe. Besides, if the promoters wanted to act with justice, they should not have accepted the consent of several other people: people who possess nothing on the island that they can sell. Their reserve is on the mainland; their tribe is there and not here. Yes, we assert that it is a big mistake, a bad proceeding, to ask from someone a thing that does not belong to him, but to accept his word nevertheless. Is it their property that is being taken? Have they some interest in keeping it? Also, did those other people surrender eagerly—they still have their reserve on the mainland. Great chief, we come only now to make our report, because we have been occupied with our harvest."[164]

Choné then gave his full account of how the negotiations unfolded, as best as he could recall, from his perspective: "When the honourable chief, MacDougall, was seated in the meeting room, he expected that the natives were going to come up and shake hands with him. But they did not do so. They said to him: It is up to you who come to speak to us, to give us your hand first. He rose, gave his hand to our chiefs, then he spoke. Now, here is what he said:

"'My friends, it is time to explain to you my mission. The great queen has given complete authority to the great chief seated in Quebec, and the great chief charged me to take care of you. I am the head of the Indian Department, and in this title, I come to ask you for your little island. I have carefully considered all that concerns you, and I want to treat you properly. You know that many settlers know your island, and want to settle here; your efforts can never drive them back. If you surrender your land, you shall congratulate yourselves on the benefit that you shall gain. In the first place your generosity will be a reason for me to extend my kindness to you. Then, I will give you an authentic title that assures you forever the part of the island that you choose, far from where the Whites will settle. The rest will be sold, and the money from the sale deposited in the bank, after the surveyors have been paid. Each year, you will be paid the interest on this money. I add that the Whites will come here and settle in great numbers, and to your advantage; as they will bring all sorts of things with them. There will be farmers and merchants. Everything will be at a good price. You will not need to go far to exchange your products. Near you, you will have flour mills, sawmills, forges, etc. In a word, you will lack nothing, and you will be surrounded by all the care of the great chief. Here is what land they shall give you: 100 acres to each family, 50 to young men, and 100 to orphans over 21 years. Besides, your children will be well educated. I hear that you came with weapons (not true, interjected Choné). I too, have the forces of the great chief.

Anyone using violence against those who speak will be treated severely. Everyone is free to speak; I invite you all to speak your thoughts.'

"Itawashkash: 'One moment, I am going to consider what you have said.'

"MacDougall: 'Do not hurry, but reflect on it.'

"Pekoneiassang: 'Hurry! What have you still to consider? Make known your thoughts. Should we not keep this land for which they came to ask us? Our minds have been made up for a long time. There is nothing more to deliberate.'

"MacDougall then left, and the people remained alone to examine the propositions. The account continued thus:

"'We have again talked together, all of us who hold onto our land, and we have not thought to surrender it, for it is the only thing we have. Then, according to what they said to us: it is not just us, men, who will receive 100 little measures per family; the young men of 21 winters shall have 50, and the orphans who count also 21 winters 100. This is all that has been promised: But there are also more children, the young girls, the grandsons and the granddaughters already of 20 winters, without counting those who are born today and who shall be born in future. We don't want to harm our existing children, nor those who come after. If we abandon our island, they would not have any property. This is what we say all together!'

"The counsel ended," said Choné. "The people called McDougall, and Itawashkash said: 'My brother, I will make known to you our thoughts, after having reflected on the words that you addressed to us. It is not the first time that we have considered these things; Well! Here are my thoughts: I hold my land, I do not surrender it. What I said last autumn is still my thought and my word. Always, I also want to keep for my children this land, the little that I possess. It is here that the Great Being gave me to live, and I want to remain here. For you it is over there, on the other side of the great sea that has been given to you to live; it is there doubtless that stretches the measure (acre) that you have come to name, not here. You should leave quickly because we are now occupied with our harvest. You are disturbing us, so please hurry and finish. These are the thought of all my chiefs present here.'

"MacDougall responded: 'This is pointless! The great chief absolutely wants to have your island. In future, they will not speak to you as they have until now, all together. But they will go to find you on your land, speak to each individually, ask for his property, or accept his word, and take his property. Those who are *en bas du courant* spoke like you, and yet they have not prevented the settlers from settling among them. That is what will happen to you. The Whites will soon rush onto your land, and despite all your efforts they will make themselves masters. Now, those who do not want to accept my proposals may leave; the others may remain.'

"Then the old man Assiginak spoke, addressing the English chief: 'I give you my hand my father, I press you with all my force, and I embrace the great chief (the Queen of England).' Then turning towards his brothers: 'Oh! my little brothers, I am the first born of all of us on the island of the Otawas. I am the eldest of all the chiefs and warriors. Listen to me, you have no reason to say: My ancestor came here, I was born here. The ancestor of the Ottawa alone came to this place. My Ottawa ancestor was over there, where the sun falls, it is there that I lived, then I came to this land. Now, here are my thoughts: I am owner here, and I surrender all that I possess.'

"Jako rose while the old man Assiginak was still speaking and Ironside wanted to stop him but Jako pushed him back and said: 'Tell the old man to sit down.'

"Werbewiokivan [Ironside]: 'He has not finished.'

"Jako: 'It is not for him to speak; my chiefs want me to speak.'

"Assiginak: 'Who are you?'

"Jako: 'I am Jako; Atagiwinini is the name of the old man who raised me.'

"Assiginak: 'Your words are useless. Like the foul mud that spreads its odour on all sides, that is its value.'

"Jako: 'Assiginak, you are an old man; the time is near for you to leave this earth. Look at your grave. It is not for you to speak here. You are too old; you are not capable of dealing with the matters that we treat.'

"Then Jako addressed MacDougall, thus: 'My brother I am happy to see you today in daylight. This is what I have always wanted. I said to myself: "Would that I may see the one who is in charge, so that I understand him and he understands me." Listen my brother to what my chiefs say through me: Is it really now, when good fortune is beginning for the native, is it now that you have come to ask him for all his land! Be careful! Those natives who ceded the mainland have not yet received any of the money that you promised to pay them. You promised them four *piastres*; now, see this (Jako pointed to his pants, explained Choné): they cost me four *piastres*, but I did not get them with what you gave for my land. It is the sugar that I take from the trees on my little island that gave them to me. Look at me, Brother. I am a chief from the mainland that my father ceded to the Great Woman-Chief. If my father had come here, he would have spoken. I am not ashamed to reveal my misery to you. One thing amazes me. It is that the Great Woman-Chief comes to ask us for our property! Is she so poor? Does she not have abundant treasures over there in the land they call England? But we who have abandoned our property, we are unfortunate! Brother, understand my thoughts and those of my chiefs: We do not surrender any of our land. If there are among us are some of contrary mind, their words are nothing; the majority alone must decide. Brother, if you offered me something of yours, I would accept it; but if you were offering me something that is already mine, I would not listen to you. I will stop, as it is late. When the light returns, it will be the Day of the Prayers (Sunday, noted Choné) the day occupied only with the things of the Great Being. Hence, your mission will still not have been completed.'

"Sakiwinebi: 'This Assiginak, who is sitting there, speaks with an incredible pride. I know him very well, and I know his origin. He is a slave! He has lied saying: I am Ottawa.'

"The natives, who knew the situation, raised their voices and said: 'You speak the truth. He is a slave!' But Assiginak's son spoke: 'Sakiwinebi, you must respect my father. Have you forgotten that he is already looking at his grave. Your words are shameful.'

"Sakiwinebi: 'Why has he spoken thus! He came close to receiving some blows! I am right in treating him as he deserves.'

"Assiginak's son: 'Anyway, it is not what my father says that will take place; but what all the people decide.'

Choné continued: "The meeting ended late on Saturday night; the natives then recounted the events of the next day: Sunday morning several of us withdrew to Wikwemikong for prayers; the other chiefs remained at Manitowaning. From all parts of the island of the Otawas, men were there in great numbers; all held firmly to their land. But now as to what happened on Sunday night: Since the officials could not obtain the consent of the chiefs, they distributed firewater to some of them, who then lost self-control and surrendered. The next day, they went to find Mijakevangé [Maishegonggai], who told them that the Great Chief's envoy had called them and had said to them: 'If you obey me, you shall be first chief, esteemed by all the Whites and forever happy.' They were few in number and intended to separate from us. We had not learned all that," Choné said bitterly, "until our return from Wikwemikong. Can one find more unworthy conduct? Intoxicate the chiefs or promise them honours to extract their consent! And who are those who ceded? They are known: they are the ones capable of anything, the libertines, the robbers, the ambitious, men without pity for their brothers.

"However, when we all—residents of Wikwemikong—heard about the defection of our brothers, Wakekijik, one of our chiefs, rose and said: 'All you men of Wikwemikong, answer: Do you hold on to your land? Do you wish to keep it? Those who are firm in their decision, lift up your hand and say in one strong voice: Yes, we hold on to it, we keep it. Yes! etc.' Wakekijik said a second time: 'Is it your decision? Hold up your land? Will you keep it?' And all responded in one stronger voice: 'Yes, we affirm it.' Wakekijik said a third time: 'My friends do not decide lightly; your resolution, is it taken, is it final?' And all cried with all their force: 'Yes, yes, we want to keep our land. And to better know our thoughts, we add: Perhaps there is among us those who are of a contrary opinion; Oh! Good, it is necessary that they declare it.' Wakekijik spoke again and said: 'Come now, those who do not think like us, show yourself. And you, Tekoman [Tehkummah], you have been known for a long time. You have said nothing, though you have been often asked; but you do want to give up our island! If anyone wants to put themselves on your side, then go over there near him.' Only one person got up and joined him. 'Let those who are convinced and firm in their resolution gather around me.' And all came around him.

"It was past noon when this event ended and the English official returned," said Choné. "Those who had abandoned us were there also. MacDougall sat down in the speaker's chair, and said to us, the residents of Wikwemikong: 'I had resolved not to talk to you, but since I see you have returned in such numbers, I will say one more word: Do you want to accept my propositions? I have brought money, and I have borrowed from the Great Chief himself; I will give it to you if you give up your island. What do you think? Give me your answer.'

"Jako: 'My brother, here are the thoughts from my chiefs: Our elders have spoken of a perfectly beautiful bird; it is with its feather that I want to caress your ears, so that you listen to my words. Of course, I am happy to see you, for you are handsome, very beautiful, and your face is perfectly white, as also your heart is very pure. Well, listen to me. We will never want to give in to those who give you our land; we will always treat them like our brothers. But for us, residents of Wikwemikong, our resolution is taken: we do not want to surrender. Later, if what you have promised to the other chiefs is realized, if they are happy and paid faithfully, we will examine if we must accept the propositions. These are the thoughts of my chiefs.'

"Then the non-Believing chiefs rose successively; first Mijakevangé [Maishegonggai], then Kijikobinesi, Bebaniesse, Itawikisie [Itawashkash] and Bemigewanessikang. They spoke thus to the Great Chief's envoy: 'I accept your proposals, and I surrender what I possess.' Then they marked the part of the island that they were selling. But their names should not have been accepted because they all had their reserves on the mainland, and not here," Choné pointed out. "They do not have the right to give up that which does not belong to them. It is therefore a serious error and an unworthy thing to have accepted a thing that was not theirs to give. Itawashkash, Wakaasi and Debassigue spoke in their turn, and surrendered their property; then they asked that the men of Wikwemikong be allowed to keep their land. They requested us to treat them always as friends. 'It would not be good," Choné said they added, "if you acted otherwise, because the priest has always recommended that we love one another. Then came Tekoman's [Tehkummah's] turn; he surrendered like the others, but they should not have listened to him. He has not been chief for three years; his surrender," Choné concluded, "was worthless."

Choné said that when all the ceding chiefs had spoken, MacDougall rose: "My Native brothers, I am happy to see that you love each other as brothers. For those of you who come from Wikwemikong, you shall have what you desire; you remain proprietors of your land from the middle of Manitowaning Bay to Atchitamaiganing at the entrance to the lake. I add one thing that I ask you to note: Since we leave you more then you need, you must welcome those who come to you and who do not have land. For those who have accepted my propositions, I thank them. They know that I will be faithful to my promises. If up until now you have not received the money that you should for the cession of the mainland, it is because the Government has not extracted the benefits hoped for; but this time, you will draw each year what will be due you. How much? Perhaps two, perhaps three *piastres*. Tomorrow at ten o'clock you will meet the Superintendent. There, your names will be registered and the money that I have brought will be distributed to you."

"Thus finished the council," said Choné. "The next day, the ceding chiefs returned to the Superintendent. Alas. What disappointment! He promised them much and they expected to receive much; however each received only one *piastre*. Grief overcame them and they began to weep."[165]

Choné, disgusted by the whole affair, immediately returned to his tiny room, took up his pen and began his campaign to have the treaty annulled. He and his fellow priests were convinced the treaty was detrimental to their people and to their missions. *Comment voulez-vous qu'ils pensent autrement?*—How could they think otherwise? God and common sense knew that *l'île Manitouline* still rightfully belonged to them, not to this deceitful government. *Certainement*, no-one could deny this inalienable truth.

Chapter 4
Manitoulin Island and Reverend Peter Jacobs

Peter Jacobs
Peter Jacobs usually rose with the sun, rushed around all day and retired exhausted at sunset. But he was awake long before sunrise on Thursday, 2 October 1862. He eased himself out of bed with the stealth of a warrior and the consideration of a newlywed.

Within minutes he was dressed in what he knew she would say was underdressed for autumn and was walking lightly but quickly on the track that led to the woods. He needed to compose his thoughts before the day began for the others.

This was an auspicious day, and the beginning of a few important days in what so far was the best year of his life. But an anxious feeling had gradually overcome him over the past few days, resulting in his inability to sleep.

Once in the woods he slowed down and began to talk to the Lord. He soon felt calm enough to tackle the jumble of troubling thoughts racing around inside his head. By the time the warm rays of the rising sun filtered through the leaves he had prepared himself for the day ahead. He headed back into the village.

Some late-blooming yellow and white blooms caught his eye. He stooped and collected a handful, careful not to damage their roots, and then raced home to present them to his wife.

Today was the first anniversary of Peter and Susan Jacobs' marriage. Their first-*month* anniversary, actually; they had been united in holy matrimony exactly 30 days earlier. Peter still could not believe his good fortune. Truly, he had never expected that Miss Susan Cooper would have ever considered him, yet alone consent to marry him and leave her comfortable home in Mimico for a poor frame house in Manitowaning.

Susan was the third daughter of Reverend H.C. Cooper, the Church of England rector of Christ Church in Mimico, Etobicoke Township, Canada West. Peter and Reverend Cooper had met at one of the annual church synod meetings in Toronto. The senior minister had taken a paternal interest in the young *Anishinaabe*[166] missionary and introduced him to his colleagues and family. He personally conducted the marriage service between his daughter Susan and Peter on the second day of September 1862. Perhaps Cooper recognized someone who, like himself, had overcome prejudice and obstacles to serve God. Henry Cholwell Cooper, B.A., had been born in Dublin, Ireland, in 1806. He was the eldest but illegitimate son of Horace David Cholwell St. Paul, 1st Baronet St. Paul, and Henrietta Campbell Cupples. St. Paul created three families simultaneously by means of one marriage and two concurrent relationships. Henry Cholwell Cooper graduated university, worked as a curate, immigrated to

Canada and served for many years as the rector of Christ Church in Mimico.

His new son-in-law Peter Jacobs (c1832-1864) was the son of Pahtahsega, an Ojibwe who was a well-known Wesleyan Methodist missionary, and Elizabeth Anderson. Called Reverend Peter Jacobs, Pahtahsega had been orphaned and had witnessed alcoholism as a young child. He believed education and Christianization were the only ways for his people to survive. He worked with the native people of the Hudson's Bay territories in the 1830s and 1840s. He also lectured in Canada and England. He was unique among the clergy in promoting both Methodist and Anglican missions. His children were all educated and then placed in *Anishinaabe* communities as teachers and missionaries.[167] Peter, Jr., was educated and later taught at the Church of England's Bishop of Rupert's Land school near Lake Winnipeg prior to his ordination.

So just after sunrise on 2 October, Peter Jacobs rushed into their little home, thrust the humble bouquet at his wife and embraced her in what would have been described as an unusual emotional display by a normally reserved young man.

Susan was also anxious that morning. As the daughter of a very religious man, the Church had been the focus of her entire life. She had always helped her father and now she knew she could help her husband. She had in fact been even busier than he during her first month in Manitowaning. She was learning the language, meeting the residents, working in the daily and Sunday schools, assisting with sermon preparation and trying her best to improve their rustic residence.

In addition to work and concern over the mission, Susan was worried about her husband. He was not well. She had hoped to improve his health with tender care, but the anxiety of the past week only seemed to worsen his illness. He had been suffering for almost a year from frequent bouts of coughing, and sometimes his voice was so weak he could barely read the prayers or preach. Even an extended rest away from the mission that summer had not cured him.

Susan knew that the fact that the day was their "anniversary" paled in comparison to the actual importance of the day. She knew why Peter had risen so early, and recognized that he needed the solitude of the forest to meditate. This was an important day professionally for Peter, and for them as a missionary couple.

Today, the two most important people in the Indian Department were expected to leave Toronto and head for Manitoulin Island, where they would host a grand council to discuss the surrender of the island. Captain Ironside, the local superintendent, had warned Peter that they would arrive on the Friday steamboat. In addition, several hundred *Anishinaabeg* had been invited to hear the visitors. Ironside suggested that Jacobs should be prepared to tour visitors around the mission, as well as "entertain" great numbers at the Sunday church service. This would be the largest gathering the village of Manitowaning had hosted in many years, and the largest Peter Jacobs had ever witnessed on Manitoulin.

The idea of entertaining very important persons had been bothering Peter all week. He wished he had the support of his father-in-law or his former superior,

Dr. O'Meara. He was not accustomed to dignitaries. He had gradually grown comfortable among preachers and even bishops, but Indian Department agents, except for Ironside, intimidated him.

All week long *Anishinaabeg* had been arriving in Manitowaning. Many of them he recognized and had spoken to previously, but seizing on this opportunity to convince them to be baptized was daunting.

The Church of England's Manitoulin mission had been established in 1838 as part of a government-sponsored Indian settlement. Although Reverend Charles Crosbie Brough had baptized almost two hundred native people in the first three years, not as many of them had settled at Manitowaning as Brough had hoped. Dr. Frederick Augustus O'Meara took over the mission in 1841. O'Meara was fluent in the Ojibwe language and translated many documents into Ojibwe, including the Bible and New Testament. He was a persuasive fund-raiser who procured money for the construction of St Paul's Church in Manitowaning and for an assistant: Peter Jacobs.

Jacobs was ordained as a priest and hired as O'Meara's assistant in 1856. On his arrival, Jacobs recorded for his superiors his first impression of the mission: "The Indians of Manitoulin. They do not amount to more than a thousand. Their villages are for the most part situated on the shore of bays. The greater number are Roman Catholics, there is yet a considerable number of heathens, and there are those who profess to belong to the Church of England. The largest portion are Ottahwahs, who come principally from states of Michigan, in the United States, the Ojibways too in a considerable portion; there are few Pottawottamies, who come from the country about Detroit, U.S. The Ottahwahs, Ojibways and Pottawottamies speak what are called dialects of the Algonquin language. These are slightly different. The Indians, as a whole, do not pay much attention to the cultivation of the ground; raise principally Indian corn and potatoes. Some grow now wheat and oats or kitchen-garden vegetables—pumpkins, turnips, carrots, cucumbers, cabbages, onions, beans and peas. Each year they are extending gardens and devoting more attention to agriculture."[168]

Within three years of his appointment, Peter Jacobs was forced to take over the entire mission when the government stopped paying O'Meara's salary. Though the young missionary was qualified to provide education and religion, he was unqualified to provide advice on the most urgent problems of the *Anishinaabeg*—fishing licences, timber regulations and land surrenders.

The Church of England (or Anglican Church) was the only Protestant denomination the government allowed to establish a mission on Manitoulin. Unfortunately, the Anglicans were unable to support more than one missionary at a time on the island, and even this required the support of three Church organizations. Peter relied on his siblings for assistance at the mission.

Though Manitowaning was the centre of government, it was not the centre for the *Anishinaabeg*. By the 1860s Manitowaning was a deteriorating, quiet, nearly deserted village. Most *Anishinaabeg* avoided it unless they had business with the superintendent. Even its resident chiefs, though respected for past achievements, did not have a lot of credibility and were seen by residents of the island's other settlements as superintendent Ironside's men.

Acceptance and Publicity
Jacobs reminisced as he prepared to receive the visitors. Six years earlier, when he had arrived in Manitowaning as a newly ordained deacon, the mission's population was 220, including 21 non-natives. More than half the people, 135 natives and 13 non-Natives, were members of the Church. Despite his efforts, the population had not grown significantly. Every year he had persuaded a number of residents in the three settlements that he visited to accept baptism. Some were simply returning to the Church, some had left the Jesuits and some consented to be baptized by him. Unfortunately, every year a number of residents also left the mission to find work or food, or to join family elsewhere, so the population did not reflect his success.

His first task in Manitowaning had been to restart the school. Attendance had dwindled and finally stopped because of Reverend O'Meara's frequent absences to visit other missions and raise money, and the seasonal travels by the *Anishinaabe* families to their sugar bushes, gardens, and fishing and hunting grounds. Whenever they were in the village, Jacobs lured the children back to school with day and even evening classes. Now the children were again reading, writing and learning.

Like the Jesuits, the Protestant missionaries had always encouraged the children to attend school, though the language of instruction was a controversial issue. The Manitowaning children were taught in English, with Ojibwe translations. Until recently, the Wikwemikong children were taught in Ojibwe and French. Jacobs believed their lack of English-language skills put the Wikwemikong residents at a disadvantage in dealing with the government agents.

Jacobs knew that most of the island's residents wanted their children to be schooled. He urged his superiors to send teachers and preachers. When Bishop John Strachan visited Manitoulin in August 1861, Chief George Abram Ahbedahsoowa of Little Current asked the bishop to send a teacher-missionary, "one to be with us all the time, who shall teach our children those things which are taught the white children."[169] Jacobs had anxiously awaited the arrival of the bishop and proudly presented ten *Anishinaabe* for confirmation on Tuesday, 6 August.

Jacobs was very proud of the translation projects he had worked on with Dr. O'Meara. Now he was able to provide the people with New Testaments, Prayer Books and even hymn books in their own language. He had translated 44 of the 96 hymns in the Ojibwe hymn book, *Nuhguhmoowinun*. Jacobs brought 200 of the 500 copies printed by Lovell and Gibson of Toronto back to Manitoulin for distribution in July 1861. He loved giving out these books. He was especially pleased when recipients returned later and asked him questions about the ideas in the little books.

Though rumours of a surrender of Manitoulin Island were rampant by 1861, Peter Jacobs did not mention them in his reports to his superiors. Chiefs Maishegonggai and Okemah beness, who were members of his mission, were involved in the ongoing North Shore mainland land surrenders, but Jacobs did not seem to consider these transactions to be relevant to Manitoulin Island. His reports, like his work, avoided the controversial issues of fishing, timbering and surrendering. He was Ojibwe but he embraced non-Native life.

Jacobs accepted Captain Ironside's idea that the greatest obstacles to providing religion and education were the natives' scattered communities and migratory lifestyle. "If all the Indians who have been instructed and baptized here had remained in the village," Jacobs said, "we should have had a large number of them by this time; but some of them removed to other villages, some are at Garden River, some at the Little Current and Shegwaindah Bay, and some at Cape Croker and Saugeen."[170] He also accepted his mentor Reverend O'Meara's approach: since isolation of the *Anishinaabe* from White society was unachievable, surrounding them with a healthy and well-ordered White settlement was necessary.[171]

Jacobs' missionary father had concluded that Christianizing and educating the children of the Indian people through mandatory industrial schools was necessary. Though he had been successful Christianizing them in remote communities in the North-West, the distractions of non-Native society led his converts astray. Jacobs, Sr. had witnessed the Saugeen Peninsula treaty in October 1854, through which most of the Bruce (or Saugeen) Peninsula was surrendered to the government and the Indians and their missionary were settled on reservations. The Jacobs family was comprised of teachers and missionaries, and both vocations benefited from compact assemblages of *Anishinaabeg*.

Peter Jacobs, Jr., like his missionary predecessors, competed for converts with the Jesuits and even the Methodists. He attributed his lack of success to geography and to the natives themselves. He, like his superior O'Meara, claimed that the Indians at Wikwemikong appeared to be "more industrious & attend more to the cultivation of the ground than those here" because "they have many Ottawhah Indians among them," and "it is a well known fact that the Ottahwahs, of whom there is a very large number at the village above mentioned, are generally speaking more industrious, & addict themselves more to the cultivation of the ground than the Ojibwas, from among whom most of our converts are gained." Moreover, according to Jacobs, "fish are more plentiful in the waters of Smith's, or as we commonly call it, Wequamekong Bay, than in this bay. This is a great advantage that the village there has."[172]

The Wesleyan Methodist missionaries had been visiting Manitoulin since the 1830s. The Methodist *Christian Guardian* newspaper published news of native missions and championed Indian rights. Jacobs was very worried about the encroaching Methodist missionaries. He reported: "The Methodists I am afraid are beginning to interfere in this Mission. A priest came up lately, wintered among heathen Indians, and is now staying at the Little Current. I understand he has asked his Superintendent to allow him to stay there permanently. He has no members of his church there; and therefore he has no right to plant himself in one of my mission stations. We ought to be up and doing." Jacobs recommended the Church Society "send two more agents to this Mission, one to remain at the Little Current, and the other at Shegwaindah Bay, which is really halfway between this and the other place I have mentioned. The agents should act as a school-master and lay missionaries."[173] Jacobs adopted the competitive religious attitude of his predecessor Reverend O'Meara and tried to use the competition to stir his superiors into action.

All the residents of Manitowaning, including Jacobs, complied with Captain Ironside's census demands in the spring of 1861. Even if they had wanted to resist, their proximity to Ironside in the village meant the superintendent already knew their names and statistics. Jacobs was concerned that the native people were slowly dying out. He noted in one of his reports that Chief James Wahbegagkake (White Hawk) had died at the age of about 55, leaving a widow and only two of his twelve children surviving him. "It makes one sad sometimes to think how fast the Indians are disappearing in this as well as in other parts of Canada," lamented Jacobs. "Like the snow in spring are they melting away."[174]

The Protestant mission at Manitowaning was closely tied to the government. The superintendent, doctor and missionary lived, worked and socialized together by necessity. The government had paid the salaries of Jacobs' predecessors. Jacobs' close association with Ironside probably prevented the *Anishinaabeg* from discussing their complaints about the superintendent with him. Jacobs never mentioned the natives' May 1861 petitions against Ironside, even though the residents of one of his mission stations, Sheguiandah, had signed the petitions.

Rev. James Chance[175] of Garden River on the North Shore travelled with Peter Jacobs to Toronto for the annual church synod meeting in June 1861. They "had a consultation as to the best means of bringing the subject of Indian missions before the people of Toronto." Chance had suggested that Jacobs "should address the assembly in the St. Lawrence Hall, on the occasion of the public meeting." Jacobs immediately responded No; "it was only the great guns that were fired off there." Much to Jacobs' relief, Chance addressed the assembly on behalf of the Indians, and both men were able to return to their missions and announce that their missions had been discussed at the meeting.[176]

In the fall of 1861 Jacobs learned from Captain Ironside that the government was sending commissioners to negotiate a surrender of the island. Ironside assured him that it was the government's intention to deal liberally with the Indians. Jacobs was therefore not surprised when two gentlemen from Toronto and a surveyor arrived in Manitowaning. He was introduced to William Russell Bartlett, the superintendent of the Toronto office of the Indian Department, and to Charles Lindsey, who had been appointed by the government specifically for this project.

On Saturday, 5 October 1861, a council was convened in Manitowaning. All the senior chiefs and men were in attendance, about 130 Indians in total, by Jacobs' count. Four *Anishinaabeg* who had signed the 1836 treaty were also present. Peter Jacobs was asked to act as translator for the commissioners. Fortunately, they provided him with a written copy of their speech. That made his job as translator easier, more accurate and less stressful. Peter was Ojibwe, as were most of the native people from the mainland's North Shore, but many island residents were Odawa, and some were Potawatomi. Though their languages were similar, there were many small differences that did not affect normal interaction but that might be important in his translation of the foreign commissioners' words. Some of the people were dependent on his every word, while others were ready to correct or challenge him. Charles de Lamorandière, a trader from Shebawahning, was chosen by the *Anishinaabeg* to interpret their words to the commissioners.

William Bartlett spoke first. He said that he and Mr. Lindsey had been directed by the Honorable commissioner of Crown Lands, who was also the superintendent general of Indian Affairs, to come and make known to them the wishes and intentions of their Great Father the governor general regarding the island. He said he would address them in English, and then his speech would be interpreted for them.

Jacobs struggled to translate the commissioner's words. He knew some of the statements would inflame his audience:

> You are aware that in the year 1836, the Island on which we are now assembled was the subject of conflicting claims on the part of two Indian Tribes, the Ottawas and the Chippewas and the Government. A compromise was come to at a Council held at this place, on the 9th of August, 1836, between 1,500 of yourselves and your Father, Sir Francis Bond Head, then Governor of Upper Canada, by which the three contending claimants agreed that this Island should be given up for settlement by all the Indians, whom the Government might permit to come here.
>
> At that time there were 9,300 Indians, under the protection of your Great Father, who assembled at an appointed place every year in Upper Canada. It was then thought that this large number would make this Island the place of their future settlement. If they had done so, and followed your example in becoming cultivators of the soil, the intention of the Government in settling this Island with Indians would have been carried out. Unfortunately, however, your people have not availed themselves of the opportunity of collecting, as settlers, upon this Island in a body by whom a large portion of its best soil might have been cultivated.
>
> While regretting that this should be the case, your Great Father has sent us here to announce to you his determination to carry out the principle of settlement agreed upon in 1836, in the only other way that is possible. The quantity of land which, in 1836, was deemed sufficient for the wants of nearly 10,000 of your people is too great to be brought under cultivation by the limited number of you who are actually settled upon it.
>
> Your Great Father is much pleased to hear of the progress you have made in cultivating the land, and thereby securing for yourselves and your families a more certain and unfailing source of subsistence than the chase affords. Far from having any desire that you should remove from this Island on which you were invited to take up your abode, your Great Father is desirous of securing to you by the same title as that by which the White Man holds his land, the soil which your industry has made fruitful.[177]

"They were told that the island would be surveyed, that each family would get 25 acres of land and a deed and that the remaining portion of the Island would be settled by whites," recalled Jacobs, "and they were asked to acquiesce in the wishes of the Great Father, the Governor-General. Several chiefs spoke: only one fell in with the wishes of the Government, the rest boldly maintained that the Island was Indian property, and that it could not be taken from them without their consent. They said also that it was not their wish to give up a part of their land and that they could not consent to its being surveyed."[178]

"Mr. Bartlett then briefly addressed the Council, to the effect that the Commissioners from the Government could not take back bad words against the Government, and that in order to give them time to talk over and reconsider the matter, the Council would now adjourn, and meet again at 12 o'clock, Monday."[179]

When the council resumed on Monday, Peter Jacobs' translation abilities were relentlessly challenged as the second commissioner, Charles Lindsey, and Chief Itawashkash traded words. Jacobs struggled to translate accurately while attempting to minimize the aggressive tones of Lindsey's phrases. Itawashkash maintained that the chiefs had thought about the past and the future of their people, of the alliance of the three tribes, and they were determined to keep the land for their children. He insisted that the commissioners and their surveyor leave without surveying. Charles Lindsey responded at great length, insisting on the government's rights to examine the island and denying that the Indians had perfect and exclusive title to the soil. The two men repeatedly challenged each other with words. Eventually, the commissioners realized they were not going to be able to persuade the chiefs to surrender or permit a survey. When the council ended with handshakes by all, Peter was greatly relieved.

On the fundamental principle of natives sharing the island with non-Natives, though, Jacobs' position was clear: "For my part," he said, "I should be glad if the island was surveyed, and if a part of it was settled by whites. The Indians would derive several advantages from the whites living among them." Jacobs' issues were with the details, not the concept. In particular, he thought each family should get more than 25 acres, "which is plainly insufficient. They should be offered also ample remuneration for the land they are asked to surrender."[180]

Jacobs knew the 25-acre offer was meagre, but not unusual. The government wanted Manitoulin Island for non-Native settlers, and these settlers needed substantial acreage because their 100-acre lots in the southern part of the country had proven inadequate to support them. The Newash (or Owen Sound) band received 25 acres per family on the Cape Croker Reserve in 1857, and the bands on the north shore of Lake Huron received 40 acres per family at Garden River in 1859. Both those bands were also promised annual payments from the interest on the sale of their land.

Jacobs declared "the mission of the gentlemen was therefore a failure," as the chiefs maintained "that it was not their wish to give up a part of their land and that they could not consent to its being surveyed."[181]

Charles de Lamorandière had been the interpreter for the *Anishinaabeg* at the negotiations. "The native people rejected unanimously the propositions of the government," he recalled, but the government spokesman "Mr. Lindsay maintained that the island had been ceded by the government on the condition that it should be entirely populated by the natives. The Potowatomie chief rose and said: 'I was present at the Treaty of 1836. I saw with my own eyes and heard with my own ears, that this island would be exclusively reserved for the native people. If the words of an English governor are not going to be respected, we do not have anything but to regret our fate.' The other chiefs made long speeches; but they did not compare with this brief and energetic speech."[182]

The commissioners and their surveyor left Manitowaning without obtaining a surrender or a survey of the land, but Jacobs knew they would return.

A few weeks later, Jacobs was surprised to read about the surrender attempt in *The Globe*. He was even more surprised to discover the Toronto newspaper's story was not only copied but commented on by almost every newspaper in the country. Jacobs and the other residents of Manitowaning shared their copies of newspapers with each other, as they received them from friends and family. Jacobs' Anglican father-in-law and the Catholic in-laws of David Layton, the Indian Department's doctor, felt it their duty to keep their relatives up to date. Now it seemed to Jacobs that every mail carrier brought more reports on the surrender attempt.

The Globe, widely known as an anti-Conservative-government newspaper, published a lengthy article entitled "Manitoulin Islands, Justice to the Indians" on 18 October 1861. Typical of newspaper coverage in that era, its editorial stance depended on whether the publisher supported the government or not, rather than empathy for the subject. It was therefore not surprising to see an editorial critical of the Conservative government's "paltry humbug" of an offer, and of the government's employment of "hack writers" such as Charles Lindsey to "administer the bribe":

> There can be no question that the Indian titles to lands should not be allowed to stand in the way of the progress of the country. But it is equally beyond dispute that these poor people should not be compelled to surrender their claims without full compensation being given. We fear that in the arrangements proposed by the Crown Land Commissioner to the Indians of the Manitoulin, the rights of the Aborigines have not been sufficiently considered.[183]

While *The Globe* took (and relished) every opportunity to belittle the Conservative government, it nevertheless agreed with the government's fundamental position that Manitoulin Island must be ceded. Reverend Peter Jacobs was of the same opinion on this and on *The Globe*'s view that the deal must include adequate compensation for the island's *Anishinaabeg*.

The press covered the Manitoulin surrender throughout November. Some, like the *St. Thomas Weekly Dispatch*, simply copied *The Globe*'s coverage. Others, including the Methodist's *Christian Guardian* newspaper, took a strong stance against the government's action: "It is pleaded that the Indians obstruct the settlement of the country; that they do not cultivate their lands as they ought; and that the Indian Reserves would be more productive if they were sold to white settlers. Supposing all this to be true, is it a sufficient reason for injustice, and for violating of treaty? The Indians once owned the whole country, and are we now to grudge them the possession of a few wretched patches of land, because they do not cultivate it to perfection?"[184]

One week later the *Christian Guardian* declared:

> The treaty of Sir F.B. Head plainly stated that these Islands were to be "the property

of Indians," that but now the Commissioners tell the Indians that these lands are to be taken from them and sold to white settlers, and that troops will be sent to compel them to submit. In 1836, Sir F.B. Head proposed it to them as an advantage, that they would be entirely separated from the whites, but now the Commissioners tell them it will be an advantage to them to live in the neighbourhood of the white settlers![185]

The *Brockville Recorder* also took an anti-government stance:

No conquered people on the face of the earth have more cause to curse their conquerors than the Indian tribes of the American continent. Despoiled of the country through which they roamed at will, debased and demoralized by "white men's customs, driven from every spot fertile to them in fish, foul, or fur, they have dwindled down to handfuls, where thousands used to roam and flourish unmolested by the European, and the curses attendant on the march of civilization.

The present Government of Canada care so little for the rights of the people, that we are not at all surprised to hear of an attempted robbery by the Indian Department, under the direction of the Hon. Mr. Vankoughnet. It appears that some ministerial speculators have fixed their eyes on the Manitoulin Islands, which are the property of the Indians just as truly as the property held by any man in Canada is his; but they are Indians, consequently John MacDonald and his crew think it no crime to despoil them of their hunting and fishing grounds.[186]

Pro-Conservative-government newspapers and those whose readers were potential settlers carried positive articles on the prospect of land surrender. *The Canadian News*, a British newspaper, carried a report from its Upper Canada correspondent in early November. A topographical description and brief history of Manitoulin were followed by the publisher's considered opinion:

Of all the Indians in Upper Canada, only 1,430 have settled on the island in twenty-five years; the Government; propose to settle the island in the only other way that is now possible—by white people, leaving the Indians in possession of all the lands they have cultivated or can cultivate, and dealing equitably with whatever interest they may have in the island. On the first essay, the Indians did not listen willingly to the proposition of the Government, which was only intended to open up the way and is not looked upon as final. It is not anticipated that the Indians will long persist in opposition to a reasonable proposition for settling this fine island, their interests in it being reserved and protected.[187]

The *Huron Signal* reported "The idea of keeping a country, almost equal to Bruce in size and fertility, out of the market, is preposterous." While there was "a duty as well as a right, on the part of the Government, that is to protect each Indian, in his actual possessions," "the protection had been offered," the writer claimed, and "opening up the island will cause an improvement in our trade, and afford us besides good half way harbours in voyages to the mines, and often on the way also to Lakes Michigan and Superior."[188]

Clearly, the government's attempt to obtain a surrender of Manitoulin Island was controversial. The newspaper publishers eagerly filled their pages with pro- or anti-government stories. The island was still considered by some people to be an ideal, isolated retreat for *Anishinaabeg*; others regarded it as underutilized land better used by settlers. The potential surrender of the island was a contentious issue.

A series of dramatic letters to the editor of the Toronto *Globe* kept Manitoulin in the public eye during the spring of 1862. Two of the letters filled almost entire first-page columns of *The Globe*. Initially, an *Anishinaabe* identified only as "Shan" wrote from Manitoulin to defend his "countryman's rights on Manitoulin Island, against the policy now being pursued by the government with a view to forcing the poor Indians to sell the remainder of their land, which they would like to reserve for themselves and for their children." He explained:

> In the treaty of 1836, between Sir Francis Bond Head, then Governor of Upper Canada, and the Indian Chiefs, it was stipulated that the Manitoulin Island was to be the exclusive property of the Indians who would come and inhabit it. The Governor, Sir F.B.H., made an appeal to the Indians in general, including those residing in the United States territory, to come and live under the protection of their great father—the King of England, (the late King was then living).[189]

"Shan" claimed that the present government prevented the Indians from selling timber and cordwood, and that the overseer of fisheries prevented the Indians from fishing. He admitted that the Indians had agreed in a grand council to prevent a survey, but "none of them has uttered a single bad word against their Great Mother the Queen, or against the Governor General; they have this idea, that their Great Mother the Queen, through her deputy, cannot act towards them in the spirit in which the employees act here. They still believe with confidence in the old treaties." He acknowledged: "There are about twenty Chiefs now residing here. Fifteen of them are determined to maintain their rights on the Island, the remaining five are perhaps willing to sell either for promises or for a few dollars, the whole island.[190]

This letter prompted William Gibbard, the overseer of fisheries, to respond. Gibbard claimed that the "American Indians" came to the island "because they did not like to be moved many hundred miles west by the United States government" and they had no claim "beyond that of unauthorized squatters, to any part of the island." As for timber and fish, they could "fall in with the Government plan," or take up "a free deed of their land and improvements and then enter into the wood business." He declared "there will be little or no difficulty in making arrangements with all the Canadian chiefs, if the proper course is pursued."[191]

Gibbard's letter prompted a response from William Keating. Keating and Gibbard illustrate the extreme opinions about the *Anishinaabeg*: Gibbard, a former land surveyor and the current overseer of fisheries, believed the Indians wasted land and resources that should be surveyed, sold and settled or worked. Keating, also a former surveyor as well as an ex-Indian Agent, considered the Indians a resource to be utilized. Though he had used his multi-lingual fluency and surveyor's skills to benefit from Indian land, and may have had undisclosed motives for opposing a surrender, he believed Manitoulin should remain a sanctuary.

Keating expressed his disapproval of Gibbard, the fishing regulations and a surrender of Manitoulin. Keating asserted that Sir Francis Head had "assured the Indians that it should be set apart entirely for their use and for that of any of their brethren who chose to leave the United States for the purpose of taking up their abode within the limits of British territory." Keating explained that an Indian could only become a freeholder if they could speak and read another language beside their own vernacular, "an educational clause" that "would materially affect the franchise men in the vicinity of Collingwood."[192]

Gibbard responded again. He defended his actions and insisted: "this great barrier to the settlement of the North Shore should be removed, and that a tract of land equal in extent and fertility, to the County of Bruce, capable of affording a living to 20,000 people, should be opened at once for settlement; and that a few scattering Indian villages, and patches of corn and potatoes, 15 to 20 miles apart, should not be addressed any longer as an impediment to the end."[193]

The series ended abruptly with William Gibbard's second letter. If there were further exchanges they were not printed. The letters did not generate a noticeable response from the general public. Manitoulin's fate was left to the politicians to decide.

Back on Manitoulin Island, the revised wood regulations were causing problems. Manitowaning residents had been earning money by supplying wood to the steamboats since 1846, and some of them had moved to Little Current in 1854 to supply wood directly to the boats plying their main route. Peter Jacobs ignored the wood controversy, though a number of his parishioners were affected. Jacobs was *Anishinaabe* by birth and ability, able to survive and travel in the North-West; but he was non-Native in attitude. He did not seem to understand the intense feeling of ownership and stewardship over the island and its resources expressed by the Manitoulin *Anishinaabeg*. It was his North Shore Church of England colleague, Reverend James Chance, who protested the timber regulations on behalf of the *Anishinaabeg*:

> The Indians came to me for advice in response to the "Notice" issued by the Department on the 7th August 1862. They did not understand the why and the wherefore of the prohibition and why they must obtain a Licence to cut that which they had always considered as their own. I referred them to the Local Superintendent when he came to pay them their annuities, and advised them to apply for a Licence and then they would understand all about it. I am sorry to say however that no satisfactory information was given and no Licence issued. As a Missionary and one who has devoted his life to promote civilization & Christianity among the Indians I cannot but regret that a Prohibition should have been issued by the Indian Department which interferes with their habits of industry and cuts off their chief means of subsistence (during the winter) and has driven several families away from the village beyond the reach of religious instruction to resume their old occupation of hunting. If I am not asking too much I should feel exceedingly obliged to you if you would at your earliest convenience inform me why the "Notice" was issued.[194]

Peter Jacobs was sick with a nagging cough for most of the winter of 1861-62. By summer 1862 his voice was so weak he was almost unable to speak. He travelled to Cape Croker in May and to Toronto in June and August. It was a dry summer and island residents were worried about the lack of rain and how their crops would be affected. Jacobs and every island resident knew that Captain Ironside was continuing to promote the surrender of the island, despite the rejection of the October 1861 proposal. Jacobs admitted to extended absences over the summer for "longer rest, as I was not very well." His absence meant that not only did he not witness Ironside's surrender campaign, he left no other authority figure to advise the *Anishinaabeg*. Dr. Layton steadfastly restricted himself to medical advice.

Peter Jacobs returned in September accompanied by his bride, Susan Cooper. He was not surprised to learn that new government agents would be arriving within the month to present new terms of surrender. He *was* surprised, though, to learn that they would be the most important men in the Indian Department, the commissioner of Crown Lands himself and his deputy. Captain Ironside assured him that the offer was going to be generous and the mission would prosper as a result of the proposal.

The Treaty and the Protestants
At mid-day on 3 October 1862, Peter Jacobs joined Captain Ironside, Dr. Layton and four *Anishinaabe* chiefs to welcome the distinguished visitors to Manitowaning. While the superintendents strategized, Reverend Jacobs and Dr. Layton gave politician David Reesor and journalist Samuel Day a tour of Manitowaning and the surrounding area. Predictably, Day, who had just spent 36 hours with the pro-treaty superintendents, was not impressed with Manitowaning. He described it as "At one time an exclusively Protestant settlement, but it contains at present 42 Protestants, 44 Catholics, and 10 heathens. It contains the residence of the agent and of the doctor, both of whom are remunerated by the Canadian Government out of the Indian Fund. A school had been established here, but it was abandoned, although for what cause I cannot say. This village was built entirely at the expense of the Indian Department; a forge and several workshops were erected, and for a time everything prospered; but owing to various causes, not the least of which is the nomadic character of the Indian bands, it has fallen into complete decay—three-fourths of the houses being either deserted or ruins. In the centre of the village is a commodious Anglican Church (built at a cost of 4,000 dols.), which I attended on Sunday, when the service was performed partly in English and partly in Indian."[195]

Day continued: "Most of the Indians have left the village, and taken up their abode at Little Current, Garden River, Saugeen, and Cape Croker. The missionary who succeeded Dr. O'Meara, is Mr. Jacobs, a half-breed, whose father, a converted Indian, gained some notoriety as a preacher among the Wesleyans. At Manitowaning and its neighbourhood, the number of Indians who are members of the Church of England amount to sixty-six. Those at Shezwaindot Bay, fourteen miles to the north-west, number merely fourteen; whilst those at Little Current do not exceed fifty-one. ... Twenty children attend the evening school, and nearly an equal number the Sunday school, in both of which Mrs. Jacobs, the missionary's energetic young wife, takes a warm interest. ... Mr. Jacobs, although zealous and attentive to his duties, yet lacks other qualities essential to success as a missionary to the Heathen."[196]

Evidence suggests that Day misjudged Jacobs. He was in fact a popular preacher and teacher who simply lacked the social skills to fraternize with or question the superintendents. His colleague Reverend James Chance described him as "the best educated and most accomplished young man of Indian blood I had ever met with, and his character as a Christian missionary was very estimable."[197] Jacobs had also impressed his superiors and other colleagues. The Reverend H.C. Cooper had been so impressed that he permitted Jacobs to marry his daughter.

On the other hand, Day was impressed with the island's potential. He praised the land, but criticized the natives. He noted the abundance of fish and timber, the successful corn and potato crops, and the temperate climate, but also remarked on the 1,200 native residents living in 10 small villages who were underutilizing the resources.

In contrast to the Anglican settlement at Manitowaning, the Catholic village of "Waquimakong," or at least its site and structures, impressed Day: "This village rises gracefully and gradually, upon the hill, which looks down on the magnificent bay of the same name. From it the eye reaches 18 or 20 miles over the great Lake Huron, towards Georgian Bay. The village itself is regular, and consists of several rows of houses, rising in the form of an amphitheatre, one above another." He commented on the neat log houses, the large stone church with a 100-foot-tall tower, the stone mission house, two schools and the newly constructed weaving factory and gristmill. Though he praised the village itself, he maintained his negative attitude towards the priests and *Anishinaabe* residents there.[198]

The tour of the neighbourhood given by Jacobs and the doctor reinforced his idea that Manitoulin Island was underutilized by the natives, and its greatest potential would be realized by non-Native settlers.

On Saturday, 4 October 1862, Peter Jacobs joined the throngs heading to the government storehouse. He recognized some of his parishioners among the men. Most looked serious and thoughtful. Many were wearing their best clothing. Some smoked and others just watched. He noticed the newspaperman was already writing notes.

Jacobs had been relieved to learn that Francis Assiginack was responsible for translating the speeches. Jacobs had acted as translator at the previous negotiations and had found it stressful. Nevertheless, he knew that he was one of the few people among the two or three hundred that could understand both the speaker and the translator, though even he was sometimes confused by the chief superintendent's formal phrases. Jacobs joined the visitors in the meeting room. He watched and listened attentively but silently to the speeches. The council meeting began on Saturday, was suspended over Sunday and resumed on Monday.

On Saturday, William McDougall addressed the assembly, with the assistance of Francis Assiginack. He explained the wishes of the government for the future of Manitoulin and its residents. Jacobs was greatly relieved by McDougall's firm but conciliatory tone. The young minister was not the only one who clearly recalled Charles Lindsey's aggressive threatening words one year earlier. Jacobs was also relieved to learn that the government's offer had been greatly increased, from twenty-five to one hundred acres per family. He was not particularly surprised by the response of the people. Even Captain Ironside had not expected the immediate approval of an offer, no matter what it held.

Sunday was Peter Jacobs' day. He held two church services and was very encouraged by the attendance. He reported that "A great many Roman Catholic Indians were present on each occasion. They appeared to listen very attentively. Just before the Indians separated to go to their respective villages, about fifteen Roman Catholics came into the house, and asked me for some of our books, which I gave them. Some asked for the Prayer Book, some the Testament, some our Hymn Book and some the First Book of Lessons. I was very glad to see such a desire on the part of these Indians to see and read our books. May they derive benefit from reading them. May God bless them, and lead them into the truth by means of the books they have received."[199]

Afterwards, he could only summarize the proceedings for his superiors:

> The Superintendent General of Indian Affairs in this Province, and the Deputy Superintendent General, came here a few days ago, and held a Council with the Indians who live on this Island. About 200 Indians met together at this place. Most of the chiefs were at first unwilling to accede to the proposition of the Government. After further consideration they concluded to take the terms that were offered to them. The Indians are to be paid for the land which they have surrendered and which will be sold to the whites, each head of a family is also to get 100 acres of land and a deed. That part of the Island alone, which lies to the east of Heywood sound and Manitoulin gulf, was reserved by the Chiefs there for themselves and their bands.[200]

Peter Jacobs was not surprised that a surrender of the island was achieved. The natives had initially rejected McDougall's offer, which centred on 25 acres per family, but eventually the increased acreage, combined with the suggestion that a treaty was inevitable, caused some of the people to reconsider.

Though the reporting varied, McDougall was understood to have said in his opening remarks that he would give the natives "an authentic title that assures you forever the part of the island that you choose, far from where the Whites will settle. The rest will be sold, and the money from the sale deposited in the bank, after the surveyors have been paid. Each year, you will be paid the interest on this money." Or, in this slightly more detailed version: "I shall give you an authentic title, called a deed, which shall assure you your ownership. You shall choose good land and it is there that you shall live from now on. When the survey is done they shall give you 12 months to make your choice. You may not take there where there is a river, as that would be an obstacle to construct a flourmill or a sawmill; nor in the bays that can serve as harbours for vessels. It is not there that you shall be. It is necessary to make your choice somewhere in the centre of the island. Your choice made, only then shall they sell. The Great Chief does not want to have the money from the sale; it shall be for you. What remains after paying the surveyors shall be put in the bank and the interest shall be always paid to you."[201]

Then McDougall promised the people future prosperity, including fair access to merchants and mills. He offered 100 acres to families and orphans, and 50 to single men, and promised education for the children and freedom from taxation.

Peter Jacobs and the *Anishinaabeg* focused on the 100 acres for every family, as well as land for orphans and unmarried adults. This was a great improvement over the 25-acre offer in 1861, the 25 acres the Newash (or Owen Sound) band accepted in 1857, and the 40 acres the North Shore bands accepted in 1859.

Though everyone had listened to McDougall's offer, and the deed of cession had been read aloud before it was signed, even an experienced negotiator might not have understood or foreseen the effects of the actual clauses. The deed of cession covered three pages and contained nine clauses, including one on land selection that had five sub-clauses.

For Jacobs, the most promising part of the treaty was the first sub-clause of the second clause, the collection of *Anishinaabeg* on lots "contiguous or adjacent to each other so that Indian settlements on the Island may be as compact as possible." The fourth sub-clause of the second clause also pertained to the *Anishinaabeg* settlement. Lots "contiguous to any bay or harbour, or any stream of water upon which a mill site shall be found" should be reserved in the opinion of the government for the public, village or park lots—which meant that almost every band could be removed from its current home. The conditions governing the acreage locations were restrictive and a potential hardship for fishermen, boat builders and those who sold wood to steamboats.

The provision of an annual payment of "interest which may accrue from the investment of the proceeds of sales of land" and the stipulation that "every Chief lawfully appointed shall be entitled to two portions" were not unusual concessions, though clearly there was a financial incentive for chiefs to sign their names. The treaty also stipulated payment of the resident superintendent's salary and office expenses after 100,000 acres of land were sold had the potential to curtail profits for the Manitoulin Island *Anishinaabeg*. The right to take fish was meaningless, and did not address the *Anishinaabeg*'s dispute over them requiring licenses to fish.

But it was one of the introductory "whereas" statements—"sell the other portions fit for settlement, and to invest the proceeds thereof, after deducting the expenses of survey and management, for the benefit of the Indians"—that severely curtailed profit for the Manitoulin *Anishinaabeg*. Similar clauses had been inserted into the 1857 Newash treaty as "deductions for defraying the expense of survey and the subsequent management of the sale of the land as are incidental by a general rule to all other Indian lands," and the 1861 Colpoy's Bay treaty as "after deducting cost of survey sale and other incidental expenses." But Manitoulin's size meant the survey costs were very high. In addition, the government intended to charge the cost of roads against the profits. The thousands of dollars soon spent on surveys and roads drastically affected *Anishinaabe* remuneration.

In brief, the 100 acres per family was in keeping with then-current standards.

The inability of the *Anishinaabeg* to claim water lots, and the deduction of expenses for surveying, road construction and management, were at once lucrative for the government and catastrophic for the *Anishinaabeg*.

On Tuesday, 7 October 1862, Peter Jacobs signed the deed of cession as one of nine witnesses.

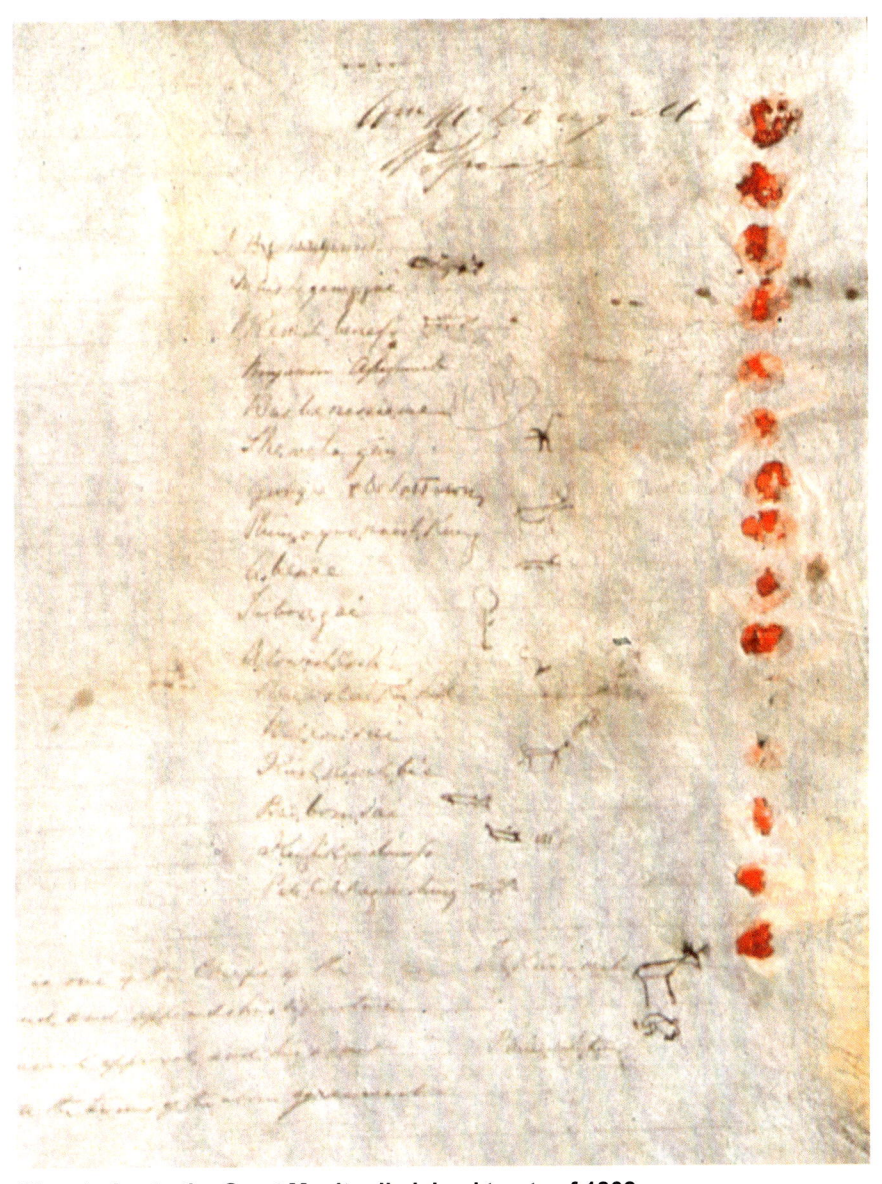

Signatories to the Great Manitoulin Island treaty of 1862
"Surrender of land by the Ottawa, Chippewa and other Indians"
Credit: Library and Archives Canada / IT 237 [detail]

The names of these signatories are transcribed in Appendix 1, pp. 167-68.

**Department of Crown Lands. The Honble W^m McDougall, Commissioner.
Plan of part of the north shore of Lake Huron shewing the subdivision of the new townships.** Scale, six miles to an inch. W.C. Chewett & Co. Lith Toronto. Department of Crown Lands, Quebec, January 1863.
W^m McDougall, Commissioner. Examined T. Devine, Head of Surveys, U.C.
Credit: Library and Archives Canada / NMC21601 [detail]

Following the October 1862 treaty that ceded most of Manitoulin Island to non-Native settlement, an existing 1862 subdivision plan of the north shore of Lake Huron was used as a base map on which surveyors' comments about the island's suitability for settlement and development were added.

Manitoulin Island / Odawa Minising / l'île Manitouline
Place Names in 1862

1 Killarney / Shebawahning
2 Little Current / Wewebijiwang / Petit Courant
3 Lonely Island / Akiwesi Minis
4 Manitowaning
5 Maple Point / Naimonakekong
6 Michigiwatinong (now M'Chigeeng)
7 North Shore
8 Providence Bay / Mindemooyasebe
9 Sheguiandah
10 Sheshegwaning
11 South Bay / Achitwaigunning
12 Sucker Creek / Aundeck Omni Akaning
13 Wikwemikong
14 Wikwemikongsing

Manitowaning, Manitoulin Island
William Armstrong, artist, 1891
979.64.3
With permission of the Royal Ontario Museum © ROM (ROM 979.64.3)

William Armstrong (1822-1914) evidently travelled and sketched views of the Great Lakes soon after his arrival in Canada in 1851. This watercolour of Manitowaning painted in 1891 appears to be a scene from the 1850s-1860s. The large red building on the shore of Manitowaning Bay is the warehouse in which several hundred people met in October 1862 to discuss the Great Manitoulin Island treaty.

Wikwemikong, Manitoulin Island
"Numbering Indians at Wequamikoong Manitoulin Island 16 Aug 1856"
William Armstrong, artist, 1908
Credit: Toronto Reference Library, Baldwin Room, JRR 2422

On the reverse of this watercolour painting's cardboard mount is the following inscription, presumably written by Armstrong:
  [Chie]f Assigenack (deserving chief) is shown naming the Indians to
  [Cap]tn Ironsides, Indian Superintendent, whose office was in building,
  [le?]ft, in a front room: Many of the Indians had to be told
  [thei]r proper names by Chief Assigenack who was provided
  [by] the government with an Undress Uniform: Two [?] HB Voyageurs
  [are] represented in Centre of picture in their pretty dress
  WA

William McDougall (1822-1905)
"Hon. William McDougall, Member of the Executive Council and Commissioner of Crown Lands"
c1862 - 1864, Quebec City, Quebec
Credit: William Ellisson / Library and Archives Canada / C-008362

Sasso Itawashkash (?-1882?)
"E-dah-wah-Skaush"
Paul Kane, artist, 1845
With permission of the Royal Ontario Museum © ROM (ROM 946.15.35)

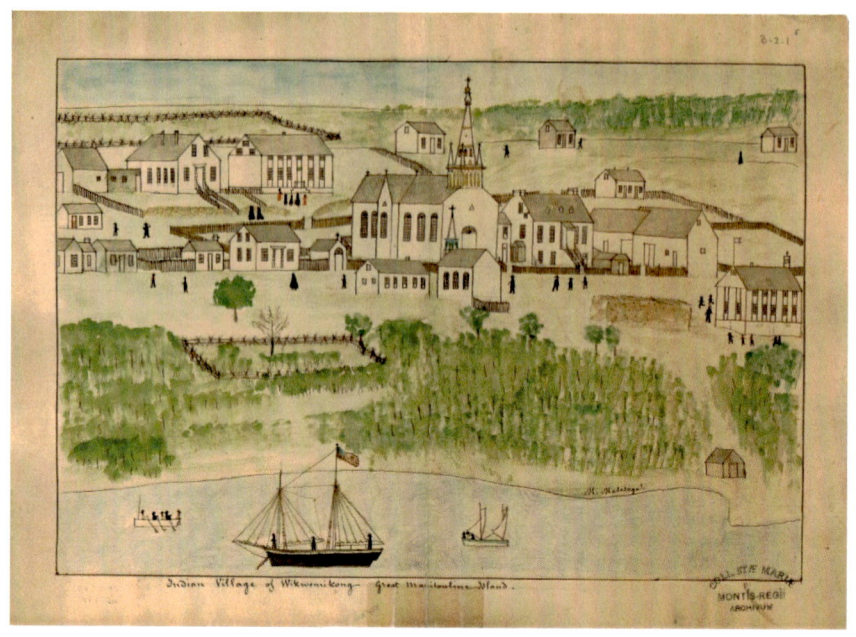

"Indian Village of Wikwemikong Great Manitouline Island"
M. Metosage, artist, c1853
Credit: Archive of the Jesuits in Canada, AJC-GLC, BO-0043-22

Jesuit missionary at Wikwemikong, August 1856
William Armstrong, artist, n.d.
Credit: Henry C. Campbell, *Early Days on the Great Lakes: The Art of William Armstrong* (Toronto: McClelland & Stewart, 1971), pp. 66-67 [detail]

This presumably is Père Joseph Hanipeaux.

Peter Jacobs, Jr. (c1832-1864) (attributed)
Tintype, private collection

This photograph was found in the papers of Church of England missionary Jabez Waters Sims' family. The unidentified person may well be Peter Jacobs, Jr., Sims' immediate predecessor at the Manitoulin Island mission.

Jean-Baptiste Assiginack (c1770-1866)
Amable Assiginack (c1788-1878)
"Portrait of Jn. Bte. Assiguinak & Amable Assiguinak"
Nicolas Point, artist, c1848-55
Credit: Archive of the Jesuits in Canada, AJC-GLC, BO-0043-25-26-20

Antoine Makons (c1819-1859)
Jean-Baptiste Atagiwinini (c1792-1867)
"Portrait of Makonss & Jn. Bte. Attaguewenini"
Nicolas Point, artist, c1848-55
Credit: Archive of the Jesuits in Canada, AJC-GLC, BO-0043-25-26-22

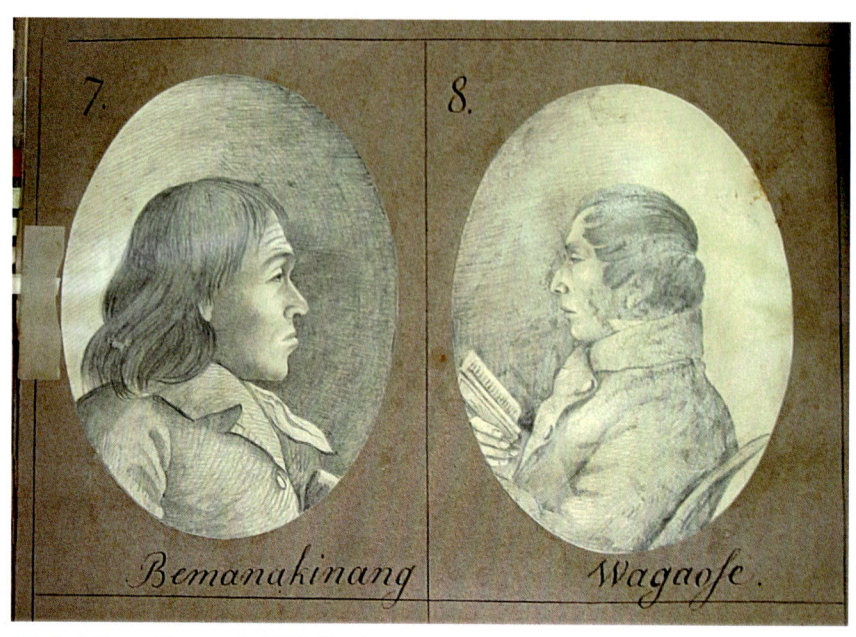

Michel Bemakinang (c1798-1878)
Wahcowsai (c1809-?)
"Portrait of Bemanakinang, and Wagaose"
Nicolas Point, artist, c1848-55
Credit: Archive of the Jesuits in Canada, AJC-GLC, BO-0043-25-26-26

William Gibbard (1818-1863)
Credit: *Annual Report of the Association of Ontario Land Surveyors,* 1920, p. 102

The steamship *Ploughboy,* at Collingwood
A.E. Young collection and other views of North America, 1858-1958
Credit: Andrew Merrilees / Library and Archives Canada / e008299992

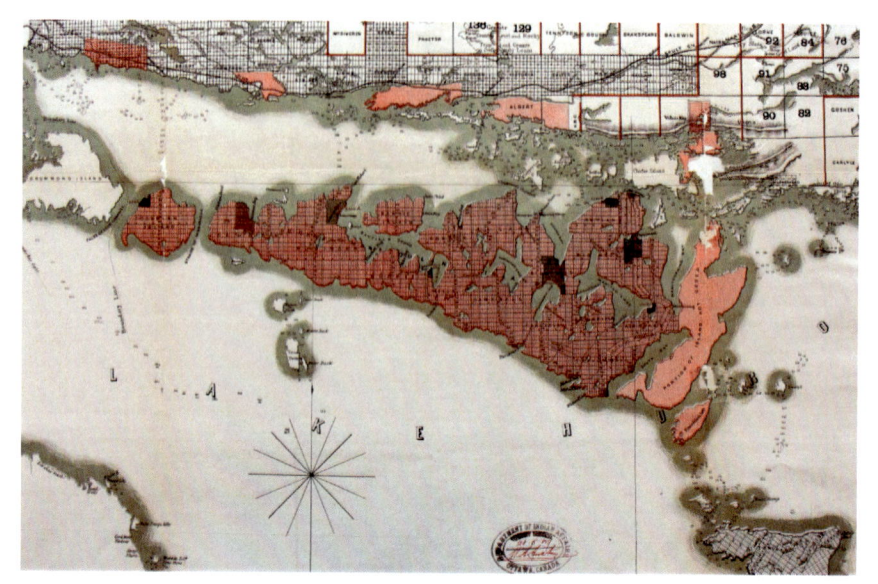

Department of Crown Lands. Honorable T.B. Pardee Commissioner. Map of the North Shore of Lake Huron. Scale, 6 Miles to an Inch. 1886. Credit: Library and Archives Canada / NMC83504 [detail]

This map created by the Ontario provincial government in 1886 shows the surveyors' subdivision grid covering the majority of Manitoulin Island. The reserves are shown in a darker tone; the unceded land is located on the eastern portion of the island.

Chapter 5
Reaction to the Treaty

The Reaction of the Press
The Globe was the first newspaper to publish a full account of the treaty, on 16 October 1862. William McDougall must have supplied the details for this strongly pro-treaty article. There was a clear change in attitude from *The Globe*'s negative October 1861coverage of Bartlett and Lindsey's failure to McDougall's success one year later. The change was due not to the improved offer, but to the change in government. The Reform government of John Sandfield Macdonald and Louis-Victor Sicotte had assumed power in May 1862. George Brown, publisher of *The Globe*, was a Reform party member who used his newspaper to promote the party and its platform. Brown and McDougall were intimate journalism, business and political colleagues.

MANITOULIN ISLAND.
MISSION OF HON. MR. MCDOUGALL.
AN IMPORTANT ARRANGEMENT EFFECTED WITH THE INDIANS.
The Commissioner of Crown Lands has returned to Toronto from his visit to the Great Manitoulin Island, having succeeded in effecting an arrangement with the Indians for the cession of their lands to the Crown for purposes of settlement. To understand what has been accomplished by Mr. McDougall, some preliminary explanations may be necessary. The Indians have been accustomed to cherish the belief that they hold the Great Manitoulin Island by a peculiarly sacred title, the great spirit Manitou having bestowed it upon them as a mark of his special favour. The Canadian Government, however, have never recognised this alleged gift of Manitou as establishing a title which they were bound to respect, and have claimed the Island, as belonging, like all the other public lands of Canada, to the Crown. In 1836, Sir Francis Bond Head, then Governor of Upper Canada, entered into negotiations with the Indian possessors of the Island, his object being to make an arrangement which would allow the Government to remove to it the Indians then residing on the mainland, in the Saugeen Peninsula, in the neighbourhood of Lake Simcoe and in other districts. He induced them to surrender their exclusive claim to the Island, to the extent of vesting it in the Government, who, it was provided, should hold it in trust for the benefit of all Indians whom they might allow to reside on it. The scheme of deporting the Indian population of the mainland to the Island has never been carried out, and on the Manitoulin Island, containing nearly a million of acres, the total population at the present time scarcely exceeds 1,200 souls. The late Government attempted to negotiate with the Indian inhabitants for the transfer of the Island, with a view to its being surveyed and sold to white settlers, and Mr. Bartlett, of the Indian Department, and Mr. Charles Lindsey were sent up last year as Commissioners, to conduct the negotiation. These gentlemen were authorized to offer the Indians, on condition of their giving up their claim, a lot of 25 acres for each family, with an additional quantity of land, the precise amount not specified,

for firewood, &c. The Indians refused to listen to the overture on such terms, and persisted in their refusal, although threatened with a visit of troops to enforce compliance. The Government did not think proper to carry out this threat, and the proposed arrangement fell to the ground. The present Government decided on proposing more liberal terms to the aboriginal inhabitants, and Mr. McDougall, having obtained an Order in Council defining the nature of the arrangement to be made, went up in person the week before last to meet the head men of the Indians, and induce them, if possible, to make an amicable surrender of their proposed rights. He was accompanied by the Hon. Mr. Reesor, M.L.C., Mr. Spragge, of the Indian Department, and Mr. Day, the correspondent of the London (England) *Morning Herald*, and took with him as interpreter an Indian youth, Assickinack, the son of one of the chiefs of the Island, who bears the same name. Young Assickinack was educated in this city at Upper Canada College, and is employed in the office of the Indian Department. The party, leaving Toronto on Thursday, the 2nd instant, took the steamer "Ploughboy" at Collingwood, and reached Manitowaning on Saturday morning. There Mr. McDougall found the principal men of the Island assembled to meet him, and proceeded to explain the terms offered by the Government, viz., to guarantee 100 acres of land to each head of a family, 50 acres to each single person over the age of 21, and to each single orphan child, and 100 acres to each orphan family of more than two children, and further to secure for the benefit of the Indians the whole proceeds of the sale of the lands, after deducting the costs of survey and management, and of constructing a few leading roads. This proposition, although much more favourable to the Indians than that made to them last year by the late Government, the chiefs were not induced to accept without some trouble. The Waquimakong tribe, comprising nearly half the population of the Island, strongly opposed any surrender of the native claims. This tribe or band occupy the eastern portion of the Island, and are under the instruction of Roman Catholic missionaries. The other Indians are for the most part Protestants, and, having separate interests from their Waquimakong brethren, were more disposed to listen to any fair offer that might be made to them. The influence of the Waquimakongs, however, was sufficiently powerful to prevent them from publicly advocating in the first instance the acceptance of the Government's offer, with one exception. Old Assickinack, the head war-chief, said to be 94 years of age, and who appeared decorated with medals which spoke of brave deeds he performed with Tecumseh in the war of 1812, delivered a harangue advising a settlement on the proposed terms. He expressed his confidence in the Queen and the Government, and said the Indians were much better off since they had come under the protection of the white man. Formerly they had to kill their game with bows and arrows, and to boil their food in stone kettles, and were very poorly clad. Now they had good clothing, blankets, guns, kettles, &c., and the shelter of good houses. This should give them confidence in the Government. For his own part he was quite satisfied with their proposition, and advised his brethren to accept it. The speech of Assickinack made quite a commotion. Some of the Waquimakongs sounded the war-whoop, and made threatening gestures, but the old chief's sons stood ready to protect him, and no violence was offered him. A Pagan Indian, however, was set up to attack him in a very abusive speech. Mr. McDougall adjourned the meeting for an hour or two, in order to give the Indians time to consider his proposal and their answer to him. At the adjourned meeting, there was still no general disposition manifested to accept the overtures of the Government. Mr. McDougall then further adjourned the meeting till Monday. He told them that he understood a portion of the Indians had been attempting to exercise intimidation over the rest, and had been threatening them with violence if they entered into the arrangement; that this could not be permitted; that those who were opposed in total to the arrangement might go away, and that those who were inclined to entertain it favourably might remain and discuss the matter further on Monday. The result was that all remained, and on Monday the Commissioner found matters in a better train for successful negotiation. The Indians finally agreed to surrender, on the terms proposed, the whole of the Island west of the portion held by the Waquimakongs, which the Commissioner conceded should be left undisturbed. The treaty was signed by all of the chiefs outside of the Waquimakong band, and also by one of the chiefs of this band, with his two *aides de camp*, the rest expressing their concurrence in the surrender. The chiefs attached to the document as their signatures various symbolic representations of the creatures of earth, air and water, constituting their individual or family distinctions, the savage aristocracy being as fond of heraldry as the proud peers of the old world. The treaty, as finally signed, contained a clause expressing the desire of the Government to have the whole Island, and leaving it open to the Waquimakongs to come into the arrangement whenever they feel so disposed. On the part of the Indians, a desire was expressed that in the future management of the Island the Government would entirely prohibit the admission of intoxicating liquor. At present there is a law prohibiting the sale of liquor to Indians, but it is constantly broken by unscrupulous traders, and the chiefs feelingly denounce the traffic as a prolific source of ruin to their young men. They desired that in future a better look out be kept for the whiskey traders, and that the traffic to the Island, whether for white man or red man, when it is opened for settlement, should be entirely prohibited. The Commissioner promised that their wishes on this head should be duly weighed by the Government. The treaty will take effect from the date of its sanction by the Governor in Council.

It is believed that there is enough good land on the Island to make five or six townships. After the survey is made, the Indians will be allowed a year to select their lands. They will not be allowed to choose lots suitable for mill sites, or situated on any harbour or bay. After they have made their selection, the remaining lands will be thrown open for sale on terms likely to encourage settlement. The Island is well timbered, in some parts with hard-wood, and in others with pine. The climate is said to be favourable for farming operations. Mr. McDougall's party saw in gardens at Manitowaning as fine tomatoes as can be found in the neighbourhood of Toronto, of large size and perfectly ripe; potatoes also of the first quality, no such thing as the potato rot having ever appeared on the Island. Melons, cucumber, &c., are found to thrive luxuriantly.[202]

Treaty witness David Reesor's newspaper *The Markham Economist* also announced the treaty on 16 October 1862: "Hon. Mr. McDougall, Crown Lands Commissioner lately made a visit to the Indians of the Islands of the Georgian Bay, for the purpose of investigating, on behalf of the Government, their grievances, and if possible to negotiate with them for some lands in their possession. After satisfying them that their rights would not hereafter be neglected by the Government, they were disposed to treat with him." A week later, *The Markham Economist* published *The Globe*'s account of the treaty.[203]

On the same day, the *Hamilton Evening Times* reported that McDougall had announced at the York Agricultural Society's annual dinner "he had just returned from a trip which had for its object to add to the agricultural wealth of the Province, by the accession of the Manitoulin Island and its opening up for the benefit of our farmers. He was glad to be able to say that he had obtained the cession of the Island from the Indians to the Government of Canada, and it would shortly be opened up. He thought there would be found upon it half a million acres of good arable land." The announcement was applauded, and the reporter suggested McDougall "deserves the thanks of the country for the energy he has displayed in the matter."

The *Huron Signal* responded enthusiastically to the treaty:

> A Step in the Right Direction.
> We are glad to see that Mr. McDougall's mission to the great Manitoulin has resulted in the attainment of the desired end, and that many thousands of acres of highly fertile land is to be open to civilization immediately. The Manitoulin is, in many respects, an important Island. Possessing a virgin soil, and being admirably situated on the highway of Western Trade, it will give comfortable and prosperous homes to numbers of settlers who will certainly visit it the moment the land is offered for sale. The climate is salubrious, and those who have lived upon it state that its vicinity to vast bodies of water has a tendency to obviate the late and early frosts incident to places much further south. This will be a great desideratum to the farming community, while its nearness to the Mining Districts of Superior, the Fisheries, and its position with regard to the navigation of Lakes Huron, Superior and the Georgian Bay, must ultimately give it a commercial importance of no mean value. And, while this is the case, it is gratifying to know that this is but another step towards Western extension. The available lands in the Indian Peninsula, Manitoulin, and the Algoma District being filled up, attention will naturally be turned to the regions beyond. We cannot expect that the great object—the opening of the North West—is to be gained in a day or a year. The work must be a gradual one, that is, until the region of sterility is reached; then a single stride ushers the indomitable Anglo-Saxon race into the fertile plains of the Far West, teeming with all, or most elements of National wealth. That stride may not be taken in our day, but gradually the climax will be reached, and it is to be hoped that men will be found equal to the momentous occasion.[204]

The pro-government press embraced the treaty as part of the Department of Crown Lands' plan to open the West through surveys and settlement. *The Quebec Mercury* had announced on 30 September that McDougall was leaving for Manitoulin Island "to meet with the Indians on Friday, to negotiate for the surrender of their title to the occupancy of the island." On 16 October, the *Mercury* reported that McDougall had "succeeded in his negotiations for the acquisition of Manitoulin Island as a field for settlement." Two days later, the *Mercury* published *The Globe's* account of the mission, but described the surrender as incomplete, "the Waquimakong tribe—numbering it is said, about half of the entire body of resident Indians—having refused" the offer.

On 21 October the *Mercury* printed a clarification: "For though half the Indians are yet to be brought to terms, the quantity of land affected by their refusal is a mere fraction of the whole." The *Mercury*'s reporter commended McDougal for "pushing forward the construction of roads through the tract of country starting at Lake Huron, with a view to their extension westward through the Superior region. Construction was to start immediately on extending the Muskoka-Parry Sound road to "a point from which Manitoulin Island will be easily reached; and again forward to a junction with the line already opened eastward from Sault Ste. Marie."

Many newspapers announced the treaty, often with excerpts from *The Globe*'s report, but coverage and attitude depended more on the newspaper's political affiliation than sympathy with the people actually living on the island. Even the British newspaper the *Canadian News, New Brunswick Herald, and British Columbian Intelligencer* reported the treaty, though it quoted only the pro-treaty *Globe*, *Mercury* and *Leader*, so British readers—potential immigrants—read only a positive land acquisition story.[205]

The Markham Economist followed its treaty negotiation reportage with an article promoting the settlement of the island. David Reesor, the newspaper's publisher and an eyewitness to the treaty, claimed to have explored Manitoulin extensively. He described it as "quite as well situated as any of the lands on the north shore of the Georgian Bay," only a few narrow channels and an island away from the mainland. Additionally, the actual channel that bordered Manitoulin was the regular steamboat route between Collingwood and Sault Ste. Marie. Positive descriptions of the island's soil, climate, harbours, timber and waterpower, which was "sufficient to supply milling and manufacturing power for 100,000 settlers," were reported. He closed with an assurance to readers that, even at "a distance of 40 miles from a white inhabitant, accompanied only by our Indian guides and interpreters, we met with only kindness and courtesy both from Christian and Pagan Indians, but more especially from the former, who were always ready to give information or assistance in any way that they had it in their power."[206]

Controversy arose over the treaty when *The Daily Spectator and Journal of Commerce* [Hamilton] broke the news that McDougall had negotiated the surrender accompanied by his brother-in-law, David Reesor, a politician and land speculator. Echoing the comments made by the *Spectator*, the Catholic *Canadian Freeman* newspaper published "The Manitoulin Injustice" on 6 November:

> Some light is beginning to dawn upon the proceedings of Mr. Commissioner McDougall in connection with the recent plunder of the poor Indian of the Manitoulin Islands. On this subject we shall have a word or two to say next week. For the present, we shall be content to quote from the Toronto correspondence of the *Hamilton Spectator*. The writer appears to be "well posted" on whatever subject he treats, and in this case he evidently speaks by the book. Be the statements true or false they are of sufficient importance to invite investigation and to urge Mr. McDougall to give such explanations as will satisfy the public and remove all suspicion of malversation in office from himself.
>
> After describing the visit of the Commissioner of Crown Lands to Manitoulin and his operations with the Indians, the correspondent of the *Spectator* proceeds to say:– Here ends the first part of the transaction, and whatever difference of opinion may prevail as to his conduct and management, the Commissioner must not be too severely judged. Never having to any one's recollection set himself up for a Talleyrand or a Nesselrode, he might still command our forbearance as a conscientious and well meaning official, for people do not expect that the so-called "heads" of departments should display any unusual amount of brains. But there is another, a darker side to this transaction—a sort of after play, which may lead people to question something more than his experience and sound judgment. The

Hon. Mr. McDougall rejoices namely in a brother-in-law, Right David Reesor; and, not having, like Clineas of old, renounced all his kindred and friends on taking office, this gentleman formed one of the suite which accompanied the Commissioner on his diplomatic mission to the island. Now, it is a fine thing, and the old song goes—"To be brother-in-law to a great, magnificent there tailed bushaw," and when a man happens to be not only a brother-in-law but a politician, an honorable, and a greedy land speculator to boot, his chances for feathering his nest are generally considered pretty good. So it happened here. When the Commissioner of Crown Lands departed by the Mackinaw boat, the Hon. Mr. Reeser (be particular about the ee, Mr. Compositor, for otherwise it might read like a razor and I do not want to be playing with edged tools!) remained on the island on some very particular business. This circumstance itself would, perhaps not have signified much: he might have staid there to bathe, fish, hunt, cultivate friendly relations with the natives, or for any other reason. By and by it leaked out, however that the Government had decided to sell the lands at Manitoulin for fifty cents the acre, and that in a quiet way, which throws an entirely new light on this subject. Mr. Reesor, if I mistake not, is a gentleman already somewhat famous for his shrewd land speculation in Bruce, and as there is an abundance of very choice land on the island, he was quite likely to take advantage of old father time by looking about here also for a snug investment on behalf of the family. Those thousand acres, (more or less, as the deeds say) at Manitowaning, which Government cleared for some apostate Indians who afterwards left this site for Waquinnikong, or some other place which nobody can pronounce without haemorrhage on the lungs, would be rather cheap at half a dollar per acre, and were certainly worth looking after. Still all these are only speculations and rumours which the Commissioner of Crown Lands will no doubt explain. For all I know to the contrary, he may have left his brother-in-law with the keen eye for "nature with her hair uncombed,"—(how do you like this poetical expression for wild lands? it is original) on the island, to see that no more Indians ran off and joined the Jesuit fathers, for whom Mr. McDougall has such an orthodox horror, especially when their influence happens to be used against him at the hustings. But, then—as old Jack Falstaff already complained—this is a very bad world to live in, and Mrs. Grundy is apt to think the worst of all that she does not understand. Now the sale of lands where the clover in many places grows knee-deep, where the soil is rich and the climate genial, at fifty cents per acre, does look a little strange. So does the circumstance that the Commissioner should have departed from the usual practice of offering the land to general competition at public auction, as the Government did in the Saugeen peninsula, by which the proceeds of the sale might be increased several hundred per cent. In fact, considering that the Government holds the relation of trustee towards the Indian, who is the real beneficiary, any other manner of bringing the land into the market would be unjust, if not absolutely illegal. Putting therefore the low price, the mode of sale, the brother-in-law, this, that, and the other, together, the Honorable Commissioner of Crown Lands should certainly notice these reports, were it only to silence those who pretend to see in them evidence of a "family compact". He may be innocent, but were he a very Spartan in virtue, such appearances will stain his reputation. Honesty, in the popular acceptance of the word, is only relative, and must stop somewhere, as the moral philosopher said when he ate the sucking pig sent to his friend.[207]

Though melodramatic, the article was accurate: David Reesor was a member of the Legislative Council of Upper Canada, a brother-in-law of McDougall and a land developer, as well as founder and editor of *The Markham Economist*.

The *St. Catharines Constitutional* initially reported that McDougall had succeeded in getting a treaty signed by "fourteen of the Chiefs for the surrender for the whole of the Islands, with the exception of the Wikwimikong and Wikwimikongsing."[208] One month later, the *Constitutional* commented on the Hamilton *Spectator*'s assertion that McDougall's brother-in-law was profiting from the Manitoulin Island surrender: "If it is true that the government permit jobbing and speculation in the choice lands of the island, they ought to be visited with the severest condemnation. The job looks all the blacker from the relationship of the parties implicated."[209]

The news that a survey of Manitoulin Island was in progress prompted *The Canadian Freeman* to publish "More About The Manitoulin Jobbery" on 4 December 1862:

> The party appointed by Commissioner McDougall to complete the fraud initiated by himself, on Sunday the 5th of October, against the Indians, reached Manitoulin Island on the 9th ulto. Their mission is, to explore and survey the tracts of land, of which the poor red men have been robbed by as base trickery and palpable swindling as the most expert black leg could employ. So shameful has been the wrongs inflicted, and so unprincipled the expedients resorted to in order to perpetrate the wrong, that we have no hesitation in affirming that, the wrong doer and his accomplices ought to be indicted before the bar of justice, in the same manner as any foot-pad or swindler arrested for robbery or for obtaining goods under false pretences. We have already published evidence sufficient to show the pseudo-treaty—which Mr. McDougall coaxed or cajoled the minority, or Protestant portion of the Indians to sign, on Sunday the 5th of October, while the Catholics were absent sanctifying the Lord's day,—to be a nullity and a "sham" in the eyes of the law. Notwithstanding this fact, it is to be feared that, the Commissioner of Crown Lands will be shielded by his position from receiving his just deserts. Nay, so far from Mr. McDougall being impeached for the Manitoulin fraud, we have every reason to surmise he will be permitted to share, without remonstrance or exposure by the press or the Legislature, the profits, which his brother-in-law, Mr. David Reesor, is about to reap from the transaction.
>
> We remonstrated against the action of the late administration last year, when Mr. Charles Lindsey of the *Leader*, and Mr. Bartlett of the Indian Department were sent as Commissioners to conduct negotiations at Manitoulin. We remember very well the loud and indignant protest of the *Globe* apropos of the flagrant injustice contemplated by the Cartier-Macdonald Ministry against the "poor Indians." What a change has come over the opinions of our contemporary, with the change of the government? If he does not yield a willing assent to "the McDougall inquiry" he has not one word to say in condemnation of it. We cannot blame the *Globe*, however, for passing over in silence the conduct of the Crown Lands Commissioner. In doing so it but follows in the track of other journals, from which we had expected something better than a tacit and cowardly connivance at wrongdoing—no matter who or in what position the guilty party.
>
> We too, like some of our confreres of the press, promised the Ministry "a fair trial," but we made no promises to pass over in silence, or refrain from condemning, any act of the Ministry, individually or collectively, that we might consider deserving of censure. To do this for any party or under any consideration is beneath the dignity and honor of the journalist. We regret the manifest dispositions of many of our contemporaries to "eat their peck of dirt" by becoming the toadies and

apologists of men like Mr. Wm. McDougall. Their fyles would show since last June a remarkable change of sentiment towards the members of the Cabinet. We have no objection to the somersaults which our contemporaries have turned if the Ministers actually merited the favorable change of opinion; but it is nauseous and disgusting to find journalists belabouring with fulsome praise—without any deserving—the very same men whom they covered, not six months ago, with the filth of their abuse. Unqualified subserviency and vassalage, such as we have indicated, must disgust the very men who are made the objects of a homage degrading alike to the recipient and to him who offers it. In our humble opinion there is no journal so serviceable to a party—be it an organ or otherwise—as the one that bestows blame and praise as occasion may demand. The carte blanche given by our contemporaries to Mr. McDougall's Manitoulin operations, have induced the foregoing remarks.

To return to our subject, which we think it almost useless to discuss any further, since we fear that the crying injustice towards the poor Indians of Manitoulin, is not likely to be prevented. Nevertheless some benefit may be derived, by imparting additional information on the matter to the public.

The *Globe* published some time ago an article on "The Mission of the Hon. Mr. McDougall in Manitoulin Island." This article is a remarkable piece of nonsense and misrepresentation. We shall follow it in our remarks.

The Canadian Freeman later retracted its claim that the treaty was concluded on Sunday. The Methodist *Christian Guardian* newspaper commented on the *Freeman*'s assertions:

The Manitoulin Indians.
The *Canadian Freeman* has a second lengthy article in strenuous opposition to the late Government arrangement respecting the Manitoulin Islands. It asserts that only about one hundred of the Manitoulin Indians are Protestants, that one hundred and fifty are Pagans, and that all the rest are Roman Catholics. It asserts more over that the recent treaty was made, as well as the former one relating to these same Islands on a Sunday; that it was made with two or three chiefs, and not with the tribes; that these chiefs accepted it under a sort of compulsion; that one of them is father to the Government Interpreter, Assiganauk, and himself receives a salary and presents from government; said that the great body of the Indians protest against the whole arrangement, as being illegally accomplished, and as being in direct violation of former treaties. The matter is plain, if the above statements are correct. Is it a duty to do justice with Indians, to keep faith with them, to regard their legal possession and title as sacred as the white man's? We feel just as anxious for justice to Roman Catholic as to Protestant Indians, and we believe the claims of justice and the obligations of solemn treaties ought to be inviolable under all circumstances. We do not know whether the above statements are correct, nor whether the treaties expressly gave the Indians a title to the whole of the Islands. The *Freeman* says the bargain was completed on Sunday while the R.C. Indians were absent at Church, while the Commissioners profess to have dealt liberally in allowing each family 100 acres of land. It has been reported, in former years, that agents were allowed a large percentage on the sales of Indian lands; there has been a great anxiety to create a fund out of which to pay the salaries of agents; and it is probable that one agent is abundantly sufficient for all the business the Department has to transact with the various Indian communities. It is an old complaint of the tribes that they were always shut out from all remedy, because all their memorials and petitions for redress of grievances had to go through the hand of these self same agents, and that

they could seldom or never reach the ear of the government. We hope there is sufficient honorable and Christian feeling among our legislators to secure a rigid investigation of Indian affairs, and to establish such principles and regulations as will protect them from injustice in all time to come. Whether they be Pagans, or Christians, Romanists or Protestants, let justice be done them. Otherwise God will have a controversy with us.[210]

The Markham Economist responded to the *Freeman*'s anti-treaty reports with "The 'Freeman' and The Manitoulin," declaring "these charges are without foundation." The author, presumably David Reesor, claimed the treaty was not signed on a Sunday, but negotiated on Saturday, the 4th of October, then adjourned until Monday the 6th. He insisted that all the Roman Catholic chiefs "on the main body of the Island, as well as all the Protestant Chiefs, freely, and of their own accord, after holding council amongst themselves, signed the Treaty. The only parties resisting were the Waquimakong Indians, a village under the immediate control and influence of Father Chenet." After describing part of the negotiations and the terms of the treaty, he alleged "the *Freeman* would prefer to see a million acres of good land withheld from settlement and practically kept under the control of two Jesuit Priests."[211]

The press evolved from discussing the treaty itself to arguing over the sale of the land. *The Quebec Mercury* defended McDougall, and claimed "not only has no sale been effected or thought of, but no proposition for the purchase of the Island has been received from the quarter named or any other." The *Berlin* [Ontario] *Telegraph* reported: "The conditions of the surrender by the Indians secure to them twelve months in which to locate the lots reserved to them. During that period, the survey will go on. And until these arrangements be completed no propositions for purchase will be entertained by the Department. Till then, gossipers about 'jobbery' and 'corruption' may hold their tongues." The Hamilton *Spectator* concluded: "It remains to be seen whether there was a bargain, our correspondent merely intimating that rumour said there was some kind of understanding about 50 cents an acre. We shall be glad to learn that no arrangement has been come to for that the purpose of disposing of the lands in question to favored individuals."[212]

The Globe reported: "It is absolutely imperative that the condition of actual settlement be attached to every purchase .... The Indian lands have been managed on different principles, however, from the Crown Lands, and in no case that we are aware of have they had the condition of actual settlement attached to their sale." The reporter concluded by asserting that "the Catholic priest on the island has been making exertions, through powerful influence of the Roman Catholic Bishops in Lower Canada, to secure the sale of the lands by auction without actual settlement conditions."[213]

Reesor's *Markham Economist* tackled the sale and price of Manitoulin land. He alleged that the commissioner of Crown lands was being pressured by the Catholic priests and bishop to sell the Manitoulin land to the highest bidder without providing colonization roads and free grants for settlers. Reesor predicted the result would be land speculation, not settlement. He recommended one hundred miles of colonization roads with adjacent free grant lots, and the remainder of the land sold at 50 cents per acre to actual settlers, thus providing the Indians with valuable 100-acre lots in the middle of civilization and a generous income from land sales.[214]

On 4 December, *The Markham Economist* printed the account of the negotiations written by Samuel Day, the *London Morning Herald*'s journalist and treaty witness:

The proceedings commenced by the Commissioner shaking hands with the chiefs, according to their desire, made known through the interpreter, a son of old Assickinack, who was educated at Toronto College, and is now in the employment of the Indian Department. Mr. McDougall next essayed to state the object of his mission, and explained the intentions of the Government towards the Indians on the Island. The Indians met the proposition with a storm of indignation; the chiefs of the Wequimakong tribe being most strongly opposed to a relinquishment of their reserves. Several chiefs, or persons deputed by chiefs, delivered lengthy speeches, wherein they set forth in very poetical language and logical order, the grounds of their opposition. After every speaker had concluded, he shook hands, first with the commissioner and then with all those round the table. During the sitting of the council great excitement was manifested, and, horrible yells, and even the war whoop was given. Only poor old Assickinack was favourable to the proposed arrangement. He expressed his confidence in the Queen and the Government, and said the Indians were infinitely better off since they had come under the protection of the white man; for his part, he was satisfied with the proposition made to him, and he advised his brothers to accept it. The poor old warrior's address created wild commotion, the painted Indian placed his hand on his war-knife. But the chief's two sons stood ready to protect him. A Pagan Indian immediately stood up at the desire of his fellows and attacked the old man in very abusive speech, and, fearing lest he should come to grief, one of the officials removed him from the Council. The chiefs opposed the project with great vehemence. "As for you, brother," said one, addressing the Superintendent General, "God has given you money; as for us Indians, we have been living without it. God has given us the land to cultivate for our own use, on which we get what we want. I cannot rob my children of what belongs to them. The propositions made by the Government to us long since, have never been realized, and the poorer we are. We are not able to receive your propositions now. I wish, as poor as I am, that I would be left alone. I want only to keep the strip of land I now hold for my children, and I wish you to pity me in my state. My wish is to keep the land just as it is." Finally the Council was adjourned for a couple of hours, in order to give the chiefs an opportunity of consulting together. Upon re-assembling most of the Indian chiefs were firm in their opposition to the intentions of the Government. The possibility of entering into any negotiations seemed hopeless, and Mr. McDougall further adjourned the assembly until the following Monday, at the same time, informing the Waquimakong Indians and others who made the most formidable opposition to the projected treaty, that they may return home, as their presence was not again required. Meanwhile rumours had spread that some of the Indians came to the council armed with pistols and knives, and that acts of violence were likely to occur at the next meeting. Our party felt under a little apprehension for a time and precautionary measures were adopted in case of violence being offered. At length the leading chiefs were got together, the propositions in the proposed treaty and the intentions of the Government more lucidly explained, the result of which was, that before the second council was held, three chiefs had been brought round, an object in part effected by the immediate pecuniary advantages offered to them and each Indian of their respective bands. The council on Monday went off quietly, contrary to what had been expected; so I congratulated myself on my happy escape from being scalped—anything but a desirable process, judging from an elaborate description of the operation which I had heard on the island. The horrible fiendish face of that painted Indian I have mentioned, disturbed my repose by night, and haunted me by day. The council meeting on Monday, which was largely attended by Indians was protracted till a late hour; but everything was arranged for the signing of the treaty on the following morning. On Tuesday the majority of the chiefs, warriors, and their "aides de camp," assembled in a room in the agent's house, when the treaty, written on vellum, was laid on the table, read and interpreted. Eighteen chiefs and one or two head men appended their marks to the document, which, as specimens of Indian heraldry may be regarded as remarkable. One chief of the Waquimakong band, and two of his aides-de-camp, signed the treaty on behalf of himself alone, and to show his concurrence in the object of the Government. The heraldry of this savage aristocracy consisted of symbolic representations, such as the beaver and the bear on his back, the crane, the reindeer, the pike, and other similar creatures on earth, in air, and in water. Much merriment was occasioned at the artistic attempts of some of the chiefs, who failed most miserably in delineating the object they intended. When the treaty was duly signed and witnessed by your correspondent and others, a few hundred pounds were divided among the contracting chiefs for themselves and their bands, varying in sums, from one to two dollars, which amounts were not given as a gratuity, but as advances upon the anticipated emolument to be derived from the sale of the lands in the island.[215]

The Canadian Freeman responded to McDougall's and Day's versions of the treaty with an account "written by the Indians themselves," addressed to the governor general, and translated from French "as closely as possible to the plain and simple mode of expression peculiar to the Indians." An accompanying editorial admitted the *Freeman* had incorrectly reported "the treaty was signed on Sunday," but noted the "iniquitous transaction was finally completed through the manoeuvres which were employed on Sunday, to secure the signatures for the following day."

Account of the Conference at Manitwaning, 4th October, and what the Chief (Mr. Macdougall) said there:
He waited for the savages to go and give him the hand, when he was seated at the place of the counsel. They did not go there. They said to him: You who come here to address us, it is for you to be the first to give us the hand. It is then that he arose and came to give the hand to our chiefs; and after having given the hand he spoke:
My comrades—My Indian friends—the moment is arrived to make known to you why I am come here into your island. It is I whom the great chief has charged to have care of you. I am at the head of the Indian Department; and it is in this quality that I come to demand from you your little island. I have not entrusted any one with my commission; I come myself to bring this decision to you. I have reflected, in order to determine what could be of utility to you; I do not wish to treat you in a manner that would be injurious to you. I have made haste, notwithstanding the multiplicity of my occupations—for I have not to occupy myself with you alone, there, from whence I came; but the thought to come immediately to see you has prevailed. There is a great number of people in the surrounding country whose regards are fixed on your isle; and it is not to one place alone that their looks are thus directed, but really to a great many, in order to come there to pitch their camps. If you do not now accept what I propose, all your efforts will not be sufficient to repel the cultivators—nor mine—nor those of the great chief; and thus you will find yourselves thrust aside without any benefit. If, on the contrary, you now give me

your land, you will have to congratulate yourselves for the profit that it will bring you. This is why I have had a duty to come in haste to labor for your well being. If you do not now accept the propositions I bring to you, perhaps others will come, and treat you in a manner which will not be well for you—for, perhaps I shall not be long in power—because some of those of whom I speak have designs, without reason, it is true, to take your land from you. This is the way they reason: The great chief, named Sir F.B. Head, had decided that all the Indians of the neighbourhood should come to settle here, that which has not been done. Consequently, if we wish to consider things well, it must be said that you are not the proprietors of the island, for the condition imposed has not been fulfilled. You alone are not in sufficient number to occupy it. It is useless for you to embarrass yourselves with this fine land. There is a large number at the lower side of the streams who wish to cultivate this land; they wish to go still farther towards the west, to seek land to cultivate. As to those who came last autumn, certainly they came by commission. Some one said here that they came without commission. Assuredly they were sent; but as certainly they promised you too little. They have told you that you are not the owners of the island. Today, I do not tell you that. Assuredly you are the owners of the island. If you transfer it to me, I shall treat you perfectly well; it will be a means, a reason, to watch over your safety. I shall give you an authentic title, called a deed, which will secure to you your property. You shall choose a good farm; and it is there you will live henceforth. When the survey shall be made, they will give you twelve months to make your choice. You may not select where there is a river—it would be an obstacle to the construction of a flour-mill or saw-mill; nor in the bays which would serve as harbors for vessels. It is not there that you shall locate; it is necessary that you make your choice somewhere in the centre of the island. Your choice made, it is then only that they shall sell; and of the money which will come from the sale, the great chief does not want any for himself—it shall belong to you. Whatever will remain after the payment of the surveyors, shall be placed in bank, and the interest shall be always paid to you. If therefore, you now accept the propositions I have made; you shall be perfectly happy. The whites will come here in great number, bringing with them all kinds of things. There will be farmers and merchants. Everything will be cheap—you will no longer suffer for anything. You will no longer be obliged to go to seek for some person to exchange your products—you shall receive just payment for them. You will no longer be deceived, as formerly—you shall be, henceforth, well treated in all respects. You shall get everything with facility—everything will be brought here. There will be near you, flour-mills, saw-mills, forges—you will no longer have to go to a distance for your implements of culture. In a word, you shall be surrounded (with every comfort?) [sic] by the great chief. It is, also, very advantageous to the great chief to have your island. It is from here, especially, that he will take what is necessary to construct a road for fire-waggons on the main land, as far as the head of the current. This is what shall be given to you, respectively: Each family, 100 acres; a young man over 21 years, 50 acres; an orphan young man of 21 years, 100 acres. And the taxes which are given to the great chief, you will not give them. And your children shall be well instructed. I have learned that you have come with arms; and I also have come with the forces of the great chief. Whoever will use violence against those who shall speak, will be treated with rigor. Each one should be free to speak—all should express their thoughts. I invite whoever wishes to speak, to do so. Or, if you wish, first reflect and deliberate on the propositions I have made to you.

 Itawashkash said : First, for a little moment, I go to consider what you have said.

 The English chief said: Be not too precipitate; select well.

 Pekoneianone said: Haste! what, then, have you still to consider? Quick let him know our thought. Do we not wish, then, any longer to keep that which they come to demand from us? For a long time we have habituated ourselves to the thought that we are immovable. There remains, therefore, nothing new to consider.

(The English Chief went out for an instant)

Deliberation of the Indians.
And this is what we have further said together, we who hold to our land: Considering the words which we have heard, we have not thought for an instant to give up our land, which they come to demand from us; for we do not possess any other land—it is all that remains to us. Then, of that which they are to give us, as we have been told, only us full grown men will receive for each family, 100 acres; to young men of 21 years they promise 50 acres; and to orphan youths of 21 years they also promise 50 acres. This is all they have promised to give us—to full-grown men alone. But there is a great number of other children—young girls and boys—girls from 20 years down to 1—those who are born to-day as well as those who may be born in the future. Behold, all things we have considered and weighed, and we have not thought at all to do injury to our children now existing, or those who shall be born. If we should abandon our land, they will, absolutely, not have any property. That is what we have said to each other in assembly.

(They ask for the great English chief.)

Itawashkash said: My brother, I make known to you our thoughts—having first reflected on the words which you have addressed to us. It is not for the first time that we consider these things; no, we think of them always. This is my thought: I hold to my land—I shall not give it up. What I said last autumn, when they came to make this demand of me, is still my thought and my word today. I, also, wish always to preserve to my child this my land—the little I still possess. It is here the Great Spirit gave me to live, and I do not wish to abandon it. For you, it is there below, as the other shore of the great water, that it has been given to you to live; and it is there below, probably, that is situated the allotment which you name to us—not here. It is necessary to despatch speedily, for at present we have a great deal of labor, harvesting what we have grown. Not one of us, so far as I can see here, is idle. You retard us; you should hasten now, and finish. Such is the thought of our chiefs here present.

Words of the English Chief: Well, I have heard your thought, and all that you have said. It is useless; they will not cease to speak to you; the great chief absolutely desires to get your land. They will not speak to you any more as they have done up to the present time—in a body. They will visit each of you on your farms and make the demand of you individually. Those who will accept the proposition, their word shall be taken; the land of which they are the proprietors shall be taken. Mark well what was said by those below, at the foot of the stream—that which has been said by yourselves: It is here that the Great Spirit has given us to live. They were wrong; moreover, they ceded their land in spite of everything, although they held to it. That, also, is what shall happen to you, as it did to them. At the present time, the whites there below fill the land. That is what shall take place here. You will not be able to prevent them, despite all your efforts to keep them at a distance; I could not either, nor even the great chief. They will come here to pitch their tents, in spite of you. As to you who now hold to your land, you who come from Wikwemikong, you have only to return to your labors; nothing more will be said to you. There are, perhaps, some among you here who receive favorably what I have said, and who will accept my proposition. Let those not go. When Sunday will be passed away, I shall speak to them. There is, probably, still a little provisions here to give them to eat to-day and to-morrow.

That is what the English chief said on Saturday, and how he ended his action for a short time.

Assiginak said: I give you the hand, my brother, I press you with all my strength, and I embrace the Queen. That is what he said to the English chief. Then he spoke as follows to the savages: Well, my little brothers, my co-Ottawas, it is I who am the first-born of all, as many as we are, on the island of the Ottawas; in fact, of chiefs and braves I am the first-born. But you cannot say: My ancestor came here. You were born in many places. The ancestor of the Ottawa alone came here. For myself, my Ottawa ancestor came from there below where the sun sets; it is from there that I am come. Yonder, at Majitashky, as they say, it is there that I have dwelt; then I arrived here; and that is why I also think that I am a proprietor here; and I give up all that I possess.

Jacko arose whilst Assiginak was still speaking. Mr. Ironside (local superintendent) tried in vain to stop him, but was pushed away. Jacko said to him: Tell that old man to sit down.

Mr. Ironside replied: He has not yet said all that he has to say.

Jacko answered: It is not for him to speak. My chiefs desire that I should say what I have to say.

Assiginak asked: Who are you?

Jacko: I call myself Jacko. Atagwinini is the name of the old man who reared me.

Assiginak: Your word will not be of any service. Like your filthiness, which spreads its odor on every side, such shall be its value.

Jacko: Assiginak, you are an old man (94 years); you see the moment near at hand when you will leave this earth. Look to your grave. It is not for you to say anything here. You are too old; you are not capable of treating the matters those collected here are discussing.

Speech of Jacko to the Hon. Mr. Macdougall: My brother, truly I am perfectly pleased to see you, to-day, whilst the sky gives us light. That is what I have always desired. I thought that we should see him who is at the head, that I should hear himself speak; that he, also, would hear my thought, I whom they call Indian (*Anishinabe*). That is why I repeated yesterday evening: To him who came to speak to me first I answered, I shall not listen to you. (He alludes to the mission of Mr Lindsay, in the autumn of 1861.) My brother, now my chiefs make known to you their thought. Is it really now that the happiness of the savage is about to commence, now that you are come to demand from him his land, in its full extent? Attention, my brother; there is no mention now of what you promised to pay to those who gave up that main land. You promised them four dollars. Look here, my brother, at my pantaloons; they cost me four dollars, and it is not with the payment you made me for my land that I bought them. It is the sugar taken from the trees here in my little island that has procured them for me. This is what I say to you, my brother: Look at me, recognize me; I am myself a chief of that main land which my father ceded to the great woman chief (the Queen). It is not I who would have spoken, if my father had been able to come; he it is who would have addressed the word to you. I am not ashamed to display my misery before you, as much as it is to be seen. Truly, I am filled with astonishment. Who is this great woman chief? Is she an unfortunate, this great woman chief, as she is called? Is she not the one whose riches are overflowing in her land? And, today, how many miseries are suffered by him who has abandoned his land to her! And further, my brother, now, again, you come, to say: The great chief has sent me to demand your land from you; that great woman chief has given all her authority to the great chief whose court is in Quebec. This is what is said by my chiefs, whose word I bring to you: This land, which you come to demand from us, we shall not give it up. I singularly admire, again, what you have said. Would not this be the expression? That the small number would, perhaps be quite right to make this cession! Such a thing never takes place. It is the great number, the majority of the judges who decide what ought to be done. And now you say: There are, perhaps, some here who find good what I say, and who will accept. No; for myself, I would not refuse a gift that you would make to me from your own wealth; but mine, my property, that you wish to give to me—you! I shall never listen to you. What astonishes me much, my brother, is, that you come to me and say: Your land is excellent. For myself, who know what the land which I inhabit is, I say now: What you see here full of rocks is not good, without doubt. That is what it is in the whole of the interior; in a few places only it is good—there would not be enough for ten of your farmers, as I know the quantity of land necessary for each. Lakes are also in great number, as well as marshes and rocks. I, who call myself a savage, could never grow anything in the water nor on the rocks. Certainly, my brother, what I say to you now, it is painful to me to say. Never have I had the thought to cause the loss to the great chief of the money which he has in his purse, by saying that my land is good; as I know it, as I see it, so do I speak of it to you. I do not wish to speak long to you my brother; the days are short in this season, which the Great Spirit has given us. We cannot finish now the affair which you come to treat; it is already late. When the light shall return, it will be the day of prayer, when only the things of the Great Spirit can be treated. With the new light no one shall speak of these things.

Sakiwinebi said: That Assiginak, who is seated yonder, who expressed himself with so much vanity, I know perfectly whence he has his origin. At the time when our fathers used to go in search of scalps, they brought a man who had been seized there where the sun sets, where dwell the savages who are called Akiwewegiwame. That is whom he has for ancestor, that Assiginak. He is an Akiwewegiwame, he who sits yonder—that is, a slave. He said not the truth, when he said: I alone am truly Ottawa—The savages, who also knew the affair, said to him: What you say is true. That is really what he is.

F. Assiginak (interpreter to the Commissioner and son of the old man before mentioned) said: What good is it to speak thus to our ancient? Do you not know that he, also, sees himself near to his grave? What you said then is a disgrace to him.

Sakiwinebi said: Well, neither had he the right to say what he said. By the way, just now, little would have been necessary to cause us to quarrel about the words he made use of. What I said, I did not say without reason. I was right in what I said.

F. Assiginak: Finally, it is not what he has said that will take place, but really what all the savages together shall say; that is what shall be done.

Thus ended the conference, late in the night of the Day of Mary (Saturday).

This is what took place on Sunday night: There was a traitor named Miskomanetone. He had fire water; he gave it away to be drank. Now this is the one who carried it. A son of Assiginak carried it to his elder brother, Itawashkash, to make him drink, telling him at the same time to give up that land which we possessed in common. But he would not listen so long as he was in his senses; but did afterwards, having lost his understanding—he was drunk. It was then, it appears, that he said: I yield. That is one very bad thing which has occurred. And what have those done who served as instruments to deceive the Indians for their land and at the same time to make drunk those of whom they made the demand? He was drunk the whole night, until morning (It is thus the law against the sale of liquors to Indians was observed during those shameful transactions). When day broke, these same instruments of deception made haste to complete their task speedily. They went to Misagwange, and he told them the promises which had been made to them, thus: That they should be leading chiefs—that they would be held in consideration by the whites—that they would be honored, and be in a state of perfect welfare—and that for all time. Those are the promises made by the great chief who came (Mr. Macdougall); that is what he said to each one, having called them separately. In going to give their names, they used great haste, before we from Wikwemikong could arrive. When we did arrive, they told us that four chiefs had given their consent. One of them—Itawashkash—had, nevertheless, declared that no one could, of himself, give up the smallest thing in the island. It could only be done when our accord was unanimous. That is what had been declared by Itawashkash (son of old Assiginak). This manner of acting is certainly the more vicious, as such a cession has been received as lawful. Those who have acted thus are a small number; their conduct is known; they are those who have been suspected. We have, therefore, separated from them, holding firm to our resolution to preserve our land for ourselves and for our children present and to come, for it is all we now possess. Yes, certainly, we are the owners. It is here that our ancestors have always lived, from the beginning till to-day. That is the title for our property. And our fathers, some of whom still live, also brought reinforcements to the war. When the war was ended, you gave this land to them. That is a second title to our incontestible ownership.

On Monday, when the people of Wikwemikong came back, Mr. Macdougall renewed his proposals and promises.

Jacko, their speaker, answered in the name of all the others: We have no ill feeling against those who have given up their claims to the island; but, for ourselves, absolutely we do not wish to give up our land. Only, if, in the future, we see those others perfectly happy and punctually paid, perhaps the thought will come to us also to accept your present propositions. This, then, is the action we have taken, we inhabitants of Wikwemikong: When we saw that we could not do anything, one of our chiefs—Wakekijig—arose and said: All you men of Wikwemikong, I ask you now, Is your thought still as you have expressed it in the past? Shall we hold to our land, which we possess in common? If such is your thought, you have only to raise your arm, in order to answer—Such is still our thought, we hold to it. All raised their arms, saying at the same time, Such is still our thought, and we shall hold to it firmly. Wakekijig said: Once more I ask you: Do you still think the same? Such is our thought, and we affirm it—we shall hold to it firmly. Their accent became bolder. Wakekijig said: Still again I ask you, Is that what you think? Do not decide lightly. Then all, in a still more elevated tone, cried out, saying, With all our strength we will hold to it; we will not abandon it. After that, we thought we had not yet done enough. One thing came to mind, in order the better to make known our thought; for, perhaps, we said, there were still some amongst us who thought differently. Wakekijig said, therefore: Consequently, let us do one thing more; perhaps there are still many amongst you who think differently. Do not act in that manner; do not conceal anything now. Make clear your thought. As to Tekoman [Tehkummah] (a deposed chief), he has been known for a long time; he has surrendered our island. He has never said so, although for a length of time the question has been put to him. Are there any who side with him? Let them place themselves yonder where he is. Only one went to join him. Let those who hold to their land come to my side. And all those who hold to their land went to his side.

The discussion was thus finished when the English chief entered. It was past noon.

Address of the English Chief—On Saturday night, I told you who come from Wikwemikong, that I would not say anything further to you. To-day, when I see you in a large number, I think it my duty again to address a few words to you; but I shall not repeat what I said the first time I spoke to you. I think you have well reflected on what I said to you. I beg of you, therefore, to listen to my words, and to receive the propositions that I bring to you. I bring also a little money; I wish to give it to you, to render binding our common contract. The money that I bring is from the great chief. I have borrowed it from him. Later, I shall return it, when they will have sold this island. Have I not heard again that you came armed the first time? That is not well. When I learned that you had acted in that manner, I was anxious to speak to you on the subject, today; but, having seen your interpreter, he told me the cause of it. That is why I do not wish to say anything more to you about that affair.

Discourse of Jacko—My brother, whom I love much, my chiefs make known to you their thought on what they have heard from you. Well, my brother, our ancients have spoken of a perfectly beautiful bird. It is with the plumage of this bird that I wish to brush the dust from your ears, so that you may hear well what I desire to say to you. My brother, truly I am pleased to see you now, since it has been permitted to you to see here your brothers, who inhabit this island. The Great Spirit—He Who made all things, Who made the sun, and the stars, and all that we behold—it is He who has permitted you to see us to-day. My brother, really I am pleased to contemplate you. You have a fine appearance; you are perfectly handsome; also perfectly white; and also perfectly white is your heart. Oh! no; I cannot at all think that which you say; you would not preserve it in your heart. It is known, truly it is known, whence it all came—it is the work of the evil being. Now, therefore, entirely and perfectly regretting all that, we crush it all under our feet—never in the future shall we think of it, of that noise which, it is evident, has reached your ears. That is what my chiefs say to you, they for whom I speak. Well, my brother, assuredly I am satisfied now that those my brothers, have thought it their duty to give up their extremely fine land. For myself, I shall never bear them ill-will for so doing; I am content that they have accepted your propositions. Well, my brother, it is easy to know you again. Your appearance is, perfect, as we now see you; and then, also, your dignity. You are not a man to say anything lightly. Now, therefore, I make known to you the thought of all us—as many as we be—inhabitants of Wikwemikong: We absolutely do not wish to give up our land. But, in the future, should we see that to those who have given up their land to you there will come all that you have promised them, namely, perfect welfare in everything, and also your payment; if you pay them always hereafter as you have promised; assuredly, if your words be true, the thought may come to us, also, to accept your present propositions.

Mijakwange [Maishegonggai] said: I also make known my thought. I accept your propositions I cede to you all that I am master of, I and those with me who are of the Anglican persuasion (priere Anglaise)—that is to say, from the centre of Manitwaning bay to the lower part of the entrance to Otebetawaigamig bay. In like manner, you will provide for my children wherever you may see them in misery. Is it not so? In like manner, also, you promise happiness. These things you said when you demanded my land from me; and now I do not see anything of that which you promised me. Perhaps it is only now we are going to see this happiness. That is all I have to say.

Here is one, Mijakwange, who has his reserve on the main land; his tribe is also there. Here, on the island of the Ottawas, they had no right to receive his cession, when he said, I cede. Did he alone, then, possess what he gave up? Why did he speak thus? Is it because he has a refuge on the main land? It is the same with Kigikobinesi and Bebamisse and Jetawikisis [Edawe Kesis]. It is on the main land they have their reserve—not here. It was a great wrong to demand the island from them, and to take their word, when they said: I cede. They are from Manitowaning.

Itawashkash said: I make known to you my thought. Your proposition appears good to me. I accept it, and cede all that I possess. But should anything of value result from it, all of us on the island shall profit by it. For myself, I choose my reserve yonder at the great channel.

The English Chief said to him: Provided there is any land to give, it is there you shall remain, whatever may occur.

Itawashkash: As to our brothers of Wikwemikong, let them retain possession of what they have.

Debassige: Well, my brother, the Great Spirit sees me now standing before you to speak. Your proposition appears good to me, also, and I accept it; and I make my reserve where I reside.

The English Chief: You and the others cannot remain there; you are an obstacle. You shall be elsewhere.

Debassige: As to by brother there, an Ottawa of Wikwemikong, let him remain in possession of what he now has.

Tekoman [Tehkummah]: Well, my brother, I make known to you my thought. Your propositions appear good. I accept them. For a long time I have known them, and my thought has always been to accept. See my chief standing there (Mr. Ironside, local superintendent). It is he who made it known to you a long time ago. You will give me, therefore, a strong writing (a title) so that I may be actually the owner of the land you will give me.

The English Chief then spoke to him, and said: The land beside Wikwemikong is not given up. Come to this side, and then they shall give you a title.

Again, with respect to Tekoman [Tehkummah]: He is not at all considered as a chief by the Indians. It is now three winters since he was deposed in assembly by the Indians. They should not, therefore, receive his cession.

Bemigwaneshkang said: I, my brother, also make known to you my thought. Long ago I resigned the main land, and I do not see that it is at all as you promised me it should be. Then you promised faithfully to pay, and now there is nothing about it. Further, I afterwards ceded my reserve, and I have never been paid. They said to me: The great woman chief demands it from you, and the great chief also. That is why I ceded it. And now, again, you come to promise that you will pay very well. Well, I accept your propositions. My father, also, was a chief, and it was down at Quebec, I think, that he received the title of chief. That is why I make my voice heard here. As to those, my brothers, the Ottawas, let them remain in possession of the land which belongs to them; and I hope that henceforth we shall be good friends, as we have been in the past.

This Bemigwaneshkang and Ebins are persons who have their reserve on the main land. They are not such proprietors here that they could give away the island of the Ottawas. This, then, is another wrong action. Their young people (their tribe) are on the main land.

Wakaosse said: I, also, make known to you my thought. I shall not say different to the others. I find your propositions perfectly good, and I accept them. But I also make my reserve where I am settled in the interior. However, it will not be immediately that shall arrive this happiness, of which you promise to the savages the enjoyment for all time. As to our brothers of Wikwemikong, here present, leave them in possession of what they now have. That is my thought.

He is truly an Ottawa. He is the original possessor of this land.

Webinesimi said: I, also, make my reserve here, in my own ground; for all around there is nothing but stones.

Discourse of the English Chief—My Indian brothers, I have listened to you. I have heard what you said. I am glad to see that you fraternize so well. With respect to you from Wikwemikong, it shall be as you desire it now; you shall be the possessors of your land, from the middle of the bay of Manitwaning to that of Otebetawaigamig, at the entrance to the bay, and a valid title shall also be given to you. Still, there is a difficulty. But it may be solved. I will do all in my power for you, that it may be so. Now, this is what you have to do. It you see any one come here who has not any land, you shall receive and succor him. I have proposed to those who regulate the affairs, that they give you a valid title. You have still too much land for your number. I have consulted a surveyor about it—you have still too much. But, as I understand from you, perhaps in the future you will cede it, should you see in prosperity those who to-day have given up their land. To you they will not give any of the price paid for the island. Of all those who receive payment for this island, not one shall remain in the reserve. As to you who have accepted the propositions I have made, I thank you. I shall do all I have promised to you. And there shall remain here for all time a document, by which will be known our mutual contract. With respect to what you say about the cession of the main land—that you have not received what was promised you—perhaps the reason is, because the advantage expected has not been gained from it. Perhaps they have not had any profit from it, and that is why they have not done what, it appears, they promised. I tell you now, I cannot fix the sum which will be paid to you. If, however, it be possible, you shall receive, perhaps one dollar, perhaps two, perhaps even three, each year. To-morrow, at 10 o'clock, you will come to the Superintendent's office, and it is only there that I shall know what can be given to each of you, and you shall attach your names.

Jacko said: Well, my brother, my chiefs wish to say something again to you. They thank you for the words they have heard, by which they have the true knowledge that they are the proprietors of their land. I shall do what you have asked. Now, with a good heart, I shall throw my door wide open; I shall receive with great good will my fellow Indian, whoever he may be, whom I see wandering in misery. One word more my brother; To those who have given their land to you today, I do not envy the good payment you make them. What I ask is, that you take away the obstacle which prevents me drawing profit from what is on my land, so that I may sell firewood to procure the things of which I have need. That is the thought of my chiefs, for whom I speak.

The English Chief answered: My Indian brothers, I have not the authority to take away that obstacle; it is the great chief who has passed that law, by which you are prevented selling your wood. However, I shall be able to have it abrogated. Those who regulate the affairs of the country will deal with this, I cannot tell you in advance if they will succeed. What will be the thought of the great chief? ... If he wishes, the obstacle will be removed.

Those who gave up their land, repent having done so. They shed tears of regret.

This is what took place the next day. Money was given to them. On seeing what was given to each, they were vexed. The chiefs who had given up their land cried with sorrow. They received one dollar each. They thought they would receive many—and, in fact, that is what they had been promised.[216]

Many newspapers followed their treaty and land sale reports with positive stories about the survey. The *Hamilton Evening Times* printed the "Exploration of Manitoulin Island," from the Kingston *British American* correspondent's account, in February 1863. The article described John Stoughton Dennis' exploratory survey: "Of an area of 448,000 acres explored, 221,330 are represented as good lands; allowing five persons to every 100 acres, it is presumed the ceded portion of the island would sustain an agricultural population of 11,000 persons, or over 2,000 heads of families." Island soil, timber, mill sites, inland fishing, harbours and colonization roads were praised and settlement was promoted:

It appears that no difficulty occurred with the Indians during the exploration. They even expressed themselves well pleased with the steps taken to develop the resources of the Island. They have cleared, at present, 2,400 acres of land on the portion of the island ceded by them. They have one year allowed them to make selection of the lands they are to retain. Early in the Spring, the department, it is understood, will cause a thorough survey of the part of the Island to be put in the market, which will be divided into five or six townships. A great many inquiries are being made in relation to the lands in the Manitoulin; and as it is now demonstrated that the Island is fertile, a rush will undoubtedly be made the moment it comes in the market. As some wealthy residents of the old districts have manifested a desire to locate themselves on the Island, it is to be hoped that the Department will dispose of lands there in such a manner as to meet the views of those who propose to devote themselves to farming on a large scale.

From an Upper Canada point of view, the throwing open of this region to settlers, will be western extension of the most practical kind, and while, no doubt, many will proceed thither from the older settlements, it will present an inviting field for immigrants from Europe.

Lying in the tracts of communication between Lakes Huron and Superior, it is certainly desirable that the Manitoulin should be peopled, and turned to purposes of civilization, instead of remaining the mere hunting grounds of the Indian.[217]

The Canadian Freeman maintained:

> 1st. The Indians are the proprietors of Manitoulin, and their property does not depend on the "considerations of some transitory statesmen," to use the language of Mr. Macdougall; it rests on a title acknowledged in every country, civilized and barbarian—the title of possession from time immemorial. The subsequent treaties made with the Indians, even the last, that of 1836—all acknowledged that title.
>
> 2ndly. The property is common to all the Indians of the island, and cannot be disposed of by a small minority ....
>
> 3rdly. These last transactions were preceded by the most unjust vexations, and accompanied by shameful threats, such as If the Indians do not give up their property willingly with some benefit; they will be forced to do so without any benefit at all.[218]

In February and March 1863, respectively, the *Kingston Daily News* and the British *Canadian News* both published copies of the "Protest of the Indians of Wikwemikong" that had been sent to the governor general the previous November, though neither newspaper included the complete account of the negotiations or an editorial comment.[219]

Rumours of liquor at the treaty surfaced in Parliament in mid-February when Thomas Roberts Ferguson, Member for Simcoe South, rose in the Legislative Assembly to report that David Reesor had told him "that someone with him (the Commissioner of Crown Lands) had promised grog to mollify the Indians, who were found at first rather impracticable, and the grog had accomplished what could not be done without it." Two days later, on 20 February, William McDougall replied to the accusation. He read a statement from Reesor, stating:

> I need hardly say that this statement of Mr. Ferguson is entirely incorrect. In conversation with him he made the charge that the Indians had been given whiskey

to induce them to surrender the Island of Manitoulin on unfair terms. In reply, I told him that I was not aware that the Indians had received liquor of any kind during the time that negotiations were going on; that if they did get any, it must have been from traders and entirely without our knowledge.

What I did say, however, speaking of the intemperate tendencies of the Indians, was, that some time after the council was over (more than a week after you had left the Island), and while I was waiting at Little Current for the return of the steamer from Fort William, all, or nearly all the Indians of that village became intoxicated, having, as I was told, procured liquor in the night from a trading vessel.

McDougall suggested he had witnesses to "contradict this base accusation," including "Mr. Wilson, Crown Land Agent at Sault Ste. Marie; Mr. Gibbard, Inspector of Fisheries; ... Mr. S. Phillips Day, a political friend of gentlemen opposite and correspondent of an English Newspaper; Mr. Deputy Superintendent Spragge and several others." McDougall described the treaty as being much more favourable to the Indians than the previous government's offer. He claimed that only one band dissented, and they had been left in possession of their own part of the island with the privilege of availing themselves of the treaty in the future.[220]

In a letter to the editor of *The Globe*, fishery inspector William Gibbard defended the commissioner against the allegations regarding liquor:

Communication. Mr. McDougall and the Indian Treaty. (To the Editor of the *Globe*) Sir,—In yesterdays *Globe*, I noticed a reference made to me by the Honble. Commissioner of Crown Lands, in reply to the accusation made by Mr. Ferguson.

I was present at the Indian treaty alluded to from first to last, and brought away with me in my boat, the Commissioner, Mr. Day, Mr. McNabb, and Mr. Reesor, junr.

I can assent, that not a single drop of liquor was given to the Indians by any one to the best of my belief, nor was a single Indian during the whole time in the slightest degree intoxicated, or bearing any appearance of having had liquor. I can also assert that there was not a liquor trader within 20 miles—and I believe not within 30 miles—during the whole time the Commissioner was at Manitowaning. From first to last, there was not the slightest foundation given by any of the twelve white persons who were present for the fabrication of such a charge. I was under the Commissioner's orders, and received from him on the spot, positive instructions to arrest at once any person trading in liquor. At the Council and before the treaty was signed, complaint was made by the Wek-wi-me-kong Indians to the Commissioner against whiskey traders, and request made that he would take steps to check the trade. In consequence of this request, I received from the Commissioner distinct instructions for my guidance during last fall and coming season, to take certain steps, and adopt certain measures for the more effectual checking of this horrid, debasing traffic. I believe, during my absence from the Council room, that the Commissioner also promised the Indians he would, either by Act of Parliament or by order of the Governor in Council, introduce such new regulations as would tend effectually to remedy the abuses complained of in the neighbourhood of the great Manitoulin Island.

From repeated conversations held with the Commissioner on the subject of this and other matters connected with the Indians, I am satisfied that they have no greater friend, and that no greater enemy to the whiskey traders ever visited the Manitoulin Island.

I am Sir, your obedient servant.
WM. GIBBARD, Officer in charge of Fishery and Revenue Boat for Lakes Huron and Superior. Collingwood, Feb. 28 1863.[221]

Reverend Peter Jacobs tried to explain the negative press reports to his superiors: "There are now 153 Indians in this Mission who are members of our church. There have always been Roman Catholics at Manitowaning. The church was not built by the Government & it cost $2440. Some Indians have left Wikwemikong the principal Roman Catholic village on the island, as well as Manitowaning, & reside elsewhere."[222]

The Manitoulin stories, though numerous and controversial in Canadian terms, paled in comparison to news from the United States of America. The "Indian Revolt" in Minnesota, which had erupted in August 1862, led to 37 days of fighting, 500 American and 60 Dakota deaths, and almost 400 trials. Thirty-eight Dakota warriors were hung in December, and four months later Congress ordered the Dakota moved to South Dakota. Despite the relocation, the Sioux Wars continued for almost three decades, until the Battle of Wounded Knee in 1890.

The Reactions of the *Anishinaabeg*, the Government and the Missionaries
Though the immediate reaction of the *Anishinaabeg* is unknown, the majority of island residents must have been surprised to learn that a treaty had been signed. By all accounts, near-unanimous agreement to retain forever the Island of the Odawa had been confirmed at several grand councils.

Even the two or three hundred men who attended the negotiations must have been surprised to learn that a surrender had been made. Some of them suspected that the people of Manitowaning and Wewebijiwang could be persuaded by the agent, but no one, not even Ironside, would have predicted that Itawashkash and Paimoquonaishkung would succumb to the demands of the government. They were not only the most senior central and western island chiefs, but also the most vocal opponents of surrender and of the government.

Not surprisingly, the chiefs who surrendered were criticized by their people because they had yielded without consulting their bands and despite decisions made in councils that Manitoulin Island would never be given up. Bands and families were divided by their opinions on the cession, with elders generally in favour due to their loyalty to the Crown, and younger *Anishinaabeg* generally against after witnessing government interference in the fish and wood trade.[223]

Father Choné described those who signed the treaty as disappointed, ashamed and crying, while "others were menaced by their own children of being killed for having thus sacrificed the last resources of their posterity."[224] The chiefs explained their sudden change of heart: "They made us afraid, they said to us that people will take our land anyway, without any benefit for us; so we thought that it would be better to cede and receive something."[225] Father Hanipaux visited the missions on the island in November 1862 and found "the poor Catholics in a state of desolation having given up their Island."[226]

Though Wikwemikong *Anishinaabeg* appeared to have escaped the treaty, upon reflection they concluded that McDougall had obtained the majority of the island from the minority of the population, and had obtained it from chiefs who did not have the authority from their people to act; moreover, some of these chiefs already owned reserves on the mainland. This did not leave Wikwemikong in a particularly secure position. But the Wikwemikong *Anishinaabeg* were unable to react until they completed their harvest. This task, essential for winter survival, had been interrupted two years in a row by land surrender negotiations.

Their harvest finished, the Wikwemikong people assembled on 3 November 1862 to record their complaints about the treaty. They drafted a three-page document in Ojibwe in which they complained to the governor that the island of "otawaminis" had been surrendered by chiefs who did not own it. They asserted that Abence, Maishegonggai, Paimoquonaishkung, Shewetagun, Taibosegai, Itawashkash and Wahcowsai did not have the right to give up the island. Though the document bore the names of thirteen Wikwemikong chiefs, it is not known if it was translated or sent to the governor.[227]

About two weeks later, on 15 November, they wrote a much longer petition to the governor in which they described the October negotiations in detail. They insisted the treaty was an unfair contract signed by chiefs who did not own the island; that the chiefs had not consulted their bands; and that the chiefs who signed had reserves on the mainland. Their account followed a brief request:

Wikwemikong, 15 November 1862
Protest from the Indians of Wikwemikong, Peninsula of Manitoulin Island, against what occurred at Manitowaning, on the 4, 5, 6 and 7th of last October (the Mission of the Hon. McDougall)
To His Excellency the Governor General

You, who are the great Chief, who occupies the highest position and who fulfils the role of the Great Spirit here on earth, to exert your authority over all the men in the limits of the land called Canada. The Great Spirit believes that like him, your good heart is noble and pure. He believes that you also have a compassionate and generous heart to carefully protect those who are under your responsibility and authority, that is to say that you vigilantly watch everywhere on this land that you govern so that no one makes gauche regulations and also that no one suffers too much harm without being subjected to the application of your laws.

You therefore, Great Chief, whose character is of the highest integrity, we address our words to you. We place this paper before you so that you may understand and may carefully examine what has taken place here in Manitowaning; know everything that was tainted in execution of the contract of sale. No honourable man could say: this is a genuine contract if he knew exactly what occurred and that is why we bring it to your attention, so that you may examine it yourself. As for us, we have seen the course of all the things that have taken place and cannot say: this is a genuine treaty. On the contrary as we have seen and experienced it, all we can say is that this whole affair is a true deception.

If they had wanted to make something valid they should not have accepted the word of those who said: I cede (the land); as no one can by himself, was he chief, transfer a thing that we all hold. If we had all consented, only then would a true treaty have been concluded. But all have not consented; only those who have given their word. They consented as private individuals. They have not asked the advice of their respective people.

Besides, if they had wanted to act with justice they would not have accepted the consent of some. They have nothing here that they could sell. Their reserve is on the mainland. Their people are also there, not here. This is scandalous, a disgraceful proceeding, to ask someone to give a thing that does not belong to him and to accept his word. Is it their property that they ask for? And have they some stake in it to keep it? Also were they all ready to cede because they have a refuge on their reserve on the mainland? Have they harmed the owners by making them lose their property?

We are making our report to you only now because we have been occupied with our harvest.

Account of the meeting held at Manitowaning, on the 4th of October, and of what the Chief (Hon. McDougall) said there. ...[228]

Father Choné translated the Ojibwe document into French and sent it to the governor via the Catholic vicar-general and to *The Canadian Freeman* newspaper.

Louis Tehkummah, Charles Kitche Baptiste and Megwance were then expelled from Wikwemikong for assenting to the treaty.[229] The non-ceding people insisted they were simply complying with McDougall's offer to Tehkummah: "the land beside Wikwemikong is not surrendered; come to this side, then they shall give you a title," and "of all those who receive the payment for this island, not a single one shall remain in the reserve; as those who are there shall have only land."[230]

Tehkummah learned first-hand that "the determination we came to some time ago to rid all those who should approve of the giving up of our land" was to be enforced, and if he did not leave the village he would be removed. Kitche Baptiste was notified by Chief Wakekijik: "We have come to take you to Manatowaning—you must go there and live with those who have given up their land."[231] Megwance claimed that "ever since I gave my opinion in favor of the propositions made here in October last by the Commissioners, in reference to the surrender to the government of our land, I have been a marked man, and in consequence my stay in the neighbourhood of Wequemikong was rendered very unpleasant. Every day, almost, reports came to me that I was to be driven away from my home for my alleged offence."[232]

All three exiled men complained to Ironside, who reported the situation to Spragge. In response, the three families were offered houses in Manitowaning and a small amount of money.[233]

The Wikwemikong band revised its regulations after the treaty, declaring that neither the band nor its members would conduct any further business with the government. Anyone who disobeyed the ruling would be expelled from the community.[234]

When fishery inspector and treaty witness William Gibbard visited Wikwemikong on 31 October, the people and the priests saw him as a direct link to McDougall and showered him with complaints about the treaty. Three weeks later, in Michigiwatinong, Gibbard "heard stories of acts of violence either committed, or about to be, at Manitoowauning, and of armed bands from Wekwimikong, going to Manitoowauning with hostile views." He rushed there to assist in "the enforcement of the law," but no violence occurred. He reported to McDougall that the Wikwemikong priests and chiefs were determined to "drive away from their homes, all those, who in any way countenanced the late treaty." He advised punishing the activists to prevent further violence.[235]

Captain Ironside also reacted to the treaty. He apparently punished the Wikwemikong *Anishinaabeg* for their refusal to participate in the census and the treaty, and for their expulsion of treaty supporters from the community. He removed the names of some of the Wikwemikong people from the 1850 Robinson Huron treaty annuity list. Chiefs Thomas Kinojameg, Louis Wakekijik and Francis Metosage, their families, and many others, largely members of the Atagiwinini band, were struck off the list. Ironside had warned them that he "would have to recommend to you the withholding, for a time, their share of the annuities" if they did not participate in the 1861 census; whether he also threatened to withhold annuity money for their opposition to the treaty is unrecorded.[236]

Ironside also enforced the wood regulations. On 28 October he sold wood belonging to Chief Wakekijik to the captain of a steamboat without reimbursing the chief. He claimed to be acting on orders from the governor.

Father Choné complained about the treaty to his superior, Vicar-General Charles-Félix Cazeau. Cazeau forwarded Choné's letter to the Indian Department, where it was translated as:

> Peace to thee. I cannot refrain from thinking in reading over the letter which you were kind enough to send me, that Mr. Spragge has taken advantage of your good faith to abuse it; although he is a very courteous man, who may have his convictions as a man of the world and as an employee of the Government, these convictions are certainly without foundation, and I cannot share them. These gentlemen, Messrs Spragge and McDougall, came to settle in a definite matter the affairs of our Indians. But what have the Government people to do with business such as that for which they came here? What have they to settle in this business of their allies and proprietors who live quietly on their properties? Allies and proprietors, these gentlemen have recognized and expressed it in their speeches.
>
> What have they settled? They have taken from the Indian his land, giving to each head of a family 100 acres and to each boy under 10 years 50 acres. They have expelled him from his villages, thereby putting him to the necessity of choosing elsewhere, that is to say of taking new lands wherever the government will allow them, good or bad, because there is more bad then good land in the island, and for that he is to have the interest of the money accruing from the sale of his lands, when the surveyors shall have been paid. They say that this is advantageous to the Indians who derives no profit from his land. If they get 25s each every year it will be a great deal.
>
> How did they gain over the Indians? The assembly took place on a Saturday. The first answer to the Hon. Mr. McDougall's speech was an unanimous refusal, some Chiefs stayed over Sunday with many others; this day they were worked upon by means of the threats and promises which the Honorable Speaker had expressed in his speech. The assent of the minority was obtained on Monday, and the bargain was considered as concluded. The whole of the Treaty!!! was done with the assent of a certain number of Chiefs or pretended Chiefs. An immense majority of Indians are opposed to it. Is this to be believed? It is the fact. The Honorable Mr. McDougall being discountenanced by the first response of the Indians told them, since I cannot treat with a majority I will address myself to some of you only. This brought forth

from an Indian an answer which must have been rather humiliating for a government man and the signers of the treaty, when on Tuesday, upon the spot, they saw the results of these promises, and that they were obliged to abandon their villages, cried and shut themselves up. Poor Indian! He is doomed to destruction: still I must hasten to say it, the inhabitants of this part of the island (which forms a peninsula) have refused their consent. Therefore this part was left to them. They would not sully their hands by giving them to receive such a degrading and insignificant compensation ($2 for Chiefs and $1 for others). Those who received the money cannot live on that part of the island. This shall be a monument of the iniquity of the treaty. I am afraid of becoming tiresome—I stop—There is sufficient to judge of the case.[237]

Spragge responded immediately to counter the priest's claims. Rather than being expelled, he insisted, the Indians would enjoy under the treaty "a liberty of selection so exempt from injurious restrictions that in selecting the Farm lots which are to be permanently secured to them they are limited to no locality." The restriction on landing places and mill sites was only so they could be developed and sold "advantageously for the Indians," Spragge asserted. "The Inhabitants of the Western portion were very nearly unanimous in desiring that the portion of the Island should be opened for Settlement and that after reserving the quantity expressed in the Agreement for each family the rest should be sold and the money realized be placed at Interest for their benefit. The Inhabitants of the Eastern portion were for the most part (but there were dissentients among them) opposed to opening the Island for settlement and one of their duly appointed representatives, named Jacques claimed for them the exclusive right to the Eastern part." Spragge concluded "that when the whole merits of the Case are understood it will be fairly acknowledged that a most generous arrangement has been made on behalf of the Government with the Indians."[238]

Spragge's reply infuriated Choné, prompting him to protest to higher authorities and to the newspapers. Father Auguste Kohler, the Wikwemikong superior, was also surprised to learn that a treaty had been concluded. He accused the government of highway robbery, and predicted that Manitoulin would change, just as Bruce Mines (near Sault Ste. Marie) had changed following non-Native settlement:

> The forests have partially disappeared under the axe of the lumbermen and steam machines, houses of aristocratic merchants, and a mass of houses occupied by miners and adventurers of all sorts now rise in the veins of copper that they hid from the eyes of speculators.
> Blasphemies have replaced the songs of birds and taverns the wigwams of our poor natives. ... This is also what will soon happen on our dear Manitoulin where only a fifth of their island remains for the natives, the rest having been taken away in spite of the rights of the people and the sacred treaties. The two largest villages (after Holy Cross) where we had well-built chapels with a house for the missionary are going to be abandoned. The residents shall no longer have the right to settle there, nor to choose the mouths of rivers or ports where the Whites can make settlements for their residence.
> Each head of a family shall have 100 acres of land and all male children more than ten years of age, 50 acres. They have been given one year to choose a new site where they must collect together. I truly do not know where they will find it, except

by occupying swamps and rocks, as the island is covered with lakes, one of which is 5 leagues long and one third [of the land] is no good for farming.[239]

John Stoughton Dennis, the surveyor dispatched by William McDougall, spent November on Manitoulin Island. Despite hearing rumours of unrest from William Gibbard, Dennis reported positively:

> I have only to state, that of necessity—I came frequently in contact with the Indians on the portion of the island surrendered, and they were not only very friendly, and gave me every assistance, but without an exception, expressed their satisfaction with the arrangements made through yourself with the Government, with the view of throwing open the Island for settlement.[240]

Ironside maintained that all treaty opposition originated with the Jesuits. When he transmitted New Year's greetings from the chiefs of Michigiwatinong and Manitowaning to Spragge in January 1863, he maintained they were content with the treaty and anxious for its enactment. He noted, though, that they had requested land for their children in addition to "the 200 acres" held by heads of families. Content or not, they had obviously misunderstood if they believed they were receiving 200 acres: the treaty specified 100 acres per family. Even Ironside may have been confused about the acreage due, as he had discussed quantities from 25 to 150 acres during the previous two years.[241]

There is no doubt the chiefs' greetings were sincere. A New Year's Day visit to the superintendent and missionary was an annual event. It was a day of friendship, with a feast and speeches. What is significant, though, is that only three chiefs are listed; this celebration in the past often attracted several hundred residents and their chiefs.

Deputy Superintendent Spragge commented on the treaty in his annual report. He declared that it would benefit the *Anishinaabeg* and the country:

> The present condition and appearance of the Manitoulin Indians as a whole (to which of course there are exceptions) contrast unfavourably with the other Upper Canada Indians, who have settled upon their lands and reaped some of the advantages of civilization. The former all ill-attired, not healthy, nor vigorous in appearance, nor temperate in their habits, and deprived of many comforts with which a large proportion of the class referred to, are provided.
>
> An exploration of the Island has been made, under the charge of Deputy Surveyor J.S. Dennis, and the result has shown that there is a fair average of land of good quality suitable for settlement in this central portion of the Island. Numerous applications for the purchase of land have already been received, and there is every indication that when subdivided into lots the island will be rapidly settled by a respectable agricultural population.
>
> One of the great drawbacks under which the mining interests suffer, is the expense of obtaining supplies, and the distance from which they must be brought. The settlement of so extensive a tract as the Great Manitoulin Island, equal to an ordinary County, will speedily tend to lesson, and finally to remove these disadvantages. And in looking to the interests of the Indians themselves, and to the ample and permanent provision made for them as agriculturalists, it will I think, be admitted that the Province has good cause for satisfaction that this new region has

been opened for settlement.[242]

The people of Atchitawaiganing (South Bay East) wrote a petition to the governor general against the McDougall treaty in January 1863.[243]

In February, Chief Taibosegai received a letter that Ironside attributed to Father Hanipaux. The letter urged Taibosegai and Itawashkash to write the governor general and request the annulment of the treaty. Taibosegai delivered the letter to Ironside, who forwarded a copy to Spragge:

Wekwamekong, 20th February 1863
Tabahsega,
I write you a few lines about something which I want you to know, all ye people who live at Mechegewudenong & Sheshegwauning. This is it. The Governor General who lives at Quebec & all his Council are indeed intending to speak about this evil surrender of the land. It is on this account that one of the Bishops (or Chief Ministers) at Quebec has written to us, saying "I wish that the Roman Catholic Indian Chiefs, who surrendered the lands, would inform the Governor General how they were cheated, & made to consent to the surrender of their land & how all the warriors were not satisfied with what was done. Let them then request the Governor General to annul the wicked surrender." The Bishop says that they will have a favourable hearing, if they thus request the Governor General.

I wish that you chiefs & also Adahwushkaush [Itawashkash] would quickly prepare a paper. And when you have got it ready, send it to me, & we shall send it to the Bishop, who shall then himself deliver it into the hands of the Governor General. This is all. May God help you, to do that well. If you want paper, the schoolmaster will lend you some, & I shall afterwards return him that. I am Nesahwahqwud, Priest.

It would be a good thing if you made out the letter. I mean you who are chiefs at Mechegewudenong. And those who go to Sheshegwauning might deliver the letter to Adahwaushkaushe for him to sign his name to it. I hope that this will be done soon.[244]

By March 1863, anxiety among the *Anishinaabeg* had increased. According to Captain Ironside, Chief Itawashkash claimed:

Whilst Pere Hanipeaux was at Sheshegwaning he took the names of all the residents there without first giving them the reason for his doing so. This very unusual proceeding the Indians it appears, did not at all like, and they therefore asked him the meaning of it when the Priest replied, angrily, "It is customary for us to, occasionally, take the census of our people for the information of the Church." As they, however, strongly suspected that their names were intended to be used for a purpose other than that than stated by the Priest they protested against his taking the list away with him but to no purpose. The Chief requested me to say to you that he and his people adhere to the treaty no matter what the Priests may say to the contrary.[245]

Despite Ironside's claim of treaty approval, in May 1863 the residents of Michigiwatinong and Sheshegwaning wrote petitions to the governor general that demanded the treaty be cancelled. They claimed that persons who were not authorized to represent them had signed the treaty, and had done so under threats of expulsion and punishment and the inevitability of governmental action.

On 23 May, the Michigiwatinong *Anishinaabeg* asked the governor general to return their land. The petition was written in Ojibwe and signed by 21 men, including two of the four Michigiwatinong men who signed the treaty. The two other treaty signatories, Taibosegai and Paimoquonaishkung, added postscripts but did not want to sign the document.

Petition of the men of Mitchikiwatinong
To his Excellency the Governor General.
Our great Father, Great chief residing in Quebec, holding the place of Great Spirit here on earth, governing the men of this land called Canada, where you are the first one. Our Great Father, here is what the Great Spirit wants you to be: as he has the power everywhere, in the sky and on the earth. As he is infinitely just, as his heart is infinitely beautiful, as his heart is full of peace, accord, kindness, charity, joy and gratitude and it always will be as it was from the beginning. Our Great Father this is what the Great Spirit wants you to be. And indeed you also have this strength, this power and this justice. Your heart has the same beauty; your heart is the centre of peace, accord, kindness, charity and joy. Certainly you have all the power that is necessary to return this land to us that they came and took from us through speeches last autumn. For it is true that our Chiefs have been seduced and have been frightened. They said to them: If you do not cede it, the Great Chief shall drive you away. They shall take your land from you in another way and you will not be able to prevent them (the whites), no matter what you do. The Great chief himself will not be able to. That is what they said to us; how they frightened us.

Now, we will tell you who we are. We are the residents of Mitchikiwatinong (a village situated on the ceded part). All of us, we were not satisfied (with what was done), and still today, we do not have the slightest desire to consent, nor our women either to what was executed by our chiefs. Besides, they themselves, our chiefs, find nothing good in what they have done. They made them afraid and that was why they did it.

And now we declare to you, taking God as witness, in his name, we declare the truth to you. And first we say to you: everything that our brothers of Wikwemikong have made known is true. No one can say that it is not the truth. With our eyes we have seen all that has happened. We have been at the scene; here in Manitowaning last autumn.

Secondly, this is how they treated us, as one treats a child that has no sense yet— they try to make him afraid, to have what he has, when he does not want to give it on demand. When he is frightened he abandons the object because of this fear. This is how they treated us, we all who have been seduced and frightened.

Thirdly. This is what they said to us to frighten us: I come with all the power of the Great Chief; anyone who does or says anything to those who surrender the land shall be punished. Besides if you do not give up your land, you shall be driven away. The Great Chief shall drive you away. Besides they will not leave you alone because the Great Chief absolutely wants to have your land. If you do not give it up, if you hold it tightly, they will have no difficulty to take it from you. You will not be able to prevent it whatever effort you make; neither I nor the Great Chief can prevent it. That is what the English Chief (Hon. McDougall) said to frighten us.

Fourthly. We, who they call soldiers (the men composing the band), were not notified by our Chiefs when they wanted to give up the land. We are not only the masters, we are the owners. We do not give it up. And our chiefs cannot give up our property. Certainly, we speak the truth, as we know our thoughts well. Other people cannot speak our true thoughts to you. Besides our women and all our children did not consent to cede the land.

Fifthly. Our chiefs themselves, such was their well taken resolution, the thought of their future children. They decided to save them the little land that we still possess. For us, and all our women and children, this is still our resolution.

Sixthly. For us though we have not consented, though we did not want to receive the payment, our chiefs urged us and said to us: it is finished, the land is already surrendered. You cannot do anything. Thus we lost courage and spirit and took that small payment, full of grief, distress and in tears.

As for you, our Great Father, we have complete confidence that your heart is filled with kindness. We consider you like our saviour J.C. The first man and the first woman lost our well being and in its place we have been bequeathed death, all the miseries fall on us, and the eternal torments await us in hell. J.C. has withdrawn it from us and gives us back the happiness, an eternal happiness. He alone can do it, supporting God. This is how we regard you today, having lost our land by the action of those who said: I surrender it. You, our Great Father have the strength and the power necessary to restore this land to us. They are the only ones who have thought what they have said. Their families, their women and their children have not had that thought.

Now then, in the name of God, we pray you listen and accept our words: Generously return our land to us. Yes, we wish to recover it. It is the wish of everyone, of all the men here. It is the desire of our women, and of our children. We all have only one thought on this subject.

Now we place our names, in testimony of our attachment to our land, and so you understand what we hope of you. We never put our names to surrender our land.

(Note the two chiefs Ebins and Newategijig are signatories to the treaty. This petition is made in the name of all who are called the soldiers. This is why they say that they have not signed the treaty.) Note of translator.

Signed: Ebinss, Newategijig, Shabini, Anwatin, Ajawigijig, Missianakwat, Shimaganinsh, Meiawigijig, Sabire (Xavier) Ebins, Shibagijig, Nawakamigigabow, Agowisse, Michell Nigananakwet, Nigananakwat, Shibagijig, Wabane, Jan Batis Bebonaang, Ozawakigabaw, Josens Bishikiwigijig, Odoskweiab, Francois Kiwashkwa (All Catholic Christians, there are no others in the village)

Words of Bemikwaneshkang, Chief of Mitchikiwatinong.

What our young people say here is really the truth. What they say to you here is the pure truth. I am assuredly satisfied with it. And I also say to you: yes, truly they frightened me, and now I completely disapprove of what I did.

Words of Debassige, Chief of Mitchikiwatinong

I also am very satisfied with what has happened. Certainly I have never had the thought to cede, and I have never ceded the place that I live now. I shall be very satisfied that you return this land. We were frightened, that is what we say to you.

These two chiefs told me to write their words but they have not me wanted to put their names. Signed: F. Metosage (secretary)

A correct translation from the original. J.P. Choné S.J. Missionary.
Names of the treaty signatories with the French spelling.
J B. Assiginâk, Mejakwange, P. Kitchi Binesi, Benj. Assiginâk, Webinesimi, Shiwitagan, Geo. Abitasswe, Bemikwaneshkang, Ebins, Debassige, Itawashkash, Newatekijik, Wakaosse, Gashkiwabik, Bebamisse, Kijikobinesi, Batatakwishing, Tekoma.

Post Script. Bemossatang. I am astonished that someone would say that it is chief and band of Wikwemikong.[246]

On 28 May 1863 the men of Sheshegwaning also protested against the treaty. They claimed the treaty was completed before they arrived, and without their consent. Though Itawashkash was not in the village when the letter was written, his son John was the author of the 19-signature petition. A postscript added a week later by treaty signatory Chief Wakaosse [Wahcowsai] confirmed his approval of the young men's action. The document was written in Ojibwe, translated into French at Wikwemikong, and translated into English by the Indian Department.

Protest of the Indians of Shishigwaning against the treaty of Manitowaning Oct. 6th 1863 [1862]. Translation. May 28 1863. The residents of Shishigwaning. Our father, Great Chief it is very well, I am now pleased to hear that thou art disposed to hear the Indians, to know their thoughts. Certainly not, we have not been pleased. It is because they have been deceived, very gratuitously frightened, that our chiefs have parted with our island. As for us, we have not agreed with them. This then we expect of thee. That the annulments by that authority as great chief; what these bad Englishmen (*sic* Matchi Shaganashag) have come here to do.

The time when they were to sell was unknown to us. It was only when we entered the council place, that we heard them accomplishing the sale (of our land). And we were not pleased with it, and are not now. And it is for that cause that we put our names here.

Antoin Oketa, Abitagichig Wakaosse, John Atawachkach, Naganiwina, Ajawenachinss, Jak Bitasige, Abitagijig, Misiseness, Bananswe Abitagijig, Tebasan, Wabikinin, Kebeose, Michen Oketa, Seseganichkan, Wechibanawe, Metwekamichkang, Kitchi ogima, Ketagiwebi, Winiian. (All Roman Catholics of the Shishigawaning station)

The oversigned put our names in behalf of the chief of Shishigawaning. Our chief is not present; he is gone far from this place, to see his son, who has accidentally hurt himself with his gun. Perhaps he would have put his name, for I have heard him say: I will put my name. (It is the chief's son who has written this protest). And that is the reason why we have put our names. John Atawashkosh.

Wakaosse neither, is not present. He is gone far hunting. Surely he would have put his name. I am perfectly sure of it, that he would have put his name. He was very vexed, in bad humor, when the land was parted with.

There are many things which are not nice (in the transaction) and this is particularly why we are dissatisfied all of us here in Shishigwaning.

This is all. We greet thee as friend, our great father, living in Quebec.

Many residents of Shishigwaning having come here for the Procession of Corpus Christie, have brought this paper. The chief Wakaosse, in coming back from hunting, was here for the same purpose and dictated to Francis Metosage one of the secretaries of the chiefs of Wikwemikong the following:

"Wikwemikong June 7th 1863. I am very well pleased to see now here what the Indians of Shishigwaning have done. He has said the truth he who said of me: he is not pleased. Certainly I have not been pleased. And now I put here my name, now that I see here this paper. Not more than the others have I been pleased that this island had been parted with. So I make it known, I agree with the men of Wikwemikong in regard to the decision they have come to keep this island for themselves.

J Wakaosse. [treaty signatory as Wahcowsai]"
Translation J. P. Choné s.j.[247]

Father Choné wrote a letter to accompany the Sheshegwaning petition:

> His Excellency sees the Indians of different parts of the Island coming at intervals, one after another, to make known their complaint. The reason of it is that intercourse is slow, and that those residing in distant villages are informed but very late of their brothers doings, and when they know what is doing it requires a long time for them to decide. Their slowness on this point is well known; but what has added yet to that slowness is that they could hardly believe that it was possible for them to protest, so heavy was the yoke of fear under which they were kept. The truth of this assertion, which besides is a plain fact, appears from all that they have written until now to His Excellency.
> With profound respect, your Excellency's humble servant J V Choné.[248]

The residents of Wikwemikong petitioned the governor general about the timber regulations for the fourth time in May 1863. They also complained that they had not received their fall annuity payment in 1862 for their ceded ancestral property on the mainland, "the terre firma by the Otchipwais our ancestors."[249]

These three petitions were all addressed to the governor general because the *Anishinaabeg* still had no representative in the Legislative Council or Assembly. Since Captain Ironside and his superiors in the Indian Department were involved in the complaints being levelled by the *Anishinaabeg*, the governor was their only recourse.

Charles de Lamorandière, the North Shore trader who often acted as translator for Manitoulin Island residents, commented:

> The local superintendent had doubtless been ordered to make efforts to obtain the consent of the chiefs; and, during the following winter, he spoke to them separately. He used promises with some and threats with the others, and managed to divide them and to obtain the consent of several chiefs.
>
> The Hon. Mr. McDougall, then Commissioner of Crown Lands, came during the summer and made the treaty that carries his name. It was stipulated that the natives cede three-quarters of the island to the government. The signatories of the treaty have had much to regret; they have since sent petitions to obtain the revocation of the treaty; but the goal of the government was attained and the natives have not been heeded.[250]

The average Canadian settler's opinion on the treaty is unknown, but myriad land queries received by the Indian Department following the treaty indicate that many settlers wanted affordable land. W.D. Taylor of Meaford claimed that he and his friends were interested in Manitoulin Island because "Lands are held so high in this Township that it prevents any purchasing except those who have large means."[251] John J. Rafferty of King Township wrote this letter, which is typical:

> I want you to let me know when or at what time the land on the Manitoulin Island will be for sale, also if there are any white settlers there now and on what conditions the land will be sold i.e. how much will have to be cleared yearly and for how many years. By writing me and giving me the above information you will greatly oblige.[252]

Inexpensive "virgin" land was perceived to be in short supply, but there were in reality more than two million acres available for sale and settlement in Upper Canada. Though most lots were priced at seventy cents an acre, cash, or one dollar an acre on instalments, land on the north shores of lakes Huron and Superior was available at twenty cents an acre.[253]

The Manitoulin issue came before Parliament almost monthly in the spring of 1863. Father Choné's protest of 14 October 1862 had been widely circulated. Sir Narcisse-Fortunat Belleau raised the Manitoulin treaty issue in the Legislative Council of the Province of Canada on 6 March 1863. He requested that a copy of the Manitoulin treaty of 1836, "by which the possession of the Manitoulin Islands was secured to them and their heirs and successors in return for the surrender of their hunting grounds," as well as "copy of any agreement, assignment or other writing, pretended to have been made during the last six months between the Indians now residing on the said Manitoulin Islands and the Provincial Government, relating to the tenure, extent, or possession of their lands in the said Islands," be laid before the House.

On 22 April 1863, the Honorable Luc Letellier de Saint-Just asked the governor general to request copies of all orders in council and reports relative to Manitoulin Island made during 1861. The documents were printed in the government's Sessional Papers of 1863. Evidently, one would have had to be bilingual to grasp the entire picture. The English version of the Sessional Papers included copies of the 1836 treaty, the 1862 treaty, the vicar-general's letter to Spragge and Choné's letter to the vicar-general, followed by a second Return that included Vankoughnet's Manitoulin memorandum of 29 August 1861 and Bartlett and Lindsey's complete report on the attempt at cession in October 1861. But only the French version of the Sessional Papers contained the long petition written by the Wikwemikong *Anishinaabeg* on 15 November 1862 describing the negotiations.[254]

In May, when the issue returned to the Legislative Council, Narcisse-Fortunat Belleau attempted to defer the Manitoulin discussion, as some of the requested documents had not been printed. But Ulric Tessier, speaker of the Legislative Council, said

> he did not intend to oppose the motion, but he thought that under present circumstances, it would not be expedient to leave the Resolutions standing on paper, as they might create the impression that the Government had been guilty of injustice to the Manitoulin Island Indians, which was not the case. The Honorable member said it was a mistake to assume the Islands in question had been vested in the Indians in fee simple for ever, and quoted the legal instruments by which the lands had been put in possession of these aborigines. In 1861, the late Government had endeavoured to induce the Indians to give up their claims amicably, upon certain conditions which were rejected by them, and this showed at least that the Government had taken the same view of the desirability of opening out those lands for settlement for white men,—as the present Government. Then in 1862, the present Government had renewed the negotiations, offering one hundred instead of twenty-five acres to each Indian as their predecessors had done, and further to fund the money derived from the sale of the rest for the benefit of the Indians themselves. Well, part of the Island was occupied by Protestant Indians, and part by Roman

Catholic Indians, and the former had readily assented to the offer, but the latter, under the influence of evil counsellors, had steadily refused the arrangement. The upshot was that the Government had lost £100, the expense of the feast which they had given the Indians—for those people never enter upon negotiations without having first a banquet—and things remain as they were.[255]

French-speaking Catholic members of the Legislature raised the Manitoulin issue because the Jesuit missionaries appealed to the vicar-general, the Catholic Church's emissary to the government, and he approached Catholic politicians in Quebec.

The Legislative Council members let the treaty stand. Most politicians were distracted by the defeat of the Reform government in May. McDougall's party was defeated, reorganized and re-elected in May and June 1863. *The Canadian Freeman* tried to make the Manitoulin treaty an election issue, reminding electors that William McDougall was "the would be spoilator of the poor Catholic Indians of the Manitoulin Islands."[256] Nevertheless, McDougall was re-elected and continued as commissioner of Crown Lands and superintendent general of Indian Affairs.

Chapter 6
Repercussions in the Fishing Industry

Enforcement or Harassment
In the summer of 1863, a dispute over fishing territory revived treaty animosity. Fishing was still the main source of food and income for most Manitoulin Island residents. Though fishing in the northern Great Lakes had been regulated and licensed by the Crown Lands Department since 1859, the system was neither understood nor accepted by the *Anishinaabeg*. They could obtain free domestic fishing licences, in the name of their superintendent, but commercial fishing required tendering for specific locations. In theory, though, traditional *Anishinaabe* fishing grounds were not going to be licensed.

William Gibbard was the overseer of fisheries for lakes Huron and Superior. He was known as Eshkamejwanoke (The Gatherer Of Fish Guts) by the *Anishinaabeg*. His notoriety had grown exponentially since 1859, when he had simultaneously announced and enforced the new fishing regulations. That season he declared to Jesuit Father Kohler that "the Indians were a nuisance, and as such should be driven out of this part of the country,"[257] and reported to his superiors that "Manitoulin and several other islands in his territory would make splendid settlements." His annual reports criticized the *Anishinaabeg* for not fully using their fishing grounds and commended non-Native fishermen who shipped fresh and salted fish from Wikwemikong and the Isle of Coves for a ten-dollar-a-barrel profit.[258] In the spring of 1862, *The Globe* newspaper published two of Gibbard's inflammatory letters in which he endorsed the surrender of Manitoulin and criticized its *Anishinaabe* residents. "With the exception of one family on Lonely Island, and two or three others on the main island, those who follow fishing are the most miserable looking, ill-clothed, drunken, lying, stealing vagabonds of the whole band," he wrote.[259] In October 1862, he not only witnessed the treaty but gave the impression of being McDougall's right-hand man, as he patrolled for liquor traders and delivered McDougall back to terra firma.

In June 1863, Gibbard acted on his belief that the fisheries were underutilized by the "American Indians." He visited Lonely Island (*Akiwesi Minis*), a traditional fishing station of the Wikwemikong *Anishinaabeg*, and leased the south side of it to two non-Native residents of Wikwemikong. "They informed me that they had every reason to believe the Wcqwimikong Indians would as soon as the fishing season commenced drive them off the Island," Gibbard said, "and claimed my protection as old resident fishermen, under the Fishery Act. I at once gave them a licence for this season of the South half of the Island, with this understanding, that any peaceable and well-disposed Indian who did not interfere with their net grounds or building and wharves, should be allowed to fish; to this they were agreeable, and the licence was put at the nominal rate of $4."[260]

Gibbard wrote a very acerbic note to Father Kohler at Wikwemikong, asking him to inform the *Anishinaabeg* that he had leased part of Lonely Island:

> Shibaonaning, June 27 1863.
> Dear Sir,—You will oblige by notifying the Indians who are under your control, that I have leased the south half of Lonely Island—also, four miles into the Lake, all round the east, south and west sides thereof—to Philemon Proulx and Charles De La Ronde; that no Indian, or other person, will be allowed to fish on that ground, or to use the beach included in their lease, or cut wood on the same, unless driven in by bad weather, without the written permission of the lessees. By notifying your Indians, you may save them from being punished and sent to gaol, as I shall strictly enforce the law. Any complaint made will be followed up by me.
> Yours truly,
> Wm. Gibbard[261]

On Sunday, 28 June 1863, Gibbard "determined to deliver the note myself and to tell the Indians personally." He met with the priests and about a dozen *Anishinaabeg*, who assailed him with their grievances. A heated three-language debate quickly ensued over allegiance, land proprietorship and government. Gibbard eventually left.

Gibbard's action removed a primary *Anishinaabe* fishing ground and demonstrated that government control was growing. The Wikwemikong band had resolved after the treaty that it would not conduct any further business with the government. By signing a lease, the two Lonely Island lessees signalled that they supported the government and not the band. A chief was deputed to inform the lessees that they must move to the mainland.[262]

Gibbard learned of the intended eviction and returned to Lonely Island with his men. On 30 June "two boats full of men, coming round a point with great speed—drums beating and men shouting"[263] arrived on Lonely Island.

Chief Ozawanimiki delivered a letter to the lessees: "Today we ask you: is it true that you have leased this island, our property? If what they said to us is true, you are not acting properly. As long as you have lived with us, we have let you fish peacefully, at no charge, everywhere the Indians fished you also fished. Wasn't it better for you to fish as you did till now, at no cost? And now to lease the fishery from a stranger who is not the master. You are not acting properly. It shall not be so. Now then, you must leave. Go over there, onto the mainland."

Once again, Gibbard and the chief argued over ownership of the islands, governance and allegiance. Both groups eventually withdrew. The following day the *Anishinaabeg* peacefully expelled the lessees. The *Anishinaabeg* described Gibbard's actions and their reaction in a letter to the governor general.

Gibbard reported the incident to William McDougall, who replied that Gibbard, as a magistrate, alone or with the assistance of another judge, could deal with it, as "the rights of our lessees, and the majesty of the law should be vindicated in the Algoma District."

Meanwhile, on 14 July 1863 Superintendent George Ironside died. Though Ironside was not directly involved in the fisheries, his death meant that there was no government agent available to advise the *Anishinaabeg* concerning their encounter with Gibbard. Ironside had worked almost forty years for the department of Indian Affairs. He took his position seriously; his plans for the future of the *Anishinaabeg*, however, did not coincide with their own. Though part *Anishinaabe* himself, he was unable to relate to those who did not want to assimilate or embrace non-Native life. Unfortunately, during his tenure his superiors had focused on finance, legislation and land surrenders, and left him alone to supervise a huge territory threatened by an increasing number of traders, whiskey dealers and speculators.

William Gibbard returned east, where he collected 21 "special constables" to enforce the law on Manitoulin. Half of the "specials" were current or former police officers. The others included a grocer, a shoemaker, a blacksmith and assorted fishermen.

On 24 July, Gibbard and his men arrived in Wikwemikong to deliver warrants and summonses for "riotous assemblage, and terrifying and assaulting peaceable residents of Lonely Island," and to take the accused men to Sault Ste. Marie to face the charges. Once again, a heated debate erupted. And as previously, the use of three languages led to miscommunication.

The *Anishinaabeg* and the priests insisted the charges be heard by the government at Quebec, not the local magistrate at the Sault. Attempted arrests resulted in a riot. Gibbard and his men eventually withdrew. Gibbard reported to McDougall that "a much larger force" or a "legal gentleman of their own persuasion" would be required to "explain to them the illegality of their proceedings."

Father Choné and head chief Tomah Mokomanish wrote letters to the governor general complaining about Gibbard's actions.[264]

Gibbard and his men continued westward. At Bruce Mines, on the North Shore of Lake Huron, Gibbard arrested Chief Ozawanimiki for his involvement in the Lonely Island expulsion. The chief was taken to Sault Ste. Marie where he appeared before Judge Prince. David Blain, a Toronto barrister who was visiting the Sault, acted for the chief and obtained his release on bail.

Manitoulin Returns to the Headlines
The Globe was the first newspaper to announce the fishery dispute. A three-column story published on 27 July 1863 was headlined "The Manitoulin Island / Outrages by the Waquimakong Indians / Armed Force Sent to Arrest Father Kohler and Other Ringleaders." The source could only have been someone in the Crown Lands Department, probably Gibbard himself, as it included details of his June visit to Wikwemikong, his version of the Lonely Island fishing leases and the expulsion of the lessees. The coverage was anti-*Anishinaabe* and anti-Jesuit.

William Gibbard was returning eastward when *The Globe* subscribers were learning of the Manitoulin Island disturbance. He and the constables, Chief Ozawanimiki, Father Kohler and David Blain had boarded the steamboat *Ploughboy* after the trial. Early on the morning of 28 July, Gibbard vanished when the boat was between Little Current and Killarney. His disappearance was reported in the newspapers, and when his body was later found in the water, several writers suggested that Father Kohler or Chief Ozawanimiki had murdered him. As usual, the slant of the press coverage and editorial opinions was determined more by the newspapers' political affiliations than by pursuit of balanced reporting.

The Globe continued its sensational coverage on 30 July with a detailed description of Gibbard's return to Wikwemikong with the armed force, the confrontation there, the subsequent arrest of the chief, and Gibbard's disappearance. An editorial insisted that the priests who incited the Wikwemikong Indians to rebellion must be brought to justice; that the Indians "cannot be permitted to stand in the way of the advance of civilization"; and that Manitoulin "cannot be permitted to remain uncultivated, because it is Indian property."[265]

Charles de Lamorandière, who had acted as Gibbard's interpreter at Wikwemikong and Lonely Island, wrote to *The Globe* to defend the *Anishinaabeg*:

> In the first place, the manner in which the Government agents have contradicted themselves in speaking to the Indians in council since June 1860, is enough for the Indian to mistrust them; for instance, when the Hon. Judge Prince came to Manitowaning to explain the law to the Indians, he told them in Council that the island on which they were assembled was theirs—he himself had not the right to cut even a single stick. A few weeks after, Messrs. Lindsay and Bartlett came on the part of the Crown Land Department, and told the Indians in Council, that the Great Manitoulin was not theirs, &c, &c. The ensuing year, or last year, the Honorable Commissioner of Crown Lands came and told them also in Council, that the Manitoulin Island was theirs, and he wanted to purchase it, &c., &c.
>
> Why does your informant, in speaking of the banishment from Wikwemikong village last fall, of Messrs. C. de Laronde and J.B. Proulx, not mention the cause for which they were expelled? Why not mention that these two individuals were in the habit of giving spirituous liquor to the Indians, contrary to law? ...
>
> Your article would lead folks to believe that the trouble between the Government Agents and the Indians, dates from the time that the Jesuits re-entered on the Island. Your are certainly aware that the Jesuits came on the Island as missionaries in the year 1843, and the trouble commenced only in 1861, or since the whites set a covetous eye on Manitoulin island, and the Fishery Act had a good deal to do with it also.
>
> The result of the armed force sent to Wikwemikong proved a failure. When Mr. Gibbard saw that the Indians would not suffer to be handcuffed, he then commenced to parley. The Indians said that they were willing to go down if legally summoned, but would rather die than go handcuffed like criminals. Then Mr. Gibbard promised that he would not take one of them prisoners, if they would appear if summoned. They promised they would. Father Hanipeau and myself went their bail. Instead of fulfilling his promise he (Mr. Gibbard) in passing at Bruce Mines, saw one of them, named O-Zan-wau-ni-mi-ki, took him prisoner, handcuffed him, and took him up the Sault for trial. By this treacherous act the Indians are not bound to keep their word. However, the Indians are ready to go down when called for.
>
> I cannot remark without making a few remarks on the word foreigners, with which you style the Wikwemikong who left their all to come and live under the British Government by the invitation of an English Governor, Sir Francis Bond Head. You say that those Indians acknowledge no allegiance to the British

Government. This is a mistake. Their allegiance to the British dates from the first American war, in which their ancestors shed their blood in defending the British flag, and again during the years 1812, '13, and '14, their fathers fought alongside of the British soldiers, and during the rebellion of 1837 they started during the winter, accompanied by the Rev. Mr. Proulx, and went to offer their services to the Government.

When Captain Anderson was Superintendent at Manitowaning, he often advised the Indians not to allow the whites to settle in their village. They will, he said, sooner or later cause you trouble. The Indians have not followed his advice. They let Messrs. Proulx and Laronde reside among them, and now they see the result of it, and Captain Anderson's warning realized.

In conclusion, I say that I am ready at any time to refute the remainder of the falsities the article contains if I am challenged.

Charles De Lamorandiere, Killarney, Lake Huron.[266]

Le Journal de Québec covered the Manitoulin problems from an anti-treaty perspective. It carried excerpts from *The Globe* articles, but concluded:

This is the clear product of the excursion of Mr. McDougall, on Grand Manitoulin, in a time better spent at his desk, to complete his work there; this is the result of politics without depth promulgated by the *Globe* and practised by one of the radical leaders of Upper Canada. Reading the long story of the *Globe*, it is impossible not to see the spirit that animates the Clear Grits and Mr. Brown, and which animated Mr. Gibbard against the poor Indians and their religious leaders; it is impossible not to see there, from beginning to end, an excessive exaggeration, probably mixed with a multitude of assertions that justify an open inquiry, in a civilized country and far from this diabolical spirit of prejudice which presides and rules all unfortunately in certain parts of Canada.

We are far from wanting to justify the violence, if it has taken place, no more than the perusal of the poor Indians; but we await, before believing, the account in the *Globe*, of violence, anger, exasperation and outrageous words of the priests who preside over the religious teaching to the remains of the Indian race, that the government has called to Grand Manitoulin to drive them away now.

Frankly, but sadly: It is the *Globe*, always the *Globe* at work, and Mr. Brown with his fanaticism.

What did Mr. McDougall want to do! Drive the Indians away from the island! But, in going to them to make treaties with them for the cession of this island, has he not admitted their right? And if the treaties have been surreptitiously obtained from them by him and his agents, did he go to claim that they are solemnly bound, above all when almost all among them have not even signed?[267]

Three days later, *Le Journal de Québec* noted that its competitor, *The Quebec Mercury,* was attempting to "save the government of the odiousness attached to its conduct in regard to the Indians of the Great Manitoulin; but it is in vain, for the news which comes since the exaggerated version, everywhere, of the *Globe*, and, in several points, untrue, attest that Mr. Gibbard was not a man to be employed in such a mission." *Le Journal* continued: "If, as Mr. Gibbard has asserted, Father Kohler incited the Indians to sedition, and if it was criminal in the eyes of the law, why wasn't he arrested in Sault Ste. Marie where he was found with the Indian Jocko? Why wasn't he arrested on the *Ploughboy* where he was found by him and his armed force? His abstention puts the truth in doubt. ... How will this sad affair end where the government and its agents play such a lamentable role?[268]

The Globe's extensive coverage prompted David Blain, the Toronto barrister who had defended Chief Ozawanimiki, to write to its editor. It was the position of the *Anishinaabeg*, Blain explained, that the fishery had never been ceded or surrendered by them to the government:

> The Indians hold their lands as tenants in common, and it is stated that the signatures of all the parties who are as such interested, were not obtained. Admitting, however, that the Chief has authority to negotiate and conclude a treaty for his tribe, there are many Chiefs among the Manitoulin Indians, and the signatures of all were not obtained to the treaty, and, therefore, as the Indians contend, there has not been a legal surrender of all their interest in the islands. Then it is said that such of them as did sign were by the Government agents unduly and improperly influenced in different ways. They say also that when the Government were in treaty with the Indians, the latter never intended to include the Lonely Island or the fishery in dispute.

Blain questioned Gibbard's actions, and declared that the four-dollar per annum lease to Mr. Proulx would have meant starvation for the Indians who "live for about five months of the year exclusively on fish." Blain concluded: "There is no desire on the part of the Indians, so far as I could discover, to violate the law—no desire to claim a right to which they do not consider themselves entitled. They believe themselves to be the just owners of the Island and fishery, and insist upon their privilege of fishing, and upon their right to retain possession and exclude intruders."[269]

Almost all the newspapers carried articles and opinions on the fishery dispute. Many simply carried *The Globe*'s articles, with their own editorials added. *The Morning Chronicle and Commercial and Shipping Gazette*, a Quebec-based pro-Conservative party newspaper, asserted that the commissioner of Crown Lands on behalf of the government was guilty of a "double act of injustice and inhumanity" in negotiations with the Indians of Manitoulin, and that if "Gibbard has met his death at the hands of Sawamackoo [i.e., Ozawanimiki], the blame lies solely with the Government, whose very acts courted murder, or intended to inflict it."[270] *The Morning Chronicle* continued its coverage on 3 August 1863:

> The Government finds itself in the most delectable mess. It undertook to rob the Indians of the apportioned lands—apportioned, be it observed, by a former Government, in order to obtain for settlement the land they previously held. After much reluctance they were at length induced, by promises of quiet possession of these islands, to remove thereto. To disturb them in their possession is to break faith with them, to despoil them of their property—in plain terms to rob them. To say that they are holding more land than they can occupy is no argument why a portion of it should be seized by another. If such an argument were worth anything, it is equally applicable to all who possess a super abundance; and especially so to three fourths of the land-holders in every new settlement, aye, and for that matter too, in old settlements also. But we are not to look upon the Indians as though they were an agricultural population, farming land in the usual husband-like style, and judge the

number of acres which each was able to cultivate. Such a standard would lead us to most erroneous and fearful consequences. These people live a nomadic life, and are averse to change it. Hunting, fishing, and in the district to which we just now have referred, the making of sugar, forms almost the sole means of subsistence. To confine a people so circumstanced to the cribbed and limited areas of fifty or a hundred acres is just simply to starve them—a protracted and cruel death. If state necessity compels the Government of Canada to go into an extermination of the Indian race, a less costly and much shorter way would be to send in troops and butcher them without resort to any round-about course, such as crowding them into a corner to starve."[271]

The *St. Catharines Constitutional* reported: "The fraud practised upon the poor Indians of the Manitoulin Islands by Mr. Washington [sic] McDougall, Commissioner of Crown Lands, who pretended to have made satisfactory arrangements with them for giving up their lands, is now producing its natural results. The Indians insist that they never consented to surrender their possessions and are therefore determined to hold them at all hazards against all comers." "The whole affair is a striking illustration of what trouble the country may be dragged into when dishonest imbeciles under take the management of public affairs."[272]

There was "something peculiarly Irish in the features of this case," *The Irish Canadian* noted sympathetically. "The Indians who inhabit this tract, have been subjected to grievances which, if permitted to obtain for any length of time, would drive them from their homes, or give them up a prey to the direst famine." The reporter succinctly summed up the fishery issue: "A Fishery, on the south side of Lonely Island, upon which some seven or eight hundred Indians mainly subsisted, and of which they conceive themselves the lawful proprietors, was, in a most ruthless and unaccountable manner, wrested from them by a certain Government Agent—a Mr. Gibbard."[273] The reporter concluded that he was confident the government would resolve the affair, since, "if the fishery in question belong to the Crown, the Indians are evidently not aware of it."

The Canadian Freeman printed copies of letters written by Father Choné, Chief Mokomanish and David Blain as well as editorials on the fishery incident. On 13 August, the *Freeman* devoted more than four columns to the Manitoulin Island dispute. An editorial that criticized *The Globe*'s Manitoulin articles was accompanied by copies of Father Choné's letters to the editor of *The Leader* newspaper in which Choné questioned the treaty, the ownership of Manitoulin and Lonely islands and Gibbard's actions.

Father Kohler responded to the accusations against him with a letter to the editor of *The Globe*. After sixteen years as a missionary in the Indian Missions, Kohler said, he felt obligated to declare that the attempt "to get from our poor Indians, their land, by the sole principle that 'might makes right,' was nothing less than highway robbery." He denounced the attempt to steal "a million of acres of rocky and barren soil" from "those who placed themselves by the treaty of 1836 under the protection of the British Government." Kohler concluded by declaring that the actions of the Indians, contrary to *The Globe*'s reports, were "the immediate consequences of a matter of principle" and "a question of title, which will be settled by a higher authority."[274]

Reverend Peter Jacobs at Manitowaning was unsympathetic to any breaches of the laws of the country. The Wikwemikong *Anishinaabeg* "removed two French Canadians with their families to the mainland because these had been favourable to the settlement of the island by whites," he reported. "Last summer they compelled these two families to leave Lonely Island which is about twenty miles from Wequemakong, although they had obtained a licence to fish there from the Overseer of Fisheries. For these outrages they are not punished. When an attempt was made by Mr. Gibbard and about twenty constables to arrest those who had been concerned in the last disturbance, such a show of fight was made by the Indians of Wequamekong that it was not deemed advisable to make any arrests."[275]

A Mr. R. Cooper visited Manitoulin Island in August 1863 and wrote to William McDougall from Manitowaning. He endorsed the surrender and commented on the Gibbard affair. He claimed the "Indians disliked Mr. G; who; poor man, in the discharge of what he really believed to be his duty & with a determination not to be cowed, had made many enemies among them. They certainly do not seem to lament him, & I observe an ill concealed smile on their faces when his loss is named. I sometimes broach the subject to see what they'll say, and 'He won't make no more fuss with us,' is an expression you can hear rather exultingly used more than once in a days walk or sail among the friends of Niokee [Ozawanimiki] (Yellow Thunder)."[276]

McDougall sent William F. Whitcher, the senior fishery overseer, to investigate the Gibbard affair. Whitcher reported that the Indians had expelled the lessees from Lonely Island because "they had ruled that no one residing among them should have any other dealing with the Government and its agents after the Manitowaning treaty." He explained that "the mistaken lenity which stayed prompt rebuke for the ejectments of concurring chiefs that succeeded the treaty of Oct 1862, had emboldened and misled the Indians." He described Gibbard as "a dutiful and industrious officer" whose "bearing and language were, on the one hand, very aggravating and on the other were not such as to dissuade the Indians from their purpose and calm the excitement." Of Gibbard's visit to Wikwemikong with the 21 armed constables, Whitcher reported: "I fail to perceive the necessity or object of enforcing the service of summonses by such an exhibition of force." He speculated that Gibbard probably felt that "graver instances and more serious results might ensue" if he did not stop the "summary mode of executing tribal orders and enforcing obedience to their own Council Laws without regard to the liberty of the subject or rights of private property." Whitcher recommended clarifying the ownership of the fishing islands; admonishing the Indians; reinstating the property and rights of the expelled individuals; and undertaking no further leasing of the fishing islands.[277]

Whitcher, Father Choné, Charles de Lamorandière, Tomah Mokomanish, Louis Wakekijik, Ozawanimiki and Jako Atagiwinini travelled to Quebec City for a hearing at the end of August. Whitcher and the chiefs made statements before William McDougall and the attorney general. The chiefs agreed to take any future complaints to the local superintendent or the government; McDougall agreed to leave the fisheries in the neighbourhood of Manitoulin Island "free for the use of Indians and others in common," and to apply the restrictions on cutting and selling wood to merchantable timber only.[278]

The Canadian Freeman, noting that "the fisheries around Manitoulin are not to be leased in future," trusted this meant "there is now an end to the persecution of the poor Indians."[279]

The Leader, the Toronto-based anti-Reform-government newspaper of former Manitoulin surrender negotiator Charles Lindsey, said the government's announcement that "fisheries in the neighbourhood of Manitoulin, are hereafter to be free" was a confession that the Ministry had blundered, causing "an act out of which the recent difficulties arose."[280] Apparently, *The Leader* was pro-surrender but anti-fishery—though its stance, like many newspapers', was crafted on the logic of politics, which did not necessarily follow common logic.

While the various newspapers disagreed on who was responsible, the *Anishinaabeg* or the government, they all agreed that the Manitoulin fishery dispute was precipitated by the 1862 treaty.

The fishery dispute was brought up in the Legislative Council of Canada on 24 August 1863, when Sir Narcisse-Fortunat Belleau moved:

> That an humble Address be presented to His Excellency the Governor General, praying that His Excellency will cause to be laid before the House a copy of all the instructions given to Mr. Gibbard and others who were sent to take possession of the Manitoulin Islands, or part thereof, and of the fisheries there, or relating to the division and distribution of the lands on the said Islands; also copies of reports of that gentleman or of others in possession of the Government; copies of the depositions which warrants were issued for the arrest of persons who opposed the said taking of possession or division and distribution of the lands on the said Islands; a copy of the instructions given to Mr. Whitcher, who was sent to the Manitoulin Islands lately to replace Mr Gibbard; and finally copies of the Orders on the subject of possession of the said Islands, adopted since the first of May last.

The motion was inaccurate, and was ridiculed by the political opposition and the press. Adam Fergusson Blair "stated that he had no objections to the production of such papers as were in existence but some were mentioned which had no existence, just as facts were assumed which had never occurred."[281] He explained:

> Sir Narcisse Belleau calls for documents about the Manitoulin Islands which have no existence. The mover evidently labors under the extraordinary impression that a posse of constables has been sent "to take possession of the Manitoulin Island," and that warrants have been issued for the arrest of persons "who opposed the said taking possession or division and distribution of the said island." Is this ignorance of the facts? Or is it designed to catch sympathy for the assistance of those who just now affect wonderful solicitude for the "poor Indians." There exist no such instructions; no such errand was ever even thought of; no such resistance or arrest ever took place; no such possession or distribution has ever been attempted; no person has been sent to replace Mr. Gibbard, and no Order in Council on the subject of the possession of the said islands has been adopted since May last. It suits the

purpose of mischief making to disseminate utterly untrue assumptions and versions of occurrences quite different from what any reader of the knight's motion must imagine to have taken place. All of the so called Indian difficulties have been so much magnified, distorted and misused, it would be hardly consistent now to await a truthful statement thereof, by which even Indians shall perceive a difference between responsible doings of those in authority, and the irresponsible activity of mere mischievous agitators.[282]

The motion was passed and an extensive collection of relevant documents was presented as a Return in September 1863 and printed in the Sessional Papers. Manitoulin Island coverage vanished from the newspapers in mid-September after a verdict of "wilful murder by person or persons unknown" was rendered.

William Gibbard's Troubled Waters
William Gibbard's disappearance from the steamboat *Ploughboy* was never satisfactorily explained, despite an immediate shipboard enquiry and an official inquest. The inquest jury concluded that William Gibbard was murdered "on the 28th day of July 1863, when on board the steamboat *Ploughboy* somewhere between Little Current and Shebanawning [Killarney]," and that "the said murder was committed on the main deck of the said steamboat, near the foot of the stairs on the starboard or port side of the said boat, but by whom the jury have not sufficient evidence to show."[283]

The verdict was apparently based on a facial wound and the disappearance of his money and notebook, but not other personal items, from his pockets. Though 51 witnesses testified, no one saw or heard anything. More than a dozen men had spent the evening playing cards and drinking in the saloon. Many of the passengers stepped ashore at Little Current and at Killarney. Gibbard was last seen walking on the upper deck about 3 a.m., after the boat left Little Current. He was missed at breakfast and a search was carried out.

The *Ploughboy* carried about 20 crew members and 40 passengers. On this particular voyage, the passengers included Gibbard and his 21 men, Captain Smith of the steamboat *Clifton* and his wife, barrister David Blain, Father Kohler, and one lone *Anishinaabe*, Chief Ozawanimiki. Suspicion immediately fell on the chief, who had not only threatened Gibbard but had openly acknowledged he neither liked nor respected him. Gibbard was reputed to be travelling with $2,000 to pay the Indian annuities, though the money remained in the *Ploughboy*'s safe throughout the voyage.

If murder did occur, his murderer may have been one of Gibbard's own special constables. Of the 21, just half were policemen; the rest were tradesmen and fishermen. Many of them had not approved of Gibbard's actions. Arthur Curtis, a Collingwood shoemaker, reported "the Toronto party, generally were dissatisfied with the proceedings at the Island, that is with the treatment of the clergyman." William Watts, a Collingwood fisherman, noted: "All the Toronto men, seemed to be dissatisfied with Mr. Gibbard. After Mr. Gibbard was lost, and before the investigation, I heard several of the Toronto men laughing and jeering when they heard Mr. Gibbard was missing, so were some of the Collingwood men making sport of it. I can't say the expressions they made use of." Gibbard himself admitted he did not like Police Detective James Colgan of Toronto. James Boyer, Gibbard's interpreter since 1859, had been uneasy during the whole expedition. "The last time I saw him I was frightened about him, for there were so many people at the Sault and on the boat talking against him," said Boyer. "Everybody in the boat knew Mr. Gibbard had the money with him to pay the Indians on Superior. I was afraid of the white people on the boat, not of the Indian, on Mr. Gibbard's account."

Though some passengers said Gibbard was "quite natural," others described him as sober and altered in mood. Chief Constable Adam Dudgeon reported: "His manner was much as usual; but he was not in such spirits as he was when going up." Captain Smith's wife "remarked to her husband the change in him from the time the expedition proved a failure." Barrister David Blain reported that "several witnesses spoke to his troubled state of mind," and "some of the witnesses say he walked the deck that morning in a state of abstraction, would occasionally come up, speak a few words, break off in the middle of a sentence and walk away again, then return and talk over some other topic."

Gibbard's past history had surfaced on the wharf in Sault Ste. Marie just before the *Ploughboy* sailed. Jesuit Father Louis Carrez[284] reported that Gibbard "was furious at some remarks thrown against him, in which it was revealed that he had been earlier dismissed from the English army in the Indies, he announced that he would return immediately to Quebec to make his report, and took passage on the *Plough Boy* with his men."[285] Father Kohler stated that he heard a rumour just before the *Ploughboy* sailed from the Sault wharf that Gibbard had stained the British flag by his conduct in the East Indies.

William Gibbard certainly had had a tarnished military career. Baptized on 27 March 1818, he was the fourth of thirteen children born to John and Mary Gibbard of Sharnbrook, Bedfordshire, England. John Gibbard was a justice of the peace, a major in the Bedford militia and a colonel commandant of the local militia, a man acknowledged as "landed gentry." William and his three younger brothers were destined for military careers, since their eldest brother would inherit the family assets.

At the age of 15, William spent five months at the Peterborough Cathedral Grammar School while his father contacted William Astell, a director of the East India Company, to nominate William as a cadet in the company's Artillery and Engineer Seminary. William was accepted, and upon completion of the infantry course 15 months later, John Gibbard asked Astell to help secure his son an appointment to the Bombay Army infantry. William was reluctant to continue his studies and take the artillery term; or, as his father John put it, "he represents to me that appointments to the artillery are now so few, that judging from the capacities of those above him in the college, he would not have the slightest chance of success should he stay our his fourth term."[286]

Seventeen-year-old William Gibbard was appointed to the 16th Regiment of Bombay Native Infantry. William's younger brother Leonard was serving in the Royal Navy and his brothers Henry Lee and Thomas Bayly soon followed William into the East India Army, but attained the Bombay Horse Artillery.

William's military career ended abruptly when he had four or five prisoners shot near Kowtanee, India, in 1838.[287] Though it was acknowledged at his court martial that he was young, that he believed he was acting on orders and that he had "frequently displayed activity and zeal" and "humanity and gentleness towards the natives generally," he was dismissed in 1840 and his name was struck from the army records.

William Gibbard returned home. In 1842 he inherited a thousand pounds from an aunt, and this likely prompted his emigration to Canada. By February 1844, the 26-year-old was surveying roads in Simcoe County. He worked as a surveyor until he was appointed as fishery overseer for lakes Huron and Superior in 1859. In 1863 he described himself as a Public Land Surveyor and Civil Engineer, Revenue Officer on Lakes Huron and Superior, Overseer of Fisheries, Stipendiary Magistrate for Algoma, Simcoe, Grey, Bruce, Huron and Lambton, in charge of a 28-foot keelboat manned by six men.[288] He neglected to mention his past military service.

Gibbard's conduct in the East Indies had been revealed on the wharf in Sault Ste. Marie just before the *Ploughboy* sailed. Gibbard must have known that his past troubles with natives would destroy his career and reputation once again. If nothing else, it was enough to distract him and permit someone to hit him over the head, steal his money and throw him overboard. Alternatively, a threat of blackmail, or even the disgrace alone, may have prompted him to commit suicide. Suicide would have distressed his family, but a mysterious disappearance was almost heroic (his brother Leonard was the recipient of a memorial in the family church, after being wounded and killed by pirates off the coast of Borneo while in his majesty's naval service.) It is possible that Gibbard chose to disappear rather than dishonour the family name again. It is equally possible that the unpopular and arrogant fishery inspector was killed for his money by one of his underpaid, dissatisfied special constables.

Chapter 7
The Aftermath

Renewed Protests

The fishery dispute brought Manitoulin back into the headlines. It also reminded the *Anishinaabeg* and the priests that the treaty threatened their way of life.

Father Choné accompanied the chiefs to Quebec City to discuss the fishery dispute, and remained there through mid-October. He and Vicar-General Cazeau petitioned Indian Department officials, politicians, the governor general, the press and even the joint premiers of Canada, John Sandfield Macdonald and Antoine-Aimé Dorion.

Choné wrote to William McDougall on 1 September, informing him that he was in Quebec to demand cancellation of the treaty. Choné requested an "authentic act (in writing)" for the Wikwemikong Indians that acknowledged their rights under the 1836 treaty in order to suppress "for the future all seeds of discord and that the Indians may live in peace, praising the justice of the government." He added: "You are aware that nearly the whole of the inhabitants of Manitoulin desire its cancellation. I have come here to demand it; I must therefore use alliances to have it done."[289]

Choné subsequently submitted a petition to the governor general. It was translated as:

> Petition to have the effect of annulling the Manitowaning Treaty of 6th October 1862. And an Act for reinstating the Manitoulin Island Indians in their rights and properties expressed in the Treaty of 1836.
> Excellency
> The undersigned, Missionary of the Manitoulin Island Indians, in the name of the greatest majority of the said Indians, brings forth to His Excellency's knowledge that a Treaty has been accounted as concluded on the 6th October last between the Government and a part of the said Indians, by the Hon'ble Wm. McDougall, by which it appears that the said Indians would be deprived of a portion of their property equivalent to more than four fifths.
> That the pretended treaty is illegal, useless to the Governments project and prejudicial to the Indians.
>
> First the above treaty is illegal, because
> 1. The parties were unqualified to effect a contract being respectively Guardians and Minors and it is a notorious fact that the Indians are minors of the lowest degree.
> 2. The Indians have been unjustly influenced by a great terror brought to bear upon them and by illusive promises.
> 3. There has been want of liberty in the discussion. The conditions having been imposed by the purchasing party, without even letting the other party suspect that they had a right to discuss them.

4. The Treaty is based on allegations void of truth. It is not true that these Indians have given up to the Crown their rights (under the treaty of 1836) to the said Island. There is not a word in the said Treaty insinuating it. It is not right to make people believe, as in the second allegation that the treaty is conditional. It is not true that the opposing Indians consented to the cession of all the other parts beyond the peninsula. They resigned by force as may be seen in their printed protestation & relation.

5. The Indians, the pretended grantees represent only a weak minority.

6. This minority itself is purely nominal, the Chiefs having acted against the intention of their respective tribes and consequently without authority as is established by the privileges of all nations. These intentions have had repeated manifestation in general council (see printed account)

7. These intentions have been again manifested subsequently by protestations and refutations from the pretended cessionary tribe, and signed by the principals of each tribe and also by several of the Chiefs and Chief men who signed their names on the treaty.

8. Several of the signing chiefs, Mesakwange and Bemikwanesskang, have no interest on the Island, having their reserves on the main land and consequently cannot make over what does not belong to them.

9. In the name of this minority purely nominal the Indians have been deprived of more than the four fifths of their Island, and other properties.

II. The treaty does not reach the object of the Government it is useless to its schemes.

The proposed object is to improve the country in extending colonization but

1. The Island is not fitted for colonization. The Indians themselves have said to Mess'rs the Commissioners that there was not a sufficient quantity of Land on the whole extent of the Island to form ten farms.

People knowing the Manitoulin Island and the Island of St. Joseph in the vicinity of the former to the West assert that if a preference was to be given to either of them, it would be to the Island of St Joseph for it is known that the St. Joseph Island has been well spoken of by the surveyors and that after this reputation the purchasers had strong competition over the lots at the time of the sale in 1856. What has been the result for the improvement of the country? Several of the purchasers preferred to abandon their lots and lose their first payment than to continue making the subsequent payments and to become proprietors of sand, swamps and rocks.

The St. Joseph Island is less inhabited than was before the sale.

A few colonists that a speculator had brought there, have abandoned it and in the mean time the St. Joseph Island offers facility to the trade than the former one, by its fine harbors which surround it and by its proximity to the Bruce Mines and Sault Ste Marie.

2. The Manitoulin Island is useless to the establishment of a harbour in furthering navigation. Killarney on the main land, near Manitoulin incomparably offers more facility to the establishment of a harbor of this kind.

3. There is besides a great quantity of good land on the continent, all along the North shores of Lake Huron, land not yet sold though already surveyed.

III. The treaty is prejudicial to the interests of the other party that is to the Indians, and very useless. The Government pretends to ameliorate the condition of the Indians but

1. If it procures them an annual rental of 25 cents a piece, it will be a great deal. What a compensation for their property and the tranquillity of which they deprived them!

2. The execution of the treaty will be the cause of the dispersion of the Indians and consequently of their ruin because according to the clauses of the treaty they are obliged to abandon places which they inhabit such places as harbors and mill sites but it is notorious that the Indians are not found to be found in the vicinity of lands far removed from water courses. And more over the Indian settlements are to be as contracted as possible, the consequence will be that the greatest number will have rocks and swamps.

3. It is known also that the contact of whites with the Indians tends to the destruction of the former, thus the Government which has always professed to treat the poor Indians well will have to reproach themselves with an act of cruelty quite unnecessary.

In consequence I demand of His Excellency that he please to declare that there is no necessity for persevering in the execution of the said treaty.

That the said treaty be made void and annulled and that an authentic act drawn up to reinstate the Manitoulin Indians in their rights & properties such as has been expressed by the treaty of 1836, that is to say the Manitoulin Island and the surrounding multitude of Islands.

It will be an Act of Justice and humanity.

I am with a profound respect, My Lord, the very humble & very obedient servant of Your Excellency,

J.P. Choné S.J.

Missionary to the Indians Manitoulin Island.

Quebec the 16th September 1863.[290]

The petition was forwarded to the Indian Department. On the first page William Spragge wrote: "Under what right or authority does any ecclesiastic assume to apply for an abrogation of a Treaty of Cession made for the benefit of the Indians when it concerns them not him."

The petition was read in the Legislative Assembly and Council in early October 1863. Sir Narcisse-Fortunat Belleau tabled a motion requesting copies of the letter Choné had written describing his arrest and the petitions against the McDougall treaty from the Indians of Sheshegwaning, Michigiwatinong and Atchiwaigunning. The item was carried over to the next session, where it was tabled in the Legislative Assembly in February. A return resulted in June 1864.[291] In essence, the petition was presented, read ... and filed.

William McDougall moved on. He travelled to Washington in November to discuss the Reciprocity Treaty between Great Britain and the United States. From there he accompanied Abraham Lincoln to the dedication of the Gettysburg, Pennsylvania cemetery, where he witnessed the American president's renowned address.

The *Anishinaabeg* of Manitoulin Island were occupied with their harvest and fishing throughout the autumn of 1863. The chiefs who accompanied William Whitcher to Quebec City and the chief who testified at the Gibbard inquiry in Collingwood returned in September, more-or-less victorious. The former had obtained a promise that the Manitoulin fisheries would be "left free for the use of Indians and others in common" and that the wood restrictions would apply only to merchantable timber,[292] while the latter reported the verdict of "murder by person or persons unknown."

Father Louis Carrez summarized: "It appears that the question of the fisheries was decided favourably. But as for the cession of the island, his excellency the governor sent Fr. Choné to his ministers. Mr. Macdonald spoke pleasantly; Mr. Dorion was more explicit. As the priest was saying that justice was required, he was interrupted. 'It is not a question of justice,' Mr. Dorion responded, 'the question is very simple. If the lands of the island are good, your case is lost; if they are bad, your case is won. And so, the question is settled!' It was useless to persist."[293]

Manitoulin was without a resident superintendent from mid-July until late September, when Charles Thomas Dupont[294] was appointed. In addition to assuming Ironside's duties, Dupont was supposed to manage the sales of the surrendered lands and settle the *Anishinaabeg* according to the treaty.

Dupont, a 26-year-old merchant, may not have been the best candidate to conciliate the post-treaty situation because he had implicated Father Kohler in William Gibbard's disappearance. But the job—on an isolated island notorious for opposition to the treaty and the alleged murder of Gibbard—probably attracted few applicants.[295]

Dupont was shocked by Manitowaning: "I find all the buildings with the exceptions of the Superintendent's, the Minister's & the Doctor's, & the store, are all gone or going to ruin, and I am informed that there is not much good land in the immediate neighbourhood."[296]

In September and October 1863, the *Anishinaabeg* of Wikwemikong discussed their rights under the Royal Proclamation of 1763.[297] This proclamation "Establishing New Governments in America," issued by King George III, reserved the land between Quebec and the Appalachian Mountains, the Hudson's Bay territory and the Mississippi River for the Indian people and put conditions on its purchase or settlement.

The arrival of surveyors late in the fall of 1863 prompted the bands to renew their treaty protests. A 173-signature petition was sent to the governor general demanding the annulment of the treaty. A copy of the petition was published in *The Canadian Freeman*:

> Manitoulin Island, Dec. 1, 1863.
> The Indians of Manitoulin to His Excellency the Governor General,
> MAY IT PLEASE YOUR EXCELLENCY,—In the petition which our Missionary, the Rev. Chone, addressed to you last October, he proved the unlawfulness of the treaty made at Manitouaning Oct. 6th 1862. His evidence in that point is most conclusive. Moreover, he showed that that act, even if just, is both useless to the country and injurious to the inhabitants of the island.
>
> Therefore the occupation of Manitoulin by the Government would be outrageous both to justice and humanity.
>
> We now again apply to your Excellency in the name of "the Royal Proclamation" of 1763, to declare that act unlawful and void, and to protest against any pursuance thereof. Here we quote the proclamation:
>
> That no Indian tribe should be interfered with, and that no cession of their lands should be had except freely and openly made by themselves in general council; and it is expressly forbidden to any Governor General, Commander-in-Chief, &c., to grant warrants of survey, or pass patents for any lands whatever which had not been

ceded to the Crown.

According to that proclamation, we are, as we always believed ourselves to be, the proprietors of our lands not ceded, and which we possess as a nation.

Now, no cession of the Island has been made to the Government in accordance with the conditions required by that proclamation. The evidence thereof is in your hands, and we take to witness before God the conscience of the Honourable Minister who is the author of that act.

We have already sent from all parts of the Island to his Excellency four protests against the act; and by this present one, founded on our right acknowledged and proclaimed by Royal authority, we declare that we do not consent to any work undertaken by the Government upon Manitoulin Island.

It is not in our power to oppose any violent resistance; but the justice of our cause protests in the face of the whole country, and will draw down the Divine vengeance upon the oppressors of the weak.

We appeal to a competent court, a court composed of the representatives of the people, to judge between us and the Government.

"Having been informed that surveyors, sent by the Government, have landed in the Island, we have sent a deputation to them with the following declaration:–

WIKWEMIKONG, Dec. 1st, 1863.

To the Chief Surveyor of Manitoulin Island:–

Sir, We, the proprietors of Manitoulin, hear that you come to survey our lands. We protest energetically against such an attempt upon our property. We never ceded our lands to the Government; therefore we request you to cease your work. We are respectfully, &c.[298]

Similar letters signed by residents of Wikwemikong, South Bay and Michigiwatinong were delivered to all the surveyors.[299] The Sheguiandah people refused to join the protest. Dupont reported that "A,duh,we Ke,zis [Edawe Kesis] the head man at Sha,gwa,an,dah, with several other Indians from that place, came here the day before yesterday [5 December 1863], and informed me that Wah,ka,ke,zhik, Thos. Kenosh,a,meg, Joe Peltier, and two others,—all head men of Wequemikong, had been over from thence to their place, to know if they would join in driving the surveyors off the Island, stating that now they would suffer for having surrendered their portion of the Island, as the Government would only give them rocks to live upon." Dupont advised that, in the event of any trouble arising, "strong measures should be taken with these people, as they believe and have been taught that the Government are afraid of them, that they can do what they please."[300]

Three days later, Chief Taibosegai of Michigiwatinong informed Dupont that "Father Hanipeaux the Jesuit Priest of the Wek,wem,i,kong establishment had been to them to require them to write to the Government that they had not meant & do not wish to surrender their lands, & that for their refusal to comply he has formally excommunicated them & will not admit them into the Church." A few weeks later, Dupont reported that surveyor Joseph Hobson had said Chief Taibosegai asked him to tell Dupont of "the regret that he felt from his son and two others from Mitchigawadnong having signed the protest against the survey of the Manitoulin. They put their names to it without his consent or knowledge."[301]

Dupont wrote to Taibosegai: "I am sorry to learn that your son has been led away by the bad men, who are trying to make trouble for themselves very fast." Dupont assured the chief that the men were opposing the Queen, "who pays them money, who keeps a Doctor here to take care of them, and who in this very matter of the Survey and sale of the Island is acting from love to the Indian, anxious that the land which is of no use to them, may be sold for their benefit, that they may receive more money than they do now." He advised: "do not let any of your people sign any paper or be mixed up in this matter—keep the Queen for your friend, for she will reward her friends and punish her enemies."[302]

Chief Taibosegai and his band illustrate the ongoing division in the bands. Typically, the younger men wanted the treaty annulled, while the older chiefs were determined to uphold their pledge of loyalty to the Crown. Though chiefs Taibosegai and Paimoquonaishkung had added postscripts to the May 1863 anti-treaty petition, the document was written by "our young people."

When the surveyors were visited by twenty-two *Anishinaabeg* in January 1864 and directed by them to stop surveying, Dupont acted. He convened the treaty *Anishinaabeg* and persuaded them "to promise not to act anymore with these people [the Wikwemikong *Anishinaabeg*] but to be governed by my advice." Then he met with the chiefs and head men of Wikwemikong who had maintained that "the Chiefs who signed the Treaty of surrender acted contrary to a previous understanding come to amongst themselves." The chiefs agreed "that they would not proceed to violent measures, but that having made this protest they would now leave the matter to the Government." Dupont claimed the treaty signatories had participated because of "persuasion & deception & in some cases by intimidation"—the same claim made by *Anishinaabeg* themselves to explain their participation in the treaty. Dupont concluded: "they have remained quiet, tho' they are holding continual councils & all sorts of rumors as to their intentions are afloat."[303] Spragge directed Dupont to

> point out distinctly to the Indians that the surveys which are in progress are the first step towards securing to them and to their families the farm lots of 100 Acres each to which as a condition in the Treaty of October 1862 they are entitled. ... It is of course important that the various Bands should respectively form as compact settlements as possible. And that unless the rugged and inferior quality of the land would forbid it that they individually should take up lots each closely abutting one upon another. This of course you will carefully explain to them; and likewise the clause of the treaty which provides that Landing places mill sites &c should be reserved for sale.[304]

Spragge then warned Father Hanipaux that "the laws of the Province should be respected and observed" and the Indians must not be encouraged to disturb the surveyors.[305] Father Choné responded to Spragge's "threats" by questioning Spragge's law enforcement, negotiations and resolution of grievances.[306] Choné abandoned courtesy and diplomacy for frank speech. He protested the treaty relentlessly at every level of government with letters, petitions and personal visits.

The surveyors proceeded despite the objections. Reverend Peter Jacobs described the progress to his superiors:

The survey of a portion of Manitoulin commenced last fall. Three townships have already been surveyed, and two more are being surveyed. It is supposed that not more than half of the land is good. The land will be sold to whites either this fall or next spring. ... When the surveyors commenced their work last fall, a deputation of the Wequamekong Indians went to each of their camps and told them to stop their work, saying that the island was theirs, and that they had not ceded it. The surveyors paid no attention to this, but went on with their survey. It was thought at the time that violent measures would have been adopted by the Indians. Their priests, I am sorry to say, have encouraged them in what they have done.[307]

A notice was printed in Ojibwe at Wikwemikong in early January 1864. It quoted an article on Indian rights published in *The Canadian Freeman* of 13 August 1863. The translation read:

Where by the treaty with France in 1763 Canada became a British province, a royal proclamation was issued in that same year (1763) which may be said to be the Magna Carta of the Indian rights.

By that proclamation it is declared that no Indian tribe should be interfered with, and that no cession of their lands should be had except freely and openly made by themselves in General Council and it was expressly forbidden to any Governor General, Commander in Chief etc etc to grant warrants of survey or patents for any lands whatsoever, which had not been ceded to the Crown.

Wherefore the Indian tribes were negotiated with as allies and treated with as distinct and independent nations.

After the independence of the US. had been acknowledged by England a different principle was sought to be established by congress, which maintained that the treaty with Great Britain with the fee of all the Indian Lands within the boundaries of the US. the Indian Tribes living within these boundaries remonstrated with congress against such position and sent an embassy or delegation to Washington, saying: you consider yourselves as an independent people. We the original inhabitants of the country and sovereigns of the soil, look upon ourselves as equally independent and free as any other nation etc.

In maintaining this position, the Indians were encouraged and assisted by the British government and in 1792 they sent a deputation to Lord Dorchester, Governor General at Quebek. One of the questions put to Lord Dorchester was this: "Is it true that, in making peace with the U.S. the King has given away our lands?" His Lordship assures them that such was not and could not be the case, in as much as the king never had any right to their Lands, other than such lands as had been freely ceded by themselves, with their own free consent by open and public council.[308]

Dupont forwarded the notice to Spragge, describing it as "a paper printed in the Indian language at Wequamekong on the 4th Inst. & now being circulated among the Indians in this neighbourhood, by the Priests of that Establishment." Dupont received his copy from Father Blettner, who informed him that "the whole matter of the treaty &c was about being debated in the house of Assembly, when it adjourned, and would come up again as soon as it assembled."[309]

Father Choné wrote to Dupont in mid-January: "The people of Wikwemikong want to have a meeting with their Manitowaning brothers."[310] Subsequently, on 19 January 1864, a large council was held at Manitowaning. Chiefs Wakekijik and Maishegonggai, representing Wikwemikong and Manitowaning respectively, spoke. Wakekijik claimed that many Manitoulin residents were dissatisfied. He proposed that *Anishinaabeg* should "eat out of one dish," or act together, as they had agreed in 1861.

> My brother Chiefs—I mean you who live at Manitowaning—we shall tell you what we think, and we want to hear what you think. We do not consider that this Island has yet been ceded to the Government, in as much as some of the chiefs and many of the warriors did not agree to the surrender. There are Indians at She-she-gwahning, Maple Point, Me-tche-ke-wed-e-nong, Min-de-moo-ya River, and South Bay, who are averse to the Surrender. Knowing these things, we do not cease to think of this part of the Island, and to make endeavours to retain it for all the Indians as well as the small islands around it. There is not much good land on the Manitoulin, as is well known by all of us. There would be enough land for us and our children that come after us, if we did not give up any part of it. It appears to us that you who have ceded land will get little or nothing for it. The Surveyors will have to be paid for their work, and you have already received a large amount of money. We know what will be the result when whites come & live among us. They will do the labor that is required on the Island, and will of course make money—and to you, my friends, will be given the lowest meanest work to do as servants—such as, carrying water, cutting up wood, cleaning stables, making baskets &c.
>
> When the land you have ceded shall have been divided among yourselves & white settlers, what land will your children have? Our families are increasing. The Indians are increasing in number. How can all our descendants be provided for? We have no other reserve besides this. My friends, we want to eat out of one dish as it were. We do not wish to break a part of it to give away. All of us who met together at Me-tche-ke-wed-e-nong three years ago, and held a grand Council there, agreed that we should eat out of one dish. We feel convinced that the Indians would be better off if they kept the Island for themselves, than if they surrendered a part of it. This is what the We-qua-me-kong Indians think.

Maishegonggai of Manitowaning replied:

> My friends, we do not think alike. We who live on this side consented to give up the Island to the Government, but you refused to do so. You spoke of your children and their future condition. You spoke anxiously about them. We also think of ours, and trust that they may do well, and be treated well always by the whites. We have already made a treaty with the Government, and we are not going now to throw it away. The future will tell what Indians will be better off, you who refuse to make a treaty or we who consented to make it. We have hitherto obeyed the Queen & her officers; we mean to do so still. We place ourselves in the good keeping of the Government. My friends, we are no longer independent; nor could we live as an independent people. We cannot live as our forefathers did. We are dependent on the white man for many things that are essential to our welfare. The Queen is our monarch. She has authority over us. My friends, I cannot agree with you on what you have said. I tell you plainly that I shall not aid your projects. You fight against the laws and rules laid down for your observance by the Government. You want to keep the white man away from the Island. I give you warning, Take care—you may get into trouble.
>
> My friends, this side of the Island has been ceded. Why should you any longer meddle with it, or speak about it to our Indians. You have your own reserve. Speak about that and take good care of it. My friends, you have said that the Indians who

ceded their land will be very poor in times to come. I know how the Indians live who are on small reserves below. They appear to live comfortably. They do not suffer from being surrounded by whites. They are not troubled or persecuted by them. My friends, we cannot resist the tide of emigration. The whites are coming nearer and nearer to us. They will at last surround us, but they will not drive us away before them as they have not driven away the Indians, to whom I have just referred.[311]

Chief Maishegonggai was the senior chief of the Manitowaning and Sheguiandah bands. He had been promised at the treaty negotiations that his band could return to Sheguiandah, his birthplace and the site of what he considered Manitoulin Island's best land.

Reverend Jacobs acted as interpreter at the council and reported to his superiors that "the Protestant Indians who live in the ceded portion of the island have I am glad to say, lived quietly, and have been and are still obedient to the Government. Although many attempts have been made to induce them to support the measures of their disloyal and troublesome friends on the other side, they have remained loyal."[312]

Dupont claimed the speeches proved "the unwillingness of the Indians on this side, to act with the We,qua,me,kong ones." He reported that the "Indians on the ceded part of the Island, are all anxious to see the whiteman amongst them, & would make the same treaty over again, & if many signatures have been attached to any paper to His Excellency the Governor General, stating to the contrary those at least from the ceded portion of the Island, have either been attached without consent of the owners or under a misapprehension on their parts."[313]

The *Anishinaabeg* placed an advertisement in *The Canadian Freeman* on 10 March 1864:

> WARNING NOTICE! NOTICE IS HEREBY GIVEN TO the Public that We, Indians of the Ottawa and Chippewa Tribes, sole proprietors of the Great Manitoulin Island, do wish to inform all the colonists and speculators desirous of securing lands in the aforesaid Island, that we never ceded to the Government, our rights to any portion thereof and consequently the Crown Land Department can neither cause the said Great Manitoulin to be surveyed, not put up for sale, or alienate any portion of the aforesaid Island which we posses in common, without rendering themselves guilty, with respect to us, of injustice and manifest robbery, as likewise without violating the solemn pledge of sworn treaties.
> NOTA BENE
> Some of us are falsely called American Indians. Here are the facts. When after the war of 1812, the British Empire ceded to the United States, part of her dominions in North America, we, as faithful allies, left our former homes, in order to be under the protection of the English Government. The whole country belonged to us. Consult History. We may soon appeal to our great Ally, England. We protest against having our Lands under the same regulations as the Crown Lands.
> Garden River, C.W. Feb 13, 1864.

The Indian Department considered the treaty issue closed. William McDougall finally responded to the complaints with a memorandum:

The petitioners complain that the treaty of October, 1862, was unfairly obtained, and was not assented to by a majority of the Indians.

The facts are:

1. A surrender of the Indian title to the Islands of Manitoulin was made by treaty with Sir F.B. Head in 1836. Under that treaty these Islands were to be held by the Crown in trust for the benefit of all Indians who might be "allowed" by the Crown "to reside there."

2. The treaty of 1836 was signed by 16 chiefs and head men in Council, assembled for the purpose.

3. The treaty of 1862, now complained of, was signed by 19 chiefs and head men, in general Council assembled for the purpose, and after two days deliberation.

4. These 19 constituted a large majority of the Chiefs and head men of the bands residing on the Islands.

5. The treaty was made in accordance with the terms of the 23rd Victoria, Chapter 151, entitled an "Act respecting the management of the Indian lands and property."

6. It was made by the Commissioner of Crown Lands in person accompanied by the Deputy Superintendent of Indian Affairs, the Local superintendent and numerous witnesses.

7. It has been approved and accepted by the Governor General in Council, as required by the 4th Section of the Act referred to.

8. A sum of money was paid in advance to and accepted by a majority of the Indians residing on the Island, as a portion of the purchase money expected to be realized from the sale of surveyed lands to settlers.

9. Four townships have been surveyed and will soon be open for sale under the terms of the treaty.

10. The treaty of 1862 was therefore legally made by the parties competent to make it, and cannot be annulled or cancelled on the grounds set forth in the petition.

11. The appeal to the treaty of 1836, the Royal Proclamation of 1763, and the answer of Lord Dorchester to a query put to him in 1792, are irrelevant, because the treaty of 1862 is of equal authority. It is absurd to pretend that the Indians of Manitoulin are unable to treat with the Government in 1862, because they or their ancestors made treaties of a different term in 1836, or, it may be, in 1763.

Reference is requested to the treaty (of 1862) itself; the Report of Mr. Vankoughnet, and minutes of Council thereon, of 1861; the Report of Superintendent Bartlett, and the proceedings of a Council of the Indians in October 1861, and the Report of deputy Superintendent Spragge concerning the treaty of 1862.

The Commissioner of Crown Lands has good reason to believe that the opposition to the treaty of 1862 does not emanate from Indians but is the work of a few designing white men, who have acquired control over one or two bands residing on the easterly portion of the Island. He is informed also that of these Indians, the larger number is recently from the United States, and have no rights, legal or equitable under the treaty of 1836.

He submits that the treaty of 1862 is eminently just, and will prove beneficial to the few scattered bands now residing on the Great Manitoulin. They could no longer subsist by the chase, for they had destroyed nearly all the wild animals of the Island. They cultivated only a few patches of soil and lived miserably on the produce. Unlike other bands in Upper Canada, they derived no revenue from lands sold which in the case of their neighbours, the Saugeens, amount to a sum nearly sufficient for their support. They could not and would not cultivate a tithe of the land of the Island, and had no power to sell to white men. Mining explorers, Lumbermen, and settlers, unknown and unheard of in 1836, now pass them by daily, and could not long be restrained from occupying portions of the Island. The progress of settlement and civilization as well as the interests of the Indians pointed to some new arrangement, by which three quarters of a million of acres of land, now a barren wilderness, should be made productive. The treaty secures to them all the land they need for cultivation and more. It leaves about 103,000 acres under the treaty of 1836, for the use of those who dissent from the arrangement of 1862. It gives to those who agreed to the survey and sale of the westerly part of the Island all the proceeds after deducting the cost of Survey &c.

It is not easy to see what more could be done.[314]

McDougall was replaced as commissioner of Crown Lands by Alexander Campbell when the Conservative party regained power on 30 March 1864. Campbell was immediately contacted by Father Choné, who encouraged the new commissioner to cancel the treaty concluded by his political opponents.[315]

But Campbell was not about to cancel a treaty that had been initiated by his party and had obtained 650,000 acres for settlement for which the opposition had already weathered the protests. He drafted a response and instructed staff to send it to Choné and a copy to his superior, the vicar-general. Campbell asserted that the treaty was more generous than initially proposed and noted that many of the residents had "no material rights of proprietorship for they are emigrant Indians some from the United States, & others from the portions of British territory." The "treaty is a cession of the Western portion of the Island only. And the Indians occupying that section of the Island voluntarily entered into it without of course compulsion or threats of compulsion. The Wykiwemikong Bands retain the Eastern section. They are left by the Treaty undisturbed, altho their Head Chief Tekumah and some others would have agreed to a Cession of that part also." Campbell's memo concluded: "Rev. Mr. Choné has constituted himself the channel and organ for denouncing the Treaty. But as the policy & expediency of this measure was concurred in by successive administrations of opposing Political views, And it is at the same time most favourable to the true interests of the Indian people, it would be unwise to obstruct its provisions being fully carried into operations."[316]

Sir Narcisse-Fortunat Belleau brought the Manitoulin Island issue before the Legislative Council once again, in May 1864. He requested copies of all Orders in Council for the Manitoulin Islands passed since September 1863 as well as the surveyor's instructions and reports. The documents were presented and printed in the Sessional Papers. In addition, Belleau's request of October 1863 for presentation of a copy of Father Choné's July 1863 letter to the governor general, and a copy of the protests of the Indians of Sheshegwaning, Michigiwatinong and Atchiwaigunning against the McDougall treaty, surfaced that June. Sir Étienne-Paschal Taché, the joint premier, presented the return but the government was in the midst of a controversy over an unauthorized loan, resulting in its resignation at the end of June 1864 and the government's subsequent reorganization. The new coalition government focused on the federal union of British North America.

On Manitoulin, Reverend Peter Jacobs was concerned about resettlement. He described Dupont's plan to his British sponsors:

> The Superintendent wishes the Indians of this place, of the Little Current and of Shegwaindah to live all together at Shegwaindah, where there is a large tract of good land, and where there is good fishing. I do not know whether all the Indians will agree to this arrangement. If they all lived together, their village would be quite large, and their spiritual interests could be better looked after. A church and school house would have to be built for them.[317]

Unfortunately, Jacobs died in May 1864, leaving the Protestants without a missionary on Manitoulin for the first time since 1838. Superintendent Dupont informed the Church of England officials that Manitowaning was going to become a non-Native settlement, and as a result "they will have to leave here" "in accordance with the terms of the treaty of 1862 which reserves certain village sites from the selections of the Indians of which this place forms one." He claimed they wanted to move to Sheguiandah, where the fishing was better.[318] A new missionary, Reverend Jabez Waters Sims,[319] was quickly prepared and dispatched to handle the mission's relocation.

Treaty witness Samuel P. Day's book *English America* was published in 1864. It contained extensive information about Manitoulin Island, the treaty and the fishery dispute. Day's previous "observant tourist" attitude to the treaty was now tinged with scepticism: "I cannot say that I altogether favour this wresting of the poor Indians' patrimony so remorselessly from them—for contiguity to the white man is an unfailing indication of the Indian's fate. The sacredness of a former treaty should not have been so lightly regarded. If its letter was not literally fulfilled, its spirit was sufficiently manifest to have rendered it inviolable." Day claimed Father Choné had "done more to civilise the tribes scattered about Manitoulin Island than any other missionary. He really takes a Christian interest in these wretched people, and his opposition to the ceding of the island and the alienation of the Indians' patrimony is deserving of the utmost consideration." About the events of 1863, Day concluded:

> Not only have acts of violence been perpetrated by the Wikwimekong bands upon some of their fellow Indians, who had rendered themselves obnoxious to the malcontents by sanctioning the treaty, but other persons who had obtained a fishing lease on Lonely Island have been driven from thence. In reality, therefore, the treaty is null and void. Few settlers will have the hardihood to venture their lives in purchasing any allotments or in taking up their abode on the island, even did not its inaccessible position intervene to render a white settlement in such a remote and undesirable locality impossible.
>
> Possibly an attempt might be made to expel the Indians altogether from the island; but I trust that no greed of officials or land speculators will resolve itself into such a callous act of retribution. These poor Indians have been peaceful enough hitherto. They have, time after time, ceded their hunting grounds at the behests of the Government, and retired further and further from more civilised districts into obscurity. Surely there is land enough to spare in English America—and far more eligible too—without disturbing a race fast hurrying towards extinction. Canada owes much to the Indians, for whom she has done comparatively little. Let her not add to her numerous sins of omission one of commission more heinous than all the others, by sequestering the island granted in good faith to these semi-civilised tribes.[320]

Manitoulin was ravaged by fires in the summer of 1864. The destruction of crops, timber and maple trees may have prompted the Wikwemikong *Anishinaabeg* to consider requests to extract petroleum from the oil springs located on their territory as an alternative source of revenue. Wikwemikong's unceded status prevented the government from unilaterally issuing oil licences, as it had with wood and fish, though Spragge insisted that all licences had to go through the Indian Department.[321] After lengthy negotiations, in May 1865 the Wikwemikong *Anishinaabeg* granted William Baby and his partners the exclusive right to extract petroleum. Father Choné noted that the natives had drawn up an exclusive licence with one company because they were afraid the government would take possession of the oil springs, and then the entire reserve.[322] The governor general issued a licence to explore and retrieve petroleum to William Baby's Great Manitoulin Oil Company in June 1865.[323]

Despite the distraction of petroleum negotiations, Father Choné continued to advocate for the *Anishinaabeg*. He complained to the commissioner of Crown Lands that the department's control of resources maintained "the Indians always in guardianship." He asked the commissioner to return the Island to the Indians and let them escape from the state of "infancy" in which they were held.[324]

Reunification of the Bands

The opposition to the treaty that had been expressed band by band became a unanimous *Anishinaabe* resistance in the summer of 1865. In June, a deputation representing 300 *Anishinaabe* residents of Little Current, Michigiwatinong and Sheshegwaning approached the new Protestant missionary, Reverend Sims, and asked him to help them have the treaty annulled. Sims had spent his first eight months on Manitoulin Island meeting the residents and mastering their language. Initially, he believed Dupont's assertion that the treaty had been accepted and settlement was imminent, but as Sims' familiarity with the *Anishinaabeg* increased, his support of the treaty and resettlement decreased. Surprised by the consensus of Protestants and Catholics, Sims promised to consider the issue. He suggested they approach the governor general in person:

> A deputation of Indians from Sheshegwaning & West Bay—met me at Columbus' house and said they had come down specially to see me and request me to write to the Governor General respecting their grievances and to ask for redress. A deputation from the L.C. [Little Current] Indians was also associated with them. The names are as follows—these were accompanied by several others (21 in all) Chiefs Tebahsegay—Benegoonashkum and Abeens from West Bay—representing 34 families cont'g 130 Individuals, accompanied by Megwauns, Sheemenahnuhgwud. From She-she-gwahning by Deputy—Adosskaus [Itawashkash?] sent by the Chief—Pammssahdung and Shamgwish representing 33 families or 126 persons. Columbus from the L. Current representing all the Indian families there 13 in number. They stated that they had been to Mr. Dupont frequently to ask for information respecting their permanent location. That they had been always unwilling to give up the Island. That when the Commissioners came they instructed their spokesman Assickenauk to refuse to cede the Island. That he had broken faith with them & offered to surrender his portion being over persuaded by the white people—that he had told them that it was no use to refuse to give it up and that they were all very sorry that he had acted

in this way. That they did not know what was to become of their children. That one of their number from She-she-gwahning had come last spring to see Mr. Dupont on the subject that he Mr. D. refused to see him. That there was no more than enough good land on the island for the Indians and that they did not wish to be disturbed in possession of the lands they now occupied at She-she-gwanning—at West Bay and at Little Current. And that they wished me to write to the Governor General respecting the matter. I promised to consider the matter, but that they were not to hold me responsible for the result as it was not a matter which I could settle or which I had anything to do with. I however recommended that they should appoint a deputation to wait on the Governor themselves with their own statement.[325]

Sims' statement confirms that the *Anishinaabeg* themselves, and not just the Jesuits, objected to the treaty. They evidently took Sims' advice. They convened a grand council at Wikwemikong in mid-July. A petition to the governor general was written in Ojibwe, describing how the chiefs had been intimidated and frightened into signing the treaty. The names of 17 of the 18 treaty signatories (including Tehkummah but not including Jean-Baptiste Assiginack) requested the cancellation of the treaty. The names of 19 chiefs representing about 350 men concluded the document. The document was translated as:

Wequemakong 15 July 1865
Great gathering together in Council that was made, Chiefs (Speeches or Council) whose names were put to the Treaty at Manitowaning that time 6th October 1862.

Thou who art the Great and righteous Chief we know that purposely the Great Spirit gives you power and grace to be merciful in your heart, to look carefully & well over the Country of which you are the head, that no one may be wrongfully treated. And we also know the Great Spirit is just and good. He will not promote any thing that looks bad, or any bad work. He is just and good, and merciful. We know you to be the same. You do not desire to promote or help that work which has looked bad—such as by intimidation to cause cheating.

And now as far as our feet will reach our tears run down from crying looking at our children who are to live in the future, at the same time thinking how we have been cheated when frightened.

This is how we were cheated. We were told that though we would not let our land go, yet we will not be let alone. It will be taken from us by force, altho we will not let it go now. The Great Chief is determined to take our land. This is what Wm. McDougall said to us.

So verily we were made afraid, and thought it would be so—and we are those who are said to have surrendered our land.

And now be merciful unto us, patiently hear us. This time we very carefully and honestly tell the truth, what the Great Spirit wills us. We say that we did not previously ask our men—we did not tell them—very truly we knew their thoughts, that they would not let their land go even to this day. It may be said that they also surrendered. They did not surrender, and were never disposed to do so. They even cried and grieved, when they knew what we had done. We strongly wanted them that they also might think as we did, but we did not succeed in doing so even to this day.

Wm. McDougall came and caused a very bad feeling and hatred amongst us.

Even us Chiefs looked at each other when we were doing that thing which we have done. We did not agree together nor help each other. It is only lately that we settled the friendship that we broke, and again shook hands with all together that live on this Island.

And now very carefully listen to us. This time we faithfully tell our conclusion. It is that which was done in a great Council, and it is that which we strongly hold in our mind, which is, that, the people here hold the Island forever, what we now own to hold forever for our children that are to live in future.

Now we tell you how we were intimidated, when first we were asked for this Island which we own. We were told that soldiers would come to take it away from us. This is what the first one told us when we would not surrender our land.

And again a second time Wm. McDougall told us the same thing when we would not surrender our land. He said I have power; if you don't surrender to me now, again in the summer we will come to you and soldiers will be brought, and now you who live alone we will come to you and ask you and whoever consents to me, I will receive it, and he will be Great Chief and receive great blessing. He will be great. This is what Wm McDougall told us.

And now we see plainly how we are to be poor; and we see how poor our Island is. A great deal of our Odahwa Island has been burnt. It is now well seen how it looks. Nothing else but rock appeared after the burning. We did plainly tell that it was not good. Very little has been left unburnt.

Now we say truly it would be better for us Indians to live alone because very little land is left unburnt. Even if it was sold, we never would realize twenty-five cents a year and that would not be a blessing seen.

And now we desire you who art merciful in heart, and the Ruler of the country called Canada, in the name of the Great Spirit, to break now immediately the Treaty into the making of which we were frightened & cheated, by Wm McDougall, at Manitowaning, 6th October, 1862.

All of us Chiefs as far as the Odahwah Island extends, that put their names to the frightening bargain paper (Treaty) desire you now in the name of the Great Spirit to rub out our names immediately—The whole of us that live on the Island say therefore, that we may own back again what we owned before, namely the whole Odahwa Island and all the little Islands.

Again we tell you be merciful unto us thou who hast a merciful heart. The whole of our men and our women, and our children wish to keep their land forever.

We tell the truth—they are really the ones and we stole from them by surrendering, and we strongly repent of what we have done and wish you at once to spoil entirely that which we have done for it is very bad.

Signed: Mija kwange, Ogimahbiness, Benjamen Assiginack, Webinissimi, Shiwitagan, George Abidasawe, Pemikwaneshkang, Ebins, Debassige, idawashkash, Newategishig, Wakaesse, Kashkiwabik, Bebamise, Kishigobines, Padadigoshing, Tekama

We tell you this was done in the Great Council.

You the Great Chief who sits in Quebec. You who are over all the Government, we tell you in the name of the Great Spirit that it is the truth.

These our brethren that said we surrender what was owned by all; they have done that which is very bad. They did not ask those who owned, and now they heartily repent. Do pity them and grant that they may have what they desire of you. Do now immediately destroy the treaty, for they are not many who said we surrender.

We also have the same thoughts—to destroy immediately the treaty; for there were not many who said we surrender—only 18 of them—who now strongly repent of their doing. We are many who are on the Island. We know very well what was done here at Manitowaning at that time 6th of October 1862. It is true what they say that they were frightened, those who were cheated.

We sent many papers long ago, plainly telling all that was done, and all our names this the length of Odahwa Island were on those papers—and are now again this time here.

8 Wequemikong Chiefs and 151 men. Chief of Wekwemikonsing and 32 men. Chief of Waiebitchiwang and 11 men. Chief of Mitimoienisibing and 5 men. Chief of Shishigwaning and 42 men. Chief of Atchidawaiganing and 6 men. Chief of Manitowaning and 16 men. Chief of Adjidawaiganing and 8 men. Chief of Shigwaienda and 13 men. Chief of Mitchigiwatinong and 31 men. Chief of Nemanakikong and 17 men. Chief of Ogi dakishishi and 8 men.[326]

Reverend Sims noted in his journal: "Dr. Layton called. Gave us some alarming ac[coun]ts of the intentions of the Indians now in council at Wequemakong. Mr. Dupont thinks it all moonshine."[327]

The Jesuits recorded in their Diarium: "On the invitation of the natives here, most of the chiefs of the island & a good number of young warriors have assembled to attend a council that has the goal of submitting to the Government a new protest on the treaty of 1862. They have unanimously declared that this treaty was obtained by fear. Their request is addressed to the Governor of Canada. They are asking him in the name of the sovereign to destroy this treaty & to restore them as the communal proprietors of the whole island."[328]

Superintendent Dupont reported: "a council of all the Indians on the Island, as well as members from the main land of the North Shore, & the Indian peninsula, is to be assembled at Wequamekong on the 14th instant [July 1865], to discuss some project to get the Island back."[329] Two weeks later he forwarded the resulting petition, but claimed that there were "signatures attached to this petition of many parties who to my certain knowledge did not even attend the council."[330]

Spragge replied that the Wikwemikong chiefs had no right to summon a council of all the Manitoulin Indians and they would "not be permitted to intermeddle with the affairs of the Indians occupying land in the other part of the Island or elsewhere."[331]

Resettlement

As the *Anishinaabeg* were gathering in council, Dupont was proceeding with their relocation. He proposed in July 1865 to settle them "in accordance with that clause of the treaty, which requires the Indians to select land contiguous to each other, to make only three settlements, one exclusively Protestant, a second exclusively Catholic, & a third for those who can still consent to live amicably together, whether Protestant, Catholic or Pagan."[332]

Spragge warned Dupont that "the Indians upon the surrendered portion of the Great Manitoulin Island cannot be compelled to limit themselves to the formation of three permanent settlements. Should they profess willingly consent to such an arrangement—in order that by concentrating themselves they may the better succeed in the promotion of Civilization Agriculture & Education there can be no objection to it. And with that object if they can be persuaded to it, it may be & probably will be desirable." He further cautioned, "you will have the goodness to be careful to afford to those people no just cause of complaint or attempt to insist upon their joining one or other of the three settlements which you desire to protect."[333]

Two weeks later, Spragge urged Dupont to expedite resettlement "as many applications for the purchase of lands on the Manitoulin Island are being received."[334]

Meanwhile, Church of England officials persuaded the superintendent general to reserve Manitowaning and the surrounding Assiginack Township as a Protestant *Anishinaabe* settlement, thwarting Dupont's plan for Manitowaning to become a non-Native village. Despite the reservation of land, Chief Maishegonggai announced "he and the other Indians had made up their minds to remove to Shegwunandaud."[335]

Dupont began assigning people to lots in Sheguiandah, Michigiwadinong or Sheshegwaning in October 1865. He "informed the few Indians who would not make their choice—that the year from completion of survey given them by the Treaty in which to make their choice having expired they must now settle in one of these three places." Dupont reported that the Michigiwatinong men "refused to give me their names & said 100 acres for each was not enough that they wanted a large tract of miles & finally stated that they had altered their minds since making the treaty in 1862 & had at a council held at Wequa,me,kong sent a petition to his Excellency the Governor General stating that they did not wish to cede the Island." The Sheshegwaning men and Chief Itawashkash also refused to provide their names and "stated they did not mean now to surrender the Island having changed their minds." The Little Current band initially refused to relocate, and then asked to settle on "the nearest good land to that village," but Dupont insisted they move farther out, as "the good land in the neighbourhood will also be essential to its success as a village."[336]

While Dupont negotiated resettlement, petroleum licence enquiries flowed into the department. The first licence had required lengthy negotiations and the approval of the governor general, so Dupont was instructed in September 1865 to secure the consent of the Wikwemikong residents to deal with oil speculators on their behalf.[337] Despite pressure "to expedite the subject," Dupont was unable to convene the *Anishinaabeg* until after the fall fishing and harvest.[338]

Licence negotiations were further delayed when Charles Kitche Baptiste (or Tche Batisan), one of three *Anishinaabeg* who been evicted from Wikwemikong in November 1862 for supporting the treaty, returned to Wikwemikong in December 1865. Dupont supported Kitche Baptiste's action. The Wikwemikong people resented Dupont's interference and refused to discuss petroleum until Kitche Baptiste returned to Manitowaning. Jesuit Father Martin Férard wrote from Wikwemikong to Dupont's superior. He insisted the Wikwemikong people were loyal to the Queen and the governor, but distrusted Dupont. He explained:

> When the treaty of Manitowaning was made, all the Wikwemikongs who were present there, understood that Mr. Spragge had promised to those among them who had given their names to it, would be entitled like those of the part surrendered, to their hundred acres of land, in lieu of the fields which they would lose in the reserve, by separating freely from their brothers; and it is upon that interpretation that they were forcibly removed with their property to Manitowaning. ... From immemorial times, the various bands and tribes having no individual but collective rights on their

reserves, considered themselves like collective families who the heads are the chiefs duly appointed by them and recognized by the Government; and as a father in his house has a natural right to expel a stranger or an undutiful son, so they thought they could expel from among themselves those who had betrayed the cause of the family.[339]

Dupont persuaded Dr. Layton, Reverend Sims and about 18 non-Native residents of Manitoulin Island that they were in danger. They wrote a letter to the editor of *The Globe* and a petition in January 1866. Both documents reflect Dupont's attitude, describing Wikwemikong residents as "very bitter and hostile towards the settlement of the Island" and claiming the Jesuits "created a seditious spirit among the Indians."[340] Father Férard insisted their fears were "all nonsense," that "it never came to their mind to interfere with the affairs of the whites; all they ask is to be let alone."[341]

The Kitche Baptiste expulsion was resolved in March 1866 when the governor general issued a proclamation in Ojibwe and English that restored Kitche Baptiste to his home and property in Wikwemikong and declared that all band members must be permitted to express their opinions at councils without interference or intimidation. The proclamation was distributed to bands throughout the country, as rumours that the government was intimidated by the Manitoulin Island *Anishinaabeg* had spread as far as the Sarnia, Saugeen and Cape Croker bands.[342]

Meanwhile, oil licence applications gushed in. There were thirty-two requests for the Wikwemikong Peninsula alone by March 1866. Dupont was forced to resume negotiations. Though he claimed to have obtained the "equivalent to an assent to a general issue of licences," it was actually the Wikwemikong people themselves who issued a number of leases between May and August 1866.[343] The leases, written in Ojibwe with "no white man with them," all contained a clause stipulating "the ground is not given to them, but leased only wherever they may extract the oil"; or "we only rent the land for the exploration of the Oil"; or "we do not sell the land, but lease it only for oil purposes." Clearly, the Wikwemikong *Anishinaabeg* were worried that their land could be taken from them.

The *Anishinaabeg* still believed Dupont's goal was to obtain a surrender of their land. Despite initially being cancelled by Dupont, a council was convened by the *Anishinaabeg*, who assembled without him to discuss the threat of surrender. The chiefs had the minutes of their council of 10 January 1866 recorded:

Wahkaikezhik—American Ind'ns / Wik /
This Okemah who is at Manitowaning is very wise in his efforts and is trying hard in an underhand way quietly to take from us our Reserve. We now see clearly what his intention is he wishes to cast us aside—to throw us very low.
　　Taibosegai—Mitchikewedinong.
We will never give up our land, we will hold it to the last in our hands. If you, whom we call the Wikwemikong Indians, wish at any time that we should help you against those who may try to overcome you, you will at once call to us and we from the west side (Mitchikewedinong) shall come to your assistance, and on the other

hand if we wish your assistance we will call & you shall help us.

Paimoquonaishkung approved of what Taibosegai had said.

Wikwemikong Indians—If the Okemah at Manitowaning comes over to ask from us any of our land we shall at once say No. The Chiefs of Mitchikewedinong will say the same.

Wahkaikezhik—To the Manitowaning Indians (Benj'n Assikinack & Tehkummah)—Whenever you have any thing that you wish to say you should come over here & say it, or any thing that you should like to know —come over & you will learn & we will always be your friends.

Tehkummah—I am glad that you intend to be friendly towards the rest of the Indians on the Island & am thankful to hear you say so.

Wahkaikezhik—the letter we wrote last summer had no effect because we did not get it up properly. But now this is what we will do. Each chief of a village, that is, Sheshegwahning, Mitchikewedinong, Manitowaning and Wikwemikong shall make out a paper with his name attached & these we shall send to Quebec. This is the right thing to do.

Tomah—Head Chief & a British Ind'n—did not make a speech but said that the letter had better be made out soon & sent.[344]

Clearly, the chiefs intended to cooperate and petition the governor. Once again they blamed the local agent, unable to believe that the governor would treat them so callously. A petition written in June, signed by 151 Wikwemikong *Anishinaabeg*, may have resulted from the January council. The Ojibwe petition was translated as:

Ottawa (Manitoulin) Island, Wikwemikong. 18th June 1866.
Thou, Great Chief, We put this on paper in thy presence, to make known to thee our grievances; how that Agent at Manitowaning who has the care of us, treats us. We do not want him, we don't want to have him for Agent. (for the following reasons)

1. When we go to him (for business) he does not let us enter in his house but send us somewhere else, because he is proud. Where shall I learn wisdom? doubtless from he that hates me shall give me wisdom? He (that Agent) who hates and despises the Indian!

2. He calls us Americans; this is the name he gives me as an insult.

3. The same (Agent) has sent back (to our village) Kitche Batiss to vex us, also to excite some riot among us, and to have a pretext to send to Jail our Chiefs. He always works to make us miserable. (We will never have any more to do with him.) He renders us no service.

We beseech thee to use thy power to remove that Dupont (the Agent) This is what we humbly beg of thee.

We take occasion to <u>Protest again</u> and to represent to Thee, how displeased we were, when the Ottawa (Manitoulin Island) was surrendered, and how we grieve yet for it. What took place then (the Treaty) was not right at all.

We repeat again now, that we want our Land. Please to the Great Spirit, that we may own it yet. It does not look well (right) to sell it since it is only by intimidation that our Land has been taken (from us). Although we have protested, written to thee until now even, that Thou wouldst destroy (stop) the sale (of our Land).

It was on October the 4th (to use the English calculation) 1862, that one great Chief (a commissioner) Wm. McDougall came to speak and made use of some Indians, to ask them their Lands. But they all refused (loved their Lands) on that day.

It was on October 6th 1862 that some Indians having been spoken to again, and when they had been intimidated, then only they answered (surrendered the Land).

(The Indians) were not all pleased. Some few Chiefs only (did the thing). But the majority (a very great number) were not willing at all, and are not yet even now.

We hope that when Thou shall see (know) how things (the Treaty) took place, it will suggest to thee some great determination. For, indeed we are very sorrowful for the loss of our Land, and truly we grieve much in our hearts. We shall never forget it (our Land).

Therefore we humbly beseech Thee, as the Great Chief, and as the one who loves honestly (right) to hasten to destroy (to stop) that fraud.

We subscribe our names.[345]

Dupont responded to the charges against him, insisting that business was conducted in a nearby office—though conceding he "admitted the Indians to my house" three times a year. He claimed to be following instructions in calling them "American Indians" and denying them annuity money.[346]

Despite the protests, the Crown Lands Department proceeded with the sale of Manitoulin Island land. A memorandum on the sale and settlement was written in January 1866 and approved by the Governor General in Council in April. One month later the regulations for the sale were approved.[347] On 18 June 1866, lots in the townships of Howland, Sheguiandah, Bidwell, Billings and Tehkummah were released for sale, even though the *Anishinaabeg* residents had not yet been relocated. The lots were priced at fifty cents an acre, with three years continuous residence required for a patent. Mineral or oil lands were one dollar an acre in 200-acre or 400-acre blocks.

The pressure to resolve expulsion, petroleum and relocation issues so that the land sales could occur forced Dupont to modify his resettlement plan. Still determined to create a single Protestant *Anishinaabe* settlement, he repeatedly reassigned the *Anishinaabeg* to land at Sheguiandah and Manitowaning. Reverend Sims and Charles de Lamorandière both complained that Dupont was forcing people to relocate.[348] Spragge cautioned Dupont: "the Indian families at Sheguiendah cannot be compelled to abandon the lands for which they were located. If they be removed it must be the result of their own voluntary act."[349]

Dupont announced in January 1867 that the Indians should settle at "Shegwun-an-daud."[350] The following month he applied to purchase 400 acres of the Manitowaning town site. This action cast suspicion on his resettlement efforts. Not only were department employees prohibited from purchasing Indian land, but Assiginack Township was reserved from sale to anyone. Reverend Sims filed a complaint with the department, claiming Dupont assigned land based on the interests of himself and his friends and not the Indians. Dupont complained that the Church had delayed and interfered in the establishment of reserves.

As Dupont and Sims argued over land and resettlement, the British North American colonies united as Canada on 1 July 1867. One of the "Fathers of Confederation" responsible for Canada's union was Manitoulin treaty negotiator William McDougall.

Resettlement and land sales proceeded. The *Anishinaabeg* realized that some of the verbal promises made during the treaty negotiations were worthless. Chief Baibomsai of Manitowaning was relocated to Whitefish River despite his claim that "when McDougall held the Treaty at Manitowaning he promised me land at Sheguiandah and we have often told Mr. Dupont so but he won't pay any attention to us."[351] Chief Maishegonggai of Manitowaning had been told at the treaty negotiations that "the Indians should have their pick of the best land in the Island and the white men shall have the remainder." Later, though, when Dupont was merging bands, he threatened the chief with a loss of his chieftainship if he moved to Sheguiandah. The chief and his band were assigned and then reassigned lots in Sheguiandah and Manitowaning as Dupont attempted to make one Protestant settlement.[352] George Obettossoway (Ahbedossway) said he had been told at the treaty that he "was to be alowed to keep my own house and garden [at the Little Current settlement] and remain where I was when the rest of the Indians would be removed," but Dupont insisted that he move to Sucker Creek Reserve. Obettossoway wrote to Spragge: "I have been brought up among the whites and have adapted their maner of living & mode of life .... I was Born in a house lived in a house & will never die in a wigwam in the forest I would rather a thousand time to die in battle." He related:

> This island which we occupy & in which our fathers lived & theres fathers fathers before them. Long before the foot of the white men trod on our soil or even his voise was even herd in our ears then we had no care or trouble. Afterward the white men came & we lost our peace. First they bought all the main land one place after another no sooner did we go and settle in one place then we had to get up & go to another place. They at last got all the main land round about & we wear driven into the great Lakes. So we thought if we came to this Island of which we speak of we would be at rest but no, instead of a place of rest & an assilam we found ourselves in a narrow pass with no retreat & the white men close behind. He came & asked us to sell this Island and we refused & he came again & we refused. At last Mr. McDougall came he spoke & we considered he spoke again & and a treaty was made in which certain conditions wear to be observed and rules to be complied with.[353]

George Obettossoway was relocated to the Sucker Creek Reserve, where he died in July 1870 at the age of 45 years.

The *Anishinaabeg* were not encouraged to participate in the settlement of Manitoulin Island. Instead, they were isolated on reservations, just as a generation earlier they had been isolated on the island itself.

John Arthur Manitowaussen, a resident of Sheguiandah and a sub-trader for the Michigiwadinong trader, wanted to settle as a merchant in Little Current. Despite a recommendation from the Protestant missionary asserting that he was intelligent, literate and industrious, and "in every respect a pattern to his brother Indians," Manitowaussen's application was refused and he was told to devote himself to agriculture.

Joseph Shewetagun was in the sugar bush when he learned that Superintendent Dupont had sold his four-year-old log home at Little Current. By the time he returned home, the new owner had removed the lock, cleared out the house and was remodelling it as a store. Joseph received $15 for his house, but nothing for his garden lot. He moved his wife, five children and granddaughter four miles southwest to Sucker Creek. Despite being widowed not long after relocating, by 1869 Shewetagun and his family had cleared and fenced two and a half acres of land. Joseph was recorded in the departmental census as an industrious farmer and fisherman, though his fishing must have been drastically curtailed by the forced move from the lakeshore.

Between 1867 and 1870, most of Manitoulin's *Anishinaabe* residents were assigned to specific land reservations. While Dupont did not achieve his goal of three settlements, most of the *Anishinaabeg* were moved inland away from potential harbours or settlements. Dupont was replaced by William Plummer in June 1868, and his land transactions were then investigated.

Though all the treaty signatories except Assiginack regretted signing the treaty and attempted to have the document annulled, they were relocated along with their bands. Manitowaning's residents were the most difficult to relocate, in part because of Dupont's ever-changing plans. Chief Maishegonggai was eventually permitted to return to Sheguiandah, and most of his band was persuaded to join him. Chief Okemah beness and Keghikgoobeness also joined the Sheguiandah settlement in 1867, but Baibomsai's request for land at Sheguiandah was ignored and he settled instead on the mainland, at Whitefish River. Chief Jean-Baptiste Assiginack died at Manitowaning in 1866. Despite his renown as a great warrior and orator, his pro-government attitude and pro-treaty stance turned many *Anishinaabe* against him. His son Francis Assiginack returned to Toronto after the 1862 treaty, but died in Manitowaning in November 1863, at the age of 39. Benjamin Assiginack and his family were relocated to their garden plots at Sucker Lake, which became a reserve for members of the Assiginack and Tehkummah families.

Maple Point's Chief Pahtahdagwishkung and his band moved west. They preferred isolation and tradition to Western civilization and Christianization. By 1869, this 32-member band was settled on their Lake Wolsey Ombidjiwang reserve. The band remained non-Christian and maintained traditional lifestyles until early in the 20th century.

Michigiwatinong chiefs Paimoquonaishkung and Taibosegai, and head men Abence and Naiwotaikezhik, and their band were assigned in 1865 to lots between "Honora Bay" and Lake Mindemoya. By 1869, this settlement of 295 farmers and fishermen included several families from Beausoleil Island and Cape Croker.

Chief Sakiwinebi of Mindemooyasebe did not sign the treaty. He and his band numbered five families, or 28 persons, in 1869, but they were merged with the Michigiwatinong band by the Indian Department. Between 1870 and 1875 their land was surveyed, they were reimbursed for any improvements, and they were relocated. Chief Sakiwinebi never embraced Western civilization; he died at West Bay in 1885.

Sheguiandah's residents were assigned land south of their original location on the bay, despite their request for land north and west of Bass Lake. They were joined by most of the Manitowaning residents in 1867, merging, at least on paper, Maishegonggai's and Okemah beness' bands. Within a few years some of the latter's band responded to rumours of land loss and declared: "We have nothing to do with Meshahquangas people, we want to live in our Reserve."

Several families returned to their traditional land at Whitefish River.[354]

Sheshegwaning's Chief Itawashkash and his band were allowed to remain on their traditional land, though this was due to their isolated location rather than government benevolence. By 1869, the band of 20 families was considered by the Indian Department to include the Cockburn Island 12-family band and Chief Wahcowsai's band of four families who lived at Big Hill, six miles from Sheshegwaning.

South Bay West's Chief Waibenessieme died in January 1867. By 1869, the 33-member band was under pressure from aggressive settlers. Superintendent Plummer published a warning: "To all whom it may concern. The chiefs and band of Indians resident at South Bay township of Assiginack are by the terms of the Treaty entitled to 800 acres of land as a Reserve commence at no. 15 and include lots 15,16-21 on the first concession and some other lots as shall be found necessary to complete the 800 acres. Any persons found squatting on what may be the Indians reserve will be removed therefrom without necessary compensation for improvements." The land, known as Squirrel Town, was eventually taken over by settlers.

At Wewebijiwang (or Little Current), Chief Kushkewahbic (or Columbus), Joseph Shewetagun, George Obettossoway and their neighbours did not want to leave their settlement, where they had developed a profitable trade in steamboat wood. Dupont persisted and they were persuaded to move four miles inland to Sucker Creek over the winter of 1866-67, and told to become farmers.

Wikwemikong's Chief Louis Tehkummah was expelled from Wikwemikong in November 1863 for supporting the treaty. He lived in Manitowaning until the Indian Department agreed to settle the Assiginack and Tehkummah families at Sucker Lake.

The Wikwemikong chiefs tried repeatedly to have the 1862 treaty annulled. Chief J.B. Atagiwinini died in 1867. His son Jako remained active in anti-treaty activity. Chief Louis Wakekijik and Chief Tomah Kinojameg and their families, and a number of other Wikwemikong residents, were punished for their anti-treaty activity. Their names were removed from the Robinson treaty annuity list by Superintendent Ironside in 1862, and were not reinstated until 1896.

Manitoulin land sold slowly. In May 1867, the price was reduced to 20 cents an acre, cash, with occupation and improvement required within six months of purchase.[355] In September 1868, Carnarvon, Campbell and Assiginack townships were released for sale. Allan Township was released in January 1869.[356]

While the reduced price of land may have stimulated sales, it curtailed financial benefits for *Anishinaabeg*. In spring 1870, Superintendent Plummer recommended that the price of land be returned to 50 cents an acre. He noted that the 20-cent price would "not much more than pay the cost of the survey and contingent expenses, leaving little or nothing to be divided among them or their descendants." He raised the price to 50 cents in June 1870, with the usual conditions of actual occupation and improvement.[357]

Reverend Jabez Sims expressed his concern: "The settlement of the Island by the whites has operated very much against the interests of the Indian and has tended to unsettle the minds of the Indians."[358] He reported to his sponsors: "If only the cupidity and greediness of the white man can be restrained we shall get on very well, but since the surrender of a portion of this Island (and indeed the larger portion) every white man who comes in and sees the Indian Reserve covets his poor Red brothers portion and often most wickedly and greedily appropriates what does not belong to him."[359]

The *Anishinaabeg* were distracted by petroleum, resettlement and the arrival of non-Native settlers and speculators. Almost all their correspondence over the next decades referred to the injustice of the treaties and the loss of income due to government regulation of fish, timber, oil and land. They continued to address their complaints directly to Canada's governors general because they had no elected representatives.

By 1870, many *Anishinaabeg* were resettled and thousands of acres of land had been sold—but the *Anishinaabeg* lived in poverty. Father Martin Férard blamed the treaty:

> It is a fact, which can be ascertained by undeniable evidence, that the Indians were not aware at the passing of the said Treaty, of its most important Condition and among others, of the following: that the Indians who were parties to the Treaty, should not receive any annuity eventually accruing from the sale of their lands, before all the expenses made for surveying the new Townships, cutting roads, paying annual salaries to officials, should have been refunded. Had the land been such as it was expected to be according to newspapers glowing reports, and the first price of the land, $0.50 an acre, stuck to, when it has now been reduced to $0.20; there might have been a reasonable hope, that the large number of expected settlers, would have left after all expenses paid, a handsome annuity to the poor Indians, but after four years of experience, the most sceptic must be convinced that after all, the public has been deceived about the Great Manitoulin.[360]

While Férard complained to Indian Affairs, *Anishinaabeg* from Manitoulin and the North Shore mainland prepared to gather in council at Little Current. They renewed the sacred friendship between their forefathers and asked the governor to respect "our rights to the lands." They complained that commissioners had induced them to surrender their land that was intended for their children; that the game, fishery and enfranchisement acts caused hardship; and that the islands had not been properly surrendered. Two dozen chiefs and head men signed the petition on 25 July 1870.[361] William Plummer sent the petition to Ottawa. He and his superiors were more concerned about an accompanying petition respecting an increase in annuity payments due to Robinson treaty signatories than the Manitoulin Island complaints.

Rumours about additional treaties persisted. The Whitefish River–Sheguiandah band had been subjected to repeated surrender attempts. In 1873 the band begged the new Manitoulin superintendent, J.C. Phipps, to give them a deed to their Whitefish River land. The chiefs of Michigiwatinong petitioned Phipps for assurance that their lands were secure, and repeatedly questioned their lack of financial compensation.

When the governor general, the Earl of Dufferin, visited Little Current in July 1874, the chiefs complained to him that they had not received an increase in their annuities, even though farmers and industries occupied Manitoulin Island

and the North Shore. Dufferin replied that he would look into the matter. (Coincidentally, the man behind the 1862 treaty, William Spragge, had died suddenly three months earlier in Ottawa, after an evening spent at Lady Dufferin's Rideau Hall "at-home" gathering.)

In 1880, the *Anishinaabeg* of Sucker Creek and Sheguiandah petitioned Superintendent Phipps for compensation for their post-treaty property relocation losses. Dupont had promised that they would be compensated, and some may have been, but his convoluted land transactions resulted in a complicated tangle of records. Phipps investigated and concluded that a number of *Anishinaabeg* should be compensated, but a year later, inundated with applications for compensation, he declared that it was too difficult to determine losses after fifteen years.[362]

Exactly twenty years after the treaty, William McDougall ran for election as the Member of Parliament for Manitoulin and the District of Algoma. Perhaps he counted on the new settlers rewarding him with support. *Anishinaabeg* were not permitted to vote. He lost to the Conservative incumbent Simon J. Dawson. Dawson provided his opinion of the 1862 treaty in Parliament in 1886: "Of all the treaties which white men have made with the Indians, I believe that it was the very worst treaty as regards the Indians." He also claimed that it was "most unjust in its provisions" and "resulted in the downright robbery" by paying just $1.79 per head per year.[363]

Thirty-four years after the treaty, in 1896, the Wikwemikong Ojibwe whose names had been removed from the North Shore annuity list for anti-treaty activity in 1862 were reinstated. Superintendent Benjamin W. Ross had investigated their claims and recommended that a number of families be returned to the list.[364] Finally, one treaty issue had been addressed and resolved.

Appendix 1
Transcription of the 1862 Articles of Agreement and Convention for the Surrender of the Great Manitoulin Island and the Islands Adjacent
[LAC, RG10, 1846, T9939]

Articles of Agreement and Convention made and concluded at Manitowaning, on the Great Manitoulin Island in the Province of Canada, the sixth day of October, Anno Domini 1862. Between the Hon. William McDougall, Superintendent General of Indian Affairs, and William Spragge, Deputy Superintendent of Indian Affairs, on the part of the Crown and Government of said Province, of the first part, and Mai,she,quong,gai, Okemah be,ness, J. B. Assiginock, Benjamin Assiginock, Wai,be,nesse,me, She,we,tah,gun, George Ah,be,tos,o,wai, Paim,quo,-waish,-gung, Abence, Tai,bose,gai, A,to,wish,cosh, Nai wau dai ge zhik, Wau kau a say, Kush kewaubik, Chiefs and principal men of the Ottawa, Chippewa and other Indians occupying the said Island, on behalf of the said Indians, of the second part. –

Whereas, the Indian title to said Island was surrendered to the Crown on the ninth August, Anno Domini 1836, under and by virtue of a treaty made between Sir Francis Bond Head, then Governor of Upper Canada, and the chiefs and principal men of the Ottawas and Chippewas then occupying and claiming title thereto, in order that the same might "be made the property (under their Great Fathers Control) of all Indians whom he should allow to reside thereon."

And whereas, but few Indians from the mainland, whom it was intended to transfer to the Island, have ever come to reside thereon.

And whereas, it has been deemed (with a view to the improvement of the condition of the Indians as well as the settlement and improvement of the country) expedient to assign to the Indians now upon the Island certain specified portions thereof, to be held by patent from the Crown, and to sell the other portions thereof fit for cultivation to settlers, and to invest the proceeds thereof, after deducting the expenses of Survey and management, for the benefit of the Indians.

And whereas a majority of the chiefs of certain bands residing on that portion of the Island easterly of Heywood Sound and the Manitoulin Gulf have expressed their unwillingness to accede to this proposal as respects that portion of the Island, but have assented to the same as respects all other portions thereof, and whereas the chiefs and principal men of the bands residing on the Island westerly of the said Sound and Gulf, have agreed to accede to the said proposal.

Now this agreement witnesseth that in consideration of the sum of seven hundred dollars now in hand paid (which sum is to be hereafter deducted from the proceeds of lands sold to settlers) the receipt whereof is hereby acknowledged, and in further consideration of such sums as may be realized from time to time as interest upon the purchase money of the lands to be sold for their benefit as aforesaid, the parties hereto of the second part, have, and hereby do release, surrender and give up to her majesty the Queen all the right, title, interest and claim of the parties of the second part, and of the Ottawa, Chippewa and other Indians in whose behalf they act, of, in and to the Great Manitoulin Island, and also of, in, and to the Islands adjacent, which have been deemed or claimed to be appurtenant or belonging thereto, To have and to hold the same, and every part thereof, to Her majesty, her heirs and successors forever.

And it is hereby agreed by and between the parties hereto as follows:–

Firstly. A survey of the said Manitoulin Island shall be made as soon as conveniently may be by or under the authority of the Department of Crown Lands.

Secondly. The Crown will, as soon as conveniently may be, grant by Deed for the benefit of each Indian, being the head of a family and residing on the said Island, one hundred acres of land; To each single person over twenty one years of age, residing as aforesaid, fifty acres of land; To each family of orphan children under twenty one years of age containing two or more persons, one hundred acres of land. And to each single orphan child under twenty one years of age, fifty acres of land, to be selected and located under the following rules and conditions:

Each Indian entitled to land under this agreement may make his own selection of any land on the Great Manitoulin Island, Provided $1^{stly.}$ That the lots selected shall be contiguous or adjacent to each other so that Indian settlements on the Island may be as compact as possible. 2^{ndly} That if two or more Indians claim the same lot of land the matter shall be referred to the Resident Superintendent who shall examine the case and decide between them. 3^{rdly} That selections for orphan children may be made by their friends subject to the approval of the Resident Superintendent. 4^{thly} Should any lot or lots, selected as aforesaid, be contiguous to any bay or harbour, or any stream of water upon which a mill site shall be found, and should the Government be of opinion that such lot or lots ought to be reserved for the use of the public, or for village or park lots, or such mill site be sold with a view to the erection of a mill thereon, and shall signify such its opinion through its proper agent, then the Indian who has selected, or who wishes to select such lot shall make another selection, but if he has made any improvements thereon he shall be allowed a fair compensation therefor. 5^{thly} The selections shall all be made within one year after the completion of the survey, and for that purpose plans of the survey shall be deposited with the Resident Superintendent as soon as they are approved by the Department of Crown Lands and shall be open to the inspection of all Indians entitled to make selections as aforesaid.

Thirdly. The interest which may accrue from the investment of the proceeds of sales of land as aforesaid shall be payable annually and shall be apportioned among the Indians now residing westerly of the said Sound and Gulf and their descendants per capita, but every Chief lawfully appointed shall be entitled to two portions.

Fourthly. So soon as one hundred thousand acres of the said land is sold, such portion of the salary of the Resident Superintendent and of the expenses of his office, as the Government may deem equitable, shall become a charge upon the said fund.

Fifthly. The Deeds or Patents for the lands to be selected as aforesaid shall contain such conditions for the protection of the Grantees as the Governor in Council may under the law deem requisite.

Sixthly. All the rights and privileges in respect to the taking of fish in the Lakes, Bays, Creeks and waters within and adjacent to the said Island which may be lawfully exercised and enjoyed by the white settlers thereon, may be exercised and enjoyed by the Indians.

Seventhly. That portion of the Island easterly of Heywood Sound and Manitoulin Gulf, and the Indians now residing there, are excepted from the operation of this agreement as respects Survey, sale of lots, granting Deeds to Indians, and payments in respect of monies derived from Sales in other parts of the Island, But the said Indians will remain under the protection of the Government as formerly, and the said Easterly part or division of the Island will remain open for the occupation of any Indians entitled to reside upon the Island as formerly, subject in case of dispute, to the approval of the Government.

Eighthly. Whenever a majority of the chiefs and principal men, at a council of the Indians residing easterly of the said Sound and Gulf, to be called and held for the purpose, shall declare their willingness to accede to the present agreement in all respects, and the Government shall signify its approval, then that portion of the Island shall be surveyed and dealt with in like manner as other portions thereof, and the Indians there, shall be entitled to the same privaleges in every respect, from and after the date of such approval by the Government, as those residing in other parts of the Island.

Ninthly. This agreement shall be obligatory and binding on the contracting parties as soon as the same shall be approved by the Governor in Council.

In witness whereof, the said Superintendent General of Indian Affairs, and Deputy Superintendent, and the undersigned chiefs and principal men of the Ottawa, Chippewa and other Indians, have hereto set their hands and seals at Manitowaning, the sixth day of October, in the year first above written.

Executed in the presence of (having been first read translated and explained). Geo. Ironside S.I. Affairs, S. Phillips Day, Wm. Gibbard, David S. Layton, Jos. Wilson, John H. McDougall, F. Assikinack, Peter Jacobs Ch. of Eng Missionary, McGregor Ironside.

Signed: Wm. McDougall, Wm. Spragge, J. B. Assiginack, Maishcgonggai, Okemah beness, Benjamin Assiginack, Waibenessieme, Shewetagun, George Obetossaway, Paimoquonaishkung, Abence, Taibosegai, Atowishcosh, Naiwataikezhik, Wahcowsai, Kushkewahbic, Baibomsai, Kezhikgoobeness, Pahtahdagweshing.

The undersigned is one of the Chiefs of the Wequaimekong band, and appends his signature in testimony of his general approval and his assent as an individual to all the terms of the above agreement: Tehkummah, Paimsahdang.

Appendix 2
Transcription of the 1836 Provisional Agreement for the Surrender of the Manitoulin Islands and the Islands on the North Shore of Lake Huron
[LAC, RG10, 1844, IT121]

Dated 9th August 1836.
The Chippewa, Ottawa and Sauking Indians
<u>Provisional Agreement</u> for the Surrender of the Manitoulin Islands and the Islands on the North Shore of Lake Huron and also the Sauking Territory.

My Children

Seventy snow seasons have now passed away since we met in Council at the crooked place (Niagara) at which time and place your Great Father the King and the Indians of North America tied their hands together by the Wampum of friendship –

Since that period various circumstances have occurred to separate from your Great Father many of his red children, and as an unavoidable increase of white population as well as the progress of cultivation have had the natural effect of impoverishing your hunting grounds it has become necessary that new arrangements should be entered into for the purpose of protecting you from the encroachments of the whites.

In all parts of the world farmers seek for uncultivated land as eagerly as you, my red children hunt in your forest for game. If you would cultivate your land, it would then be considered your own property in the same way as your dogs are considered among yourselves to belong to those who have reared them; but uncultivated land is like wild animals, and your Great Father who has hitherto protected You, has now great difficulty in securing it for you from the whites, who are hunting to cultivate it.

Under these circumstances I have been obliged to consider what is best to be done for the red children of the forest and I now tell you my thoughts –

It appears that these Islands on which we are now assembled in Council are, as well as all those on the North Shore of Lake Huron, alike claimed by the English, the Ottawas, and the Chippewas.

I consider that from their facilities, and from their being surrounded by innumerable fishing Islands, they might be made a most desirable place of Residence for many Indians who wish to be civilized as well as to be totally separated from the Whites; and I now tell you that your Great Father will withdraw his claim to these Islands, and allow them to be applied for that purpose.

Are you therefore, the Ottawas and Chippewas willing to relinquish your respective Claims to these Islands, and make them the property (under your

Great Father's Control) of all Indians who he shall allow to reside on them? If so, affix your marks to this my proposal.

F.B. Head
Manatowaning
August 9th 1836
[signatures or names and dodems of] J.B. Assekinack [signature], Mokomanish [x], Kimewen [bear dodem], Itawachkach [signature], Kitchem okomon [moose head dodem], Pesa ata wich [snake dodem], Paimausegai [forked stick dodem], Nainawmuttebe [eagle dodem], Mosuneko [forked stick dodem], Kewuckance [crane dodem], Shawenauseway [pike dodem], Espaniole [cock dodem], Snake [squirrel dodem], Pautunseway [eagle dodem], Paimauguneshcum [reindeer/caribou dodem], and Wagemauguin [beaver dodem]

— To the Saukings. —
My children —
You have heard the proposal I have just made to the Chippawas and Ottawas, by which it has been agreed between them and your Great Father that these Islands (Manatoulin) on which we are now assembled, should be made, in council the property (under your Great Fathers Control) of all Indians whom he shall allow to reside on them.

I now propose to you that you should surrender to your Great Father, the Sauking Territory you at present occupy and that you should repair either to this Island, or to that part of your territory, which lies on the North of Owen's Sound upon which proper houses shall be built for you, and proper assistance given to enable you to become civilized and to cultivate land which your Great Father engages for ever to protect for you from the encroachments of the whites.

~~As long as the country you at present occupy shall remain uncultivated, you will have full liberty to consider it as your hunting ground.~~ [sic]

Are you therefore the Sauking Indians willing to accede to this arrangement, if so affix your marks to this my proposal.

Manatowaning
August 9th 1836
F.B. Head
[names and dodems of] Metawabe, Alexander Kagatue Wemiwaimen, Kongiaway, Netawaush

Witness
T.G. Anderson, S.I.A.; Joseph Stinson, General Supt. of Wesleyan Missions; Adam Elliot; James Evans; F.L. Ingall, Lieut. 15th Regt Command. Detachmt; and Fulford B. Feilde, Commissariat.

Selected Bibliography

Primary Sources
Manuscript Material
  The Archive of the Jesuits in Canada, Montreal. Île Manitouline / Manitoulin Island files.
  The Archive of the Jesuits in Canada, Montreal. Paquin manuscript. Unpublished typed manuscript by Father Paquin, S.J.
  The Archive of the Jesuits in Canada, Montreal. Wikwemikong Diarium, 1844-1875, 3 vols.
  Archives of Ontario. F 983, John Strachan fonds.
  Archives of Ontario. F 277, Genealogies collection, MS 871, reel 11, Indian genealogical records by Father Joseph Specht.
  Archives of Ontario. F 968, Jesuit Archives Collection, MS 159.
  Library and Archives Canada. R92, Statistics Canada fonds, Census of Canada West (Ontario), 1851/52 and 1861 [formerly RG 31].
  Library and Archives Canada. R92, Statistics Canada fonds, Census of Canada, 1871-1911 [formerly RG 31].
  Library and Archives Canada, Religious Archives, MG 17 B1, Society for the Propagation of the Gospel in Foreign Parts (SPGFP), Missionary Reports.
  Library and Archives Canada, Religious Archives, MG 17 B4, Colonial & Continental Church Society (C&CCS), Missionary Reports.
  Library and Archives Canada, MG 20, Hudson's Bay Company, La Cloche Post journals.
  Library and Archives Canada. R216, Department of Indian Affairs and Northern Development fonds [formerly RG 10, Department of Indian Affairs fonds].
  Library and Archives Canada. R4176-0-0-E, Jabez Waters Sims fonds, Journal of the Reverend Jabez W. Sims [formerly MG 24-J51].
  Union of Ontario Indians. Roy, Kelly, and Franz M. Koennecke. "Manitoulin Island Treaties, 1836 and 1862, Incomplete Historical Narrative." Unpublished paper, 1985.

Printed Material: Official Publications
  Journals of the Legislative Assembly of the Province of Canada and their appendixes.
  Sessional Papers of Canada.

Newspapers
Brockville Recorder
The Canadian Freeman [Toronto]
Canadian News, New Brunswick Herald, and British Columbian Intelligencer [London, England]
Christian Guardian [Toronto]
The Daily Spectator and Journal of Commerce [Hamilton]
The Globe [Toronto]
Hamilton Evening Times
Huron Signal [Goderich]
The Irish Canadian [Toronto]
Le Journal de Québec
Kingston Daily News
The Leader [Toronto]
London Morning Herald [England]
The Manitoulin Expositor
The Markham Economist
The Morning Chronicle and Commercial and Shipping Gazette [Quebec]
The New York Times
Perth Courier
The Quebec Mercury
Sault Star
St. Catharines Constitutional

Secondary Sources
Barry, J.C. *Georgian Bay, the Sixth Great Lake*. Toronto: Clarke Irwin, 1968.
Blackbird, Andrew J. *History of the Ottawa and Chippewa Indians of Michigan: A Grammar on Their Language and Personal and Family History of the Author*. Ypsilanti, MI: Ypsilanti Job Print House, 1887.
Bleasdale, R. "Manitowaning, an Experiment in Indian Settlement." *Ontario History* 66 (1974): 147-57.
Cadieux, Lorenzo, S.J., and Robert Toupin, S.J., eds. "Les Robes Noires à l'Île du Manitou 1853-1870." unpublished MS, Département d'histoire, Université Laurentienne, Sudbury, 1980.
Cadieux, Lorenzo, S.J., and Robert Toupin, S.J. *Letters from Manitoulin Island: 1853-1870*. Translated by Shelley J. Pearen and William Lonc, S.J. Toronto: W. Lonc, 2007 [originally "Les Robes Noires à l'Île du Manitou 1853-1870," unpublished MS, 1980].
Cadieux, Lorenzo, S.J., *Letters from the New Canada Mission, 1843-52*. 2 vols. Translated by William Lonc, S.J. and George Topp, S.J. Toronto: W. Lonc, 2001 [originally published as *Lettres des Nouvelles Missions du Canada*].
Cosgrain, H.R., ed. *Voyage au Canada, dans le nord de l'Amérique septentrionale, fait depuis l'an 1751 à 1761, par J.C.B.* [J.C. Bonnefons, supposed author]. Quebec: Léger Brousseau, 1887.

Day, Samuel Phillips. *English America, or Pictures of Canadian Places and People*. Vol. II, London: T. Cautley Newby, 1864.

Dent, John Charles. *The Canadian Portrait Gallery*. J.P. Magurn, 1881.

Dictionary of Canadian Biography.

Hamilton, James Cleland. *Famous Algonquins: Algic Legends*. Toronto: Canadian Institute, 1899.

Hamilton, James Cleland. *The Georgian Bay*. Toronto: Carswell, 1893.

Henry, Alexander. *Travels and Adventures in Canada and the Indian Territories Between the Years 1760 and 1776 in Two Parts*. New York: Riley, 1809.

Jacobs, Peter. *Journal of the Reverend Peter Jacobs, Indian Wesleyan Missionary, from Rice Lake to the Hudson's Bay Territory; and Returning. Commencing May, 1852: With A Brief Account of His Life; and a Short History of the Wesleyan Mission to that Country*. Toronto: Anson Green, 1853.

Landon, Fred. *Lake Huron*. Indianapolis: Bobbs-Merrill, 1944.

Lee, T.E. "The discovery of the Sheguiandah site, Manitoulin Island." *Inland Sea* 10 (1954): 155-62.

Miller, J.R. *Skyscrapers Hide the Heavens*. Toronto: University of Toronto Press, 1989, rev. ed. 2001.

Molson, Karen. *The Molsons: Their Lives and Times, 1780-2000*. Willowdale: Firefly, 2001.

Patterson, E.P. *The Canadian Indian: A History Since 1500*. Don Mills, ON: Collier-Macmillan, 1972.

Pearen, Shelley J. *Exploring Manitoulin*, 3rd ed. Toronto: University of Toronto Press, 2001.

Pearen, Shelley J. and William Lonc. *Letters from Wikwemikong, 1845-1863*. Toronto: W. Lonc, 2008.

Pearen, Shelley J. and William Lonc. *Letters from the Ft. William Jesuit Mission, 1848-1862*. Toronto: W. Lonc, 2010.

Point, Nicholas, S.J. *Memoirs of the Jesuit Mission at Wikwemikong, Manitoulin Island, Mid 1800s*. Transcribed by Shelley J. Pearen. Translated by William Lonc. Toronto: W. Lonc, 2009.

Robertson, James A. and K.D Card. *Geology and Scenery, North Shore of Lake Huron Region*. Toronto. Ministry of Natural Resources, 1972, rev. ed. 1988.

Stagg, Jack. *Anglo-Indian Relations in North America and An Analysis of the Royal Proclamation of October 1763*. Ottawa, 1981.

Surtees, Robert J. *Indian Land Surrenders in Ontario, 1763-1867*. Ottawa: Indian and Northern Affairs Canada, 1984.

Surtees, Robert J. *The Robinson Treaties*. Ottawa: Indian and Northern Affairs Canada, 1986.

Surtees, Robert J. *Treaty Research Report, Manitoulin Island Treaties*. Ottawa: Indian and Northern Affairs Canada, 1986.

"A Synopsis of the History of Wikwemikong." *Through the Years* [The Recorder, Gore Bay] (Sept.1993): 4-29.

Thwaites, Reuben Gold., ed. *The Jesuit Relations and Allied Documents: Travels and Explorations of the Jesuit Missionaries in New France, 1610-1791: The Original French, Latin, and Italian Texts, with English translations and Notes.* 73 vols. Cleveland: Burrows, 1899.

Van Dusen, Conrad. *The Indian Chief: An Account of the Labours, Losses, Sufferings and Oppression of Ke-zig-ko-e-ne-ne (David Sawyer), a Chief of the Ojibbeway Indians in Canada West.* London: William Nichols, 1867.

Abbreviations used in references
C&CCS Colonial & Continental Church Society
JLAC   Journal of the Legislative Assembly of the Province of Canada
LAC   Library and Archives Canada
SPGFP   Society for the Propagation of the Gospel in Foreign Parts
SPPC   Sessional Papers of the Province of Canada

Index to Names

Abence (or Ebins), 40, 42, 43, 44, 53, 110, 115, 122, 151, 153, 160 S
Anderson, Thomas Gummersall, 4, 131
Ashagashinh (or Shageshi), 44
Assiginack, Benjamin, 28, 53, 122, 153, 157, 160 S
Assiginack, Francis, 3, 16, 19, 23, 28, 33, 43, 46, 47, 50, 53, 88, 94, 100, 102, 107, 160 W
Assiginack, Isaac, 28, 41
Assiginack, Jean-Baptiste, 19, 20, 24, 25, 28, 36, 43, 49, 50, 53, 54, 56, 70, 71, 72, 94, 102, 106, 107, 108, 122, 151, 152, 160 S
Atagiwinini, J.B., 19, 22, 44, 45, 71, 106, 161
Atagiwinini, Jako, 22, 40, 42, 44, 50, 51, 53, 71, 72, 106, 108, 109, 111, 131, 134, 161
Baby, William, 151
Baibomsai, 45, 46, 53, 54, 73, 109, 122, 153, 158, 160 S
Bartlett, William Russell, 8, 9, 10, 12, 16, 35, 36, 37, 63, 80, 81, 82, 93, 99, 125, 130, 148
Belleau, Narcisse-Fortunat, 125, 135, 141, 149
Bemossatang, 122
Blain, David, 129, 132, 133, 136, 137
Blettner, Jean, 56, 145
Boyer, James, 137
Brough, Charles Crosbie, 77
Brown, George, 93, 131
Cainooshimague, Michel, 6, 29, 34, 44, 60, 61
Campbell, Alexander, 75, 149
Carrez, Louis, 137, 142
Cartier, George-Étienne, 12, 99
Cazeau, Charles-Félix, 56, 117, 139
Chance, James, 80, 88
Choné, Jean-Pierre, 55 and throughout
Colgan, James, 137
Cooper, Henry Cholwell, 75, 88
Cooper, R., 134
Cupples, Henrietta Campbell, 75
Curtis, Arthur, 136
Dawson, Simon James, 163

Day, Samuel Phillips, 2, 3, 4, 5, 6, 12, 14, 15, 17, 18, 19, 20, 21, 22, 23, 67, 87, 88, 94, 102, 103, 113, 150 W
de Lamorandière, Charles, 9, 21, 35, 37, 47, 67, 81, 82, 124, 130, 131, 134, 158
de Laronde, Charles (or Shagwawimanitons), 128, 130, 131
de Saint-Just, Luc Letellier, 125
Debassige. *See* Taibosegai
Dennis, John Stoughton, 23, 24, 111, 119
Dorion, Antoine-Aimé, 139, 142
Dudgeon, Adam, 137
Dufferin, Earl of, 162, 163
Dupont, Charles Thomas, 142, 143, 144, 145, 147, 149, 150, 151, 152, 154, 155, 156, 157, 158, 159, 160, 161, 163
Edawe Kesis, 19, 109, 143
Elliott, Matthew, 4
Eshkamejwanoke. *See* Gibbard, William
Férard, Martin, 155, 156, 162
Ferguson, Thomas Roberts, 112, 113
Fergusson Blair, Adam Johnston, 135
Frémiot, Nicolas-Marie-Joseph, 28
Gahbow, 36
Gibbard, John, 137
Gibbard, William, 18, 19, 23, 29, 53, 85, 86, 113, 114, 116, 119, 127, 128, 129, 130, 131, 132, 133, 134, 135, 136, 137, 138, 141, 142 W
Hanipaux, Joseph-Urbain, 26, 27, 56, 57, 58, 59, 114, 120, 130, 143, 144
Hawkins, William, 8, 9, 10
head men of Michigiwatinong, Sheshegwaning and Wikwemikong (August 1862), 42
head men of Mitchikiwatinong (May 1863), 122
head men of Sheshegwaning (May 1863), 123
head men of Sheshegwaning, Mindemooyasebe, Wikwemikong and Michigiwatinong (June 1862), 40
Head, Edmund Walker, 10

Head, Francis Bond, 4, 7, 8, 10, 15, 16, 26, 36, 47, 51, 63, 81, 83, 84, 85, 86, 93, 104, 130, 148
Hobson, Joseph, 143
Ironside, Alexander McGregor, 19 W
Ironside, George, 4, 5, 6, 7, 8, 9, 10, 11, 13, 14, 15, 16, 17, 18, 19, 23, 27, 29, 30, 34, 35, 37, 40, 46, 52, 53, 55, 59, 64, 71, 76, 77, 79, 80, 87, 89, 106, 110, 114, 116, 117, 119, 120, 124, 128, 129, 142, 161 W
Itawashkash, Sasso, 25 and throughout S
Jacobs, Peter, 75 and throughout W
Jacobs, Peter, Sr. (or Pahtahsega), 18
Jacobs, Susan (née Cooper), 75, 76, 87
Jako. *See* Atagiwinini, Jako
Jennesseaux, Joseph, 58
Kamaskawittagosit (Jean-Pierre Choné), 57
Kane, Paul, 26, 46
Keating, William, 85, 86
Keghikgoobeness, Charles, 45, 46, 53, 73, 109, 122, 153, 160 S
Kinojameg, Tomah (or Mokomanish), 19, 34, 42, 44, 54, 117, 129, 133, 134, 143, 157, 161
Kitche Baptiste, Charles (or Tche Batisan), 116, 155, 156, 157
Kohler, Auguste, 56, 58, 60, 63, 118, 127, 128, 129, 130, 131, 133, 136, 137, 142
Kushkewahbic (or Columbus), 45, 53, 122, 151, 153, 161 S
Layton, David, 9, 18, 19, 83, 87, 154, 156 W
Lincoln, Abraham, 141
Lindsey, Charles, 2, 7, 8, 9, 10, 12, 13, 14, 16, 35, 37, 63, 80, 81, 82, 83, 89, 93, 99, 106, 125, 130, 135
Macdonald, John Alexander, 12, 84, 99
Macdonald, John Sandfield, 1, 12, 93, 139, 142
Madjiganikwe (Sophie), 27
Maishegonggai, 19, 36, 45, 51, 52, 53, 54, 56, 72, 73, 78, 107, 109, 115, 122, 140, 145, 146, 147, 153, 155, 159, 160 S
Makons, Antoine, 34, 44
Manitowaussen, John Arthur, 159
McDougall, John Henry, 3, 19 W

McDougall, William, 1 and throughout S
McNabb, A., 18, 19, 113
Megwance, 116, 151
Metosage, Francis, 19, 44, 54, 117, 122, 123
Miskomanatons, 51, 107
Mocotaishegun, 6, 19, 29, 34, 44, 45, 56, 60
Mokomanish (or Frederic Bebametabi), 44, 64
Molson, Martha Ann, 2
Monck, Charles Stanley, 10, 66
Nahneebahwequa, or Catherine Sutton, 33
Naiwotaikezhik, 40, 42, 43, 44, 53, 122, 153, 160 S
Niibaakhom, 44
Nishkadjiwin (Joseph), 28
Nissasuakouat (Joseph-Urbain Hanipaux), 57
O'Meara, Frederick Augustus, 77, 78, 79, 80, 87
Obettossoway, George, 19, 45, 53, 54, 122, 153, 159, 161 S
Obettossoway, George Abram, 45, 78
Oga, 44
Okemah beness, 10, 19, 29, 38, 45, 46, 53, 78, 122, 153, 160 S
Ominikamigo, Augustin, 19, 34, 42, 44, 61
Ozawanimiki, 128, 129, 130, 132, 134, 136
Pahtahdagwishkung, 46, 53, 122, 153, 160 S
Paimoquonaishkung, 19, 30, 31, 37, 38, 40, 42, 43, 52, 53, 54, 73, 110, 114, 115, 121, 122, 140, 144, 151, 153, 157, 160 S
Paimosegai, Vincent, 34, 44
Paimsahdang, 53 W
Peau de Chat, 57
Pekoneiassong, 48, 70, 104
Peltier, Joe, 143
Pennefather, Richard, 6, 7, 10
Phipps, James Charles, 162, 163
Plummer, William, 160, 161, 162
Point, Nicolas, 58, 59
Prince, John, 12, 36, 130
Proulx, Jean-Baptiste, 26, 57, 131, 132
Proulx, Philemon, 128, 130, 131
Rafferty, John J., 124

Reesor, David, 3, 19, 23, 87, 94, 95, 97, 98, 99, 101, 112, 113
Ross, Benjamin Walker, 163
Sakiwinebi, 26, 40, 42, 46, 50, 71, 107, 160
"Shan", 85
Shauwanausoway, 46
Sherwood, George, 1, 11
Shewetagun (or Salter), Joseph, 19, 45, 53, 115, 122, 153, 159, 160, 161 S
Sicotte, Louis-Victor, 1, 12, 93
Sims, Jabez Waters, 150, 151, 152, 154, 156, 158, 161
Songiteeskang (Auguste Kohler), 58
Spragge, William Prosperous, 2, 3, 4, 5, 9, 11, 12, 13, 14, 15, 17, 18, 19, 21, 23, 53, 94, 113, 116, 117, 118, 119, 120, 125, 141, 144, 145, 148, 151, 154, 155, 158, 159, 163 S
St. Paul, Horace David Cholwell, 75
Strachan, John, 78
Sunego, Brunch, 33
Taché, Étienne-Paschal, 149
Taibosegai, 19, 26, 40, 42, 43, 44, 50, 52, 53, 54, 73, 110, 115, 120, 121, 122, 143, 144, 151, 153, 156, 157, 160 S
Taylor, W.D., 124

Tecumseh, 4, 5, 94
Tehkummah (or Tekoman), Louis, 6, 19, 22, 28, 29, 30, 34, 44, 45, 51, 52, 53, 56, 60, 64, 72, 73, 108, 110, 116, 122, 149, 152, 153, 157, 160, 161 S
Tessier, Ulric, 125
The Prophet (or Tenskwatawa), 4, 5
Tomah. *See* Kinojameg, Tomah
Vankoughnet, Philip, 1, 6, 7, 8, 10, 11, 16, 84, 125, 148
Vocemassussia, or Isabella, 4
Wabanosse (John), 27, 123
Wabiwiokwan. *See* Ironside, George
Wahbegakake, James, 45, 46, 80
Wahcowsai, 26, 36, 40, 42, 46, 50, 52, 53, 73, 110, 115, 122, 123, 153, 161 S
Waibenessieme, 46, 53, 110, 122, 153, 161 S
Wakekijik, Louis, 19, 34, 40, 42, 44, 51, 54, 61, 72, 108, 116, 117, 134, 143, 145, 146, 156, 157, 161
Walcot, Charles, 6
Watts, William, 136
Whasaneese (William McDougall), 23
Whitcher, William Frederick, 134, 135, 141
Wilson, Joseph, 18, 19, 113 W

S Signatory to the Great Manitoulin Island treaty of 1862
W Witness to the Great Manitoulin Island treaty of 1862

Endnotes

[1] *Huron Signal*, 2 Oct. 1862, p. 1, quoting the [*Illustrated* ?] *London News*).
[2] Manitoulin's First Nation residents were called Indians by the government and others, though the people called themselves *Anishinaabeg*. The term "Indian" is used in this chapter to reflect the government's view at the time.
[3] Karen Molson, *The Molsons: Their Lives and Times, 1780-2000* (Willowdale, Ont.: Firefly, 2001), p. 222.
[4] Day's remarks are from a combination of two sources: his book and his newspaper account. Samuel P. Day, *English America, or Pictures of Canadian Places and People*, Vol. II (London: T. Cautley Newby, 1864); Samuel P. Day, *London Morning Herald*, 30 Oct. 1862, reprinted in *The Markham Economist*, 4 Dec. 1862. This quotation is from *English America*, p. 78.
[5] Probably one of David Reesor's nephews, either 19-year-old Robert or 17-year-old David.
[6] Day, *London Morning Herald*, 30 Oct. 1862, reprinted in *The Markham Economist*, 4 Dec. 1862.
[7] Library and Archives Canada (hereafter LAC), RG 10, 573 (Ironside to Pennefather, 27 Mar. 1858), p. 182; LAC, RG 10, 519, C13,347 (Pennefather to Governor General, 13 June 1859), p. 253. In June 1859, *Anishinaabeg* on the mainland's North Shore were persuaded to surrender reserved land that had been set aside by a treaty in 1850. George Ironside was credited with securing these surrenders. LAC, RG 10, 615, C13,387, pp. 93-94. Ironside approached three Manitoulin chiefs about surrendering their North Shore property. One, Chief Okemah beness, signed a surrender document for Whitefish River but the government rejected it for not meeting standard treaty protocol. See also LAC, RG 10, 573, C13,374 (Ironside, 17 July 1861), pp. 297-303.
[8] LAC, RG 10, 613 (Chesley to Ironside, 13 Aug. 1855), p. 1040. "It was Lord Bury's and my intention to see you and the inhospitable Island upon which you are an exile. But depend upon it you are not forgotten nor will you be in any new arrangement that may be made for the reconstruction of the Department."
[9] LAC, RG 10, 258, C12,646 (Ironside to Pennefather, 12 Mar. 1861), p156170.
[10] LAC, R92 [formerly RG 31], 1861 Census of Algoma, Canada West (film C-1091); LAC, RG 10, 621A, C13,392, p. 653.
[11] LAC, RG 10, 621A, C13,392, p. 653. Population of Wikwemikong, 652; Michigiwatinong, 121; Manitowaning and Sheshegwaning, 105 each; Naimonakekong, 72; Sheguiandah, 69; Wikwemikongsing, 67; Wewebijiwang (Petit Courant), 58; Chetowaiegunning East or Atchidawaiganing (South Bay East), 54; Chetowaiegunning West or Adjidawaiganing (South Bay West), 49; Mindimoiensibing (Providence Bay), 18; and Sheshegwanasing, 11. Note that this count is slightly different than the 1861 census count, since unofficial lists counted the residents by community, while the official lists grouped the residents all together.
[12] LAC, RG 10, 258, C12,646 (Ironside to Pennefather, 5 Mar. 1861), p. 156060.
[13] LAC, RG 10, 573, C13,374 (Ironside to Pennefather, 8 Mar. 1861), pp. 280-81.
[14] LAC, RG 10, 258, C12,646 (Ironside to Pennefather, 5 Mar. 1861), p. 156059.
[15] LAC, RG 10, 615, C13,387 (Walcot to Ironside, 30 Mar. 1861), p. 28.
[16] LAC, RG 10, 573, C13,374 (Ironside to Indian Dept., 17 July 1861), pp. 297-303.
[17] LAC, RG 10, Vol. 621A, C13,392 (Tehkummah, 7 Jan. 1863), pp. 702-4.
[18] LAC, RG 10, 252 pt. 2, C12,642 (Vankoughnet to Pennefather, 5 Jan. 1860): "It has been represented to me that the interests of the Province would be materially promoted were the Government enabled to acquire from the Indians the Manitoulin Group of

Islands"; and LAC, RG 10, 733, C13,417 (Gibbard to Vankoughnet, 19 Dec. 1859). Gibbard reported that Manitoulin and several other islands in his territory would make splendid settlements.

[19] Sessional Papers of the Province of Canada (hereafter SPPC), 1863, No. 63 (Return of copies of all orders in council and reports relating to the Manitoulin Island, during the year 1861); Vankoughnet's memorandum of 29 Aug. 1861.

[20] The 1854 surrender of the Saugeen Peninsula created reserves, including the Newash reserve at Owen Sound that was further surrendered in Feb. 1857, and the Colpoy's Bay reserve in Aug. 1861. The Robinson Huron and Superior lands surrendered in Sept. 1850 were further surrendered in June 1859 by means of three treaties negotiated by Pennefather and Ironside.

[21] LAC, RG 10, 520, C13,348 (Walcot to Bartlett, 24 Sept. 1861), pp. 408-9.

[22] LAC, RG 10, 520, C13,348 (Walcot to Bartlett, 24 Sept. 1861), pp. 408-9.

[23] *Perth Courier*, 11 Oct. 1861, p. 3.

[24] SPPC, 1863, No. 63 (Bartlett and Lindsey, 12 Oct. 1861).

[25] LAC, RG 10, 416, C9620, p. 920. Assiginack, Itawashkash, Mozumeko and Paimoquonaishkung signed the 1836 document.

[26] Charles de Lamorandière (c1816-1907) was the son of Étienne Augustin de Lamorandière, a trader who settled at Shebawahning (Killarney) about 1820. Charles taught at the Manitowaning school from 1841 to 1844, worked as a trader at Shebawahning and was regularly called to serve as an interpreter as he spoke French, English and Ojibwe. The de Lamorandière family was Roman Catholic, so Charles was trusted as an interpreter by the people and priests of Wikwemikong.

[27] SPPC, 1863, No. 63 (Bartlett and Lindsey, 12 Oct. 1861); LAC, RG 10, 722, C13,412 (Spragge Memorandum, 27 June 1862), pp. 44-49.

[28] SPPC, 1863, No. 63 (Bartlett and Lindsey, 12 Oct. 1861).

[29] LAC, RG 10, 262, C12,649 (Lindsey, 18 Oct. 1861), pp. 158465-69; LAC, RG 10, 615, C13,387 (Ironside to Spragge, 14 Aug. 1862), pp. 115-21.

[30] LAC, RG 10, 262 pt. 1, C12,649 (Ironside to Walcot, 31 Oct. 1861).

[31] In November, the United States Navy seized two confederate commissioners from a British ship, violating British neutrality. The crisis was resolved at the end of December when the prisoners were returned.

[32] LAC, RG 10, 520, C13,348 (Circular from Walcot, 15 Nov. 1861), p. 458.

[33] LAC, RG 10, 291, C12,668 (Ironside to Walcot, 16 Mar. 1862), pp. 194982-84; LAC, RG 10, 521, C13,348 (Circular from Walcot, 16 Jan. 1862), p. 17 and LAC, RG 10, 615, C13,387 (Walcot to Ironside, 16 Jan. 1862), p. 126.

[34] LAC, RG 10, 291, C12,668 (Abedosawai, 26 Feb. 1862, re: 24 Feb 1862 council), pp. 194986-87.

[35] *The Globe*, 1 Mar 1861, p. 2; 7 March 1861, p. 2; and 28 Jan. 1862, p. 2.

[36] LAC, RG 10, 291, C12,668 (Ironside to Walcot, 16 Mar. 1862), pp. 194978-81.

[37] LAC, RG 10, 295, C12,671 (Prince to the Commissioner of Crown Lands, 19 Mar. 1862), pp. 197765-67.

[38] LAC, RG 10, 722, C13,412 (Spragge memorandum, 27 June 1862), pp. 44-49.

[39] LAC, RG 10, 294, C12,671 (Spragge to McDougall, 1 July 1862), p. 197254.

[40] LAC, RG 10, 521, C13,348 (Spragge to Ironside, 11 July 1862), pp. 257-58.

[41] LAC, RG 10, 615, C13,387 (Ironside to Spragge,14 Aug. 1862), pp. 115-16, 118.

[42] LAC, RG 10, 521, C13,348 (Spragge to Ironside, 23 Aug. 1862), p. 368.

[43] LAC, RG 10, 521, C13,348 (Spragge to Ironside, 25 Aug. 1862), p. 371.

[44] *The Quebec Mercury*, advertisement, May through Sept. 1862; *The Canadian Freeman*, 18 Sept. 1862, p. 2.

⁴⁵ LAC, RG 10, 722, C13,412 (Spragge memorandum, late Aug. 1862), pp. 71-72. Spragge estimated $1,000 for 300 men and 30 chiefs, at $3 and $6 each respectively, plus $100 for expenses.
⁴⁶ LAC, RG 10, 722, C13,412 (McDougall memorandum, 12 Sept. 1862), pp. 74-77.
⁴⁷ LAC, RG 10, 521, C13,348 (Spragge to Ironside, 11 Sept. 1862), p. 415.
⁴⁸ *The Quebec Mercury*, 30 Sept. 1862, p. 2.
⁴⁹ *Canadian News, New Brunswick Herald, and British Columbian Intelligencer* [London, England], 9 Oct. 1862, pp. 229-30.
⁵⁰ Day, *English America*, p. 87.
⁵¹ F.J. Falkner, "Narrative of Sault Ste. Marie, Ontario," *Sault Star*, 20 June 1921.
⁵² Probably either Alexander McNabb, the Crown Land agent for the Saugeen Peninsula, or Archibald McNabb, the surveyor of Owen Sound.
⁵³ LAC, RG 10, 615, C13,387 (Ironside to Spragge, 7 Sept. 1862), pp. 122-24.
⁵⁴ LAC, R92, 1861 Census of Algoma, Canada West: of the 1,443 people enumerated on the island, 816 were under the age of 21 and 627 were adults (282 were adult males).
⁵⁵ SPPC, 1863, No. 5 (Report from Indian Department appended to Report of the Commissioner of Crown Lands) [William Spragge's report].
⁵⁶ Day, *English America*, pp. 104-5; Day, *London Morning Herald*, 30 Oct. 1862, reprinted in *The Markham Economist*, 4 Dec. 1862.
⁵⁷ SPPC, 1863, No. 5 (Report from Indian Department appended to Report of the Commissioner of Crown Lands) [William Spragge's report].
⁵⁸ Day, *London Morning Herald*, 30 Oct. 1862, reprinted in *The Markham Economist*, 4 Dec. 1862.
⁵⁹ Day, *London Morning Herald*, 30 Oct. 1862, reprinted in *The Markham Economist*, 4 Dec. 1862.
⁶⁰ SPPC, 1863, No. 5 (Report from Indian Department appended to Report of the Commissioner of Crown Lands) [William Spragge's report].
⁶¹ Day, *London Morning Herald*, 30 Oct. 1862, reprinted in *The Markham Economist*, 4 Dec. 1862.
⁶² Order in Council, 14 Nov. 1862, O in C B Vol. 2, p. 31, LAC, RG 10, 722, C13,412, pp. 77-79.
⁶³ LAC, RG 10, 331, C9581 (Choné to Cazeau, 1 Dec. 1862), pp. 28-31, trans. S. Pearen. Charles de Lamorandière spoke Ojibwe, French and English. He often acted as interpreter for the Wikwemikong people.
⁶⁴ Day, *English America*, pp. 108-9. In Day's *London Morning Herald* account of 1862, "three chiefs had been brought round."
⁶⁵ SPPC, 1863, No. 5 (Report from Indian Department appended to Report of the Commissioner of Crown Lands) [William Spragge's report].
⁶⁶ Day, *English America*, p. 110.
⁶⁷ Day, *English America*, p. 109.
⁶⁸ Day, *London Morning Herald*, 30 Oct. 1862, reprinted in *The Markham Economist*, 4 Dec. 1862.
⁶⁹ Day, *English America*, p. 111.
⁷⁰ Order in Council, 14 Nov. 1862, O in C B Vol. 2, p. 31, LAC, RG 10, 722, C13,412, pp. 77-79.
⁷¹ "Copy of the Report of a Committee of the honourable the Executive Council, approved by His Excellency the Governor General on the 14 November 1862."
⁷² LAC, RG 10, 359, C9595 ("Department of Crown Lands. The Honble W^m McDougall, Commissioner. Plan of part of the north shore of Lake Huron shewing the subdivision of

the new townships," Jan. 1863), pp. 182-86. A detail from this map is reproduced on pp. x-xi.

[73] LAC, RG 10, 292, C12,669, p. 195683, Mitchikiwotinong Petition in Ojibwe of 27 June 1862 in which *Ogimaa* Bemegonechkang repeats the governor's words to his forefathers.

[74] LAC, RG 10, 292, C12,669, p. 195678, Mitchikiwotinong Petition in Ojibwe of 27 June 1862.

[75] *Anishinaabeg*, "the People," is how the residents of Manitoulin referred to themselves in the 19th century. Their leaders were *ogimaag*, chiefs.

[76] Twenty-first century orthography is used here; 19th century orthography included the variations *Otawa* of *Otawa minissing*.

[77] LAC, RG 10, C13,373 (Ironside, 8 Jan. 1848).

[78] Lorenzo Cadieux, S.J., *Letters from the New Canada Mission, 1843-52*, trans. William Lonc, S.J. and George Topp, S.J., 2 vols. (Toronto: W. Lonc, 2001), letter #76 (Hanipaux to Paris, 5 July 1851), pp. 306-8.

[79] LAC, R92, 1861 Census of Algoma, Canada West; LAC, RG 10, 621A, C13,392, p. 653.

[80] By 1860, John Itawashkash of Sheshegwaning, Louis Taibosegai of Michigiwatinong and Francis Metosage of Wikwemikong—all three the sons of chiefs—were also literate.

[81] Jean-Baptiste Assiginack / Assiginak / Signack (or Blackbird) (c1770-4 Nov. 1866). His grandfather was Chief Pungowish and his brothers were Chief Apakosigan (or Pakosigan) (Smoking Weed) and Chief Makedebenessi (Black Hawk) of L'Arbre Croche. J.-B. Assiginack was born in Michigan, but also lived at Mackinac, Drummond Island, Penetanguishene and Coldwater, often working as interpreter for the government. At the 1861 treaty negotiations he claimed to be 91 years old; he signed the 1862 treaty.

[82] LAC, RG 10, 573 (Ironside to Pennefather, 27 Mar. 1858), p. 182; LAC, RG 10, 519, C13,347 (Pennefather to Governor General, 13 June 1859), p. 253.

[83] LAC, RG 10, 615, C13,387 (25 June 1859 surrender), pp. 93-94.

[84] LAC, RG 10, 258, C12,646 (Ironside to Pennefather, 5 Mar. 1861), pp. 156059-61; LAC, RG 10, 573, C13,374 (Ironside to Pennefather, 8 Mar. 1861), pp. 280-81.

[85] LAC, RG 10, Vol. 621A, C13,392 (Tehkummah, 7 Jan. 1863), pp. 702-4.

[86] LAC, R92, 1861 Census of Algoma, Canada West; RG 10, 573, C13,374 (Ironside to Indian Dept., 17 July 1861), pp. 297-303. Only 278 *Anishinaabeg* agreed to participate, whereas 1,199 refused.

[87] LAC, RG 10, Vol. 259, C12,647 (23 May 1861), p. 156720.

[88] LAC, RG 10, Vol. 259, C12,647, pp. 1566723-24 in English, pp. 156697-98 in French, and pp. 156707-10 in Ojibwe with signatures. Note: there are slight variations among the translations of all the petitions. The 1860s English translation has been used where possible.

[89] LAC, RG 10, Vol. 259, C12,647, pp. 156713-22 in English, pp. 156696-98 in French, pp. 156700-6 in Ojibwe, and pp. 1567708-10 for signatures. Ironside's response is in LAC, RG 10, 573, C13,374 (Ironside, 17 Jul. 1861), pp. 297-307. Though Ironside was able to justify his actions to his superiors, the *Anishinaabeg* clearly did not understand his methods.

[90] Mrs. Sutton lost her Indian status when she married a non-Native man, but was also denied permission to purchase her family's farmland after it was surrendered because an Indian could not purchase land. With the help of the Methodists, the Quakers and the Aborigines' Protection Society she addressed provincial legislators and the colonial secretary, and even had an audience with Queen Victoria. See LAC, RG 10, 573, C13,374 (Ironside, 17 Jul. 1861), p. 307. Ironside notes that the Indians had written to Mrs. Sutton.

[91] *Christian Guardian*, 2 Apr. 1862, p. 2 (letter dated 1 Mar. 1862).

[92] LAC, RG 10, Vol. 621A, C13,392 (Tehkummah, 7 Jan. 1863, re: summer of 1861), pp. 702-4.
[93] LAC, RG 10, Vol. 261, C12,648 (chiefs to the governor, 3 Sept. 1861), pp. 158008-10, trans. S. Pearen. Each of the 7 signatories put his father's or grandfather's name beside his name to support his claim to chieftainship.
[94] SPPC, 1863, No. 63 (Bartlett and Lindsey, 12 Oct. 1861).
[95] LAC, RG 10, 416, C9620, p. 920. Assiginack, Itawashkash, Mozumeko and Paimoquonaishkung signed the 1836 treaty.
[96] The negotiations have been recreated from SPPC, 1863, App. 63, and *The Globe*, 18 Oct. 1861.
[97] Lorenzo Cadieux, S.J., and Robert Toupin, S.J., *Letters from Manitoulin Island: 1853-1870*, trans. Shelley J. Pearen and William Lonc, S.J. (Toronto: W. Lonc, 2007), letter #35 (Choné to Scholastics of Laval, 5 June 1862), p. 200.
[98] *The Canadian Freeman*, 30 Oct. 1862, p. 2. A slightly different translation is in LAC, RG 10, 292, C12,669 (Chief Bemigonechkang to Governor General, 27 June 1862).
[99] LAC, RG 10, 262 pt. 1, C12,649 (Ironside to Walcot, 30 Oct. 1861).
[100] LAC, RG 10, 292, C12,669, pp. 195678-86. According to historian Alan Corbiere, this petition is the *Anishinaabe* recollection of the Wampum Belt given to the *Anishinaabeg* by Sir William Johnson at Niagara in 1764. The vessel mentioned is the promise to deliver Indian presents.
[101] LAC, RG 10, 292, C12,669, pp. 195688-90.
[102] Cadieux, *Letters from Manitoulin*, #35 (Choné to Scholastics of Laval, 5 June 1862), pp. 200-1. The council was established sometime between Aug. 1861 and June 1862.
[103] *The Quebec Mercury*, advertisement, May through Sept. 1862; *The Canadian Freeman*, 18 Sept. 1862, p. 2.
[104] LAC, RG 10, Vol. 292, C12,669 (29 Aug. 1862), pp. 195638-44, trans. S. Pearen.
[105] LAC, RG 10, 615, C13,387 (Ironside to Spragge, 7 Sept. 1862), pp. 122-24.
[106] James Cleland Hamilton, *Famous Algonquins: Algic Legends* (Toronto: Canadian Institute, 1899), pp. 302-3.
[107] These biographies of the chiefs would not have been possible without the assistance of Alan Corbiere, formerly of the Ojibwe Cultural Foundation, M'Chigeeng, Manitoulin Island.
[108] Paimoquonaishkung (English) / Bemikwaneshkang (French) (c1801-aft. 1871) was invited by Ironside to meet the Prince of Wales in Sarnia in Sept. 1860. He signed the 1862 treaty. In 1869 he was described as 68-year-old chief, farmer and fisherman who was steady and had lived on his lot for four years. He was descended from Kagishiwe.
[109] Louis Taibosegai (English) / Debassige or Debasseghe (French) (c1809-aft. 1871) was invited by Ironside to meet the Prince of Wales in 1860 in Sarnia. He signed the 1862 treaty. He was described in 1869 as a 60-year-old farmer and fisherman of good character and steady who had lived four years on his lot (due to treaty relocation). Louis Taibosegai, Jr. (c1824-aft. 1871) was described as a 45-year-old carpenter and farmer who reads and writes and can build boats, "a very good man." See LAC, RG 10, 1996, C11,130, file 6990.
[110] Abence (English) / Ebins (French) (c1809-aft. 1871) signed the 1862 treaty. He lived at Mitchigiwatinong from at least 1849. In 1869 he was described as a 60-year-old farmer and fisherman, of good character and steady. Like the rest of the band he was relocated following the treaty, and in 1869 had lived on his lot for only four years.
[111] Naiwotaikezhik (English) / Newatekijik (French) (c1834-aft. 1871) signed the treaty as a principal man. In 1869 he was described as a 35-year-old farmer and fisherman with steady habits, who had been living on his lot for only four years, due to treaty relocation.

[112] Tomah (or Thomas) Kinojameg or Mokomanish (c1826-aft. 1891) was the son of Michael Cainooshimague (Michel Kinojameg) (?-1861) and grandson of Frederic Bebametabi (also known as Mokomanish) (?-3 May 1853).
[113] Louis Wakekijik / Wakegijig (c1802-1889) was the son of Vincent Paimosegai / Bemassige or Essiban (1780-10 Aug 1859).
[114] Augustin Ominikamigo or Nessegigabow (1808-1892) was the son of Antoine Makons (c1780-22 Dec 1859).
[115] Francis Metosage (or Francois Maitosahge) (1819-1896) asked for reinstatement of 1850 Robinson treaty payments in 1895, which he had received for only 11 years. RG 10, 2803, file 161402, 24 Apr. 1895.
[116] Jako Atagiwinini / Joseph Jaco Tagewinini (1816-aft. 1881). J.B. Tahgaiwenne, Sr., was invited by Superintendent Ironside to be part of the Manitoulin delegation to meet the Prince of Wales in Sarnia in September 1860. Jako did not sign the 1862 treaty and his father did not attend the negotiations. Joseph Jako (Atagewinnini) was described in 1869 as a 44-year-old who farms a little, goes about peaceable, sober, likes travelling and hunting deer in winter, and of good character. Jako had at least 2 brothers: Wawawoshhoning at Sarnia and Wahbudik at Cape Croker.
[117] Louis Tehkummah (English) / Tekoma (French) / Taicummosemo (c1805-1888) was invited by Superintendent Ironside to be part of the Manitoulin delegation to meet the Prince of Wales in Sarnia in September 1860.
[118] Mocotaishegun (or Mocotai Shegun) was recorded as "Chief Mocotaishegun (Assiginack)" in census records of 1857 and 1860, probably to distinguish him from Chief Jean-Baptiste Assiginack. Both chiefs were invited by Superintendent Ironside to be part of the Manitoulin delegation to meet the Prince of Wales in Sarnia in September 1860, and were identified as favouring a surrender of Manitoulin the following year.
[119] George Obettossoway (English) / Abitasswe (French) / Ahbedossway (c1828-1870). William Kingston provided a description of him in 1853 on board the *Kaloolah*. Chief Ahbetosswai (presumably the elder) was invited by Ironside to be part of the delegation to meet the Prince of Wales in Sarnia in 1860. George Obetossaway signed the 1862 treaty as a principal man. George was described in 1869 as a 45-year-old who could read and write English.
[120] Kushkewahbic (or Columbus) (English) / Gashkiwabik (French) (c1809-1870) was invited by Ironside to be part of the delegation to meet the Prince of Wales in 1860. He was described as the 65-year-old head of an industrious family with settled habits at Sucker Creek in 1869. His brother John Mekatebin also lived at Little Current.
[121] Joseph Shewetagun (English) / Shiwitagan (or Salter) (French) (c1811-aft. 1880). Shewetahgun signed the 1862 treaty. He was described in 1869 as a 58-year-old resident of Sucker Creek Reserve, an "industrious Indian" who farms and fishes.
[122] John Maishegonggai (English) / Mejakwange (French) (c1803-1878). Mishacangay (or Meshaquangue), from Sheguaiendatch, is mentioned in the 1827-35 La Cloche Hudson's Bay Company Post journals. Chief Maishegonggai was invited by Superintendent Ironside to be part of the Manitoulin delegation to meet the Prince of Wales in Sarnia in September 1860. Maishegonggai signed the 1862 treaty. He was described as a 90-year-old farmer and fisherman of good character and steady in 1869.
[123] Okemah beness (English) / P. Kitchi Binesi (French) / Charles Ogima Biness. Chief Okemah beness signed the 1862 treaty. In 1863 he received annuity payments for 64 band members.
[124] Baibomsai (or Paibomsai) (English) / Bebamisse (French) / Pabahmasay (c1807-1875). He signed the 1862 treaty as a principal man. Baibomsai became a chief about 1865 when Okemah beness died.

[125] Charles Keghikgoobeness (English) / Kijikobinesi (French) (c1808-c1878). Kezhikgoobeness signed the 1862 treaty as a principal man. The local superintendent in 1869 described him as a 60-year-old who farms and fishes, of good character. There was also a Chief Kezhikgoobeness who lived at Wikwemikongsing on the Wikwemikong Peninsula, but he did not sign the treaty.

[126] Peter Jacobs (c1833-1864): see Chapter 4, "Manitoulin Island and Reverend Peter Jacobs."

[127] Pahtahdagwishkung (English) / Batatakwishing (French) (c1774-aft. 1871). "Patatacoushinnes" and his sons, from Point aux Erables, are listed in the 1827-35 La Cloche Hudson's Bay Company Post journals trading maple sugar and martin furs for supplies. Pahtahdagwishkung signed the 1862 treaty. Pahdahdoguishing was described as a 95-year-old blind man living with his son "Nainewaishkung" at "Obigewong" in 1869.

[128] Chief Wahcowsai (English) / Wakaosse (French) (c1809-?). Wahcowsai attended the 1836 treaty and signed the 1862 treaty. He lived at South Bay East in the 1840s. Wahcowsai was described as a 60-year-old farmer and fisherman in 1869. See Alan Corbiere, "Waakaa'ose: He Who Walks Around," *Ojibwe Cultural Foundation Newsletter* 4, Issue 7 (Oct. 2009), at www.ojibweculture.ca.

[129] Chief Sakiwinebi (c1802-1885) lived at Mindemooyasebe from about 1846. Sahgewenaibe was invited by Superintendent Ironside to be part of the Manitoulin delegation to meet the Prince of Wales in Sarnia in September 1860, though it appears Abence went in his place. "Sauguinaby, a painted warrior, wearing a robe of hawk's feathers" (*The Markham Economist*, 3 Dec. 1862) attended the 1862 treaty negotiations but did not sign the treaty. Sahkewenabe was described in 1869 as a 67-year-old with steady habits who farms and fishes a little. *The Manitoulin Expositor* noted his death in 1885, remarking on his notoriety for a bearskin Busby headdress with the insignia of the 84th regiment attached, and that he had been "one of the few pagan Indians left on the adjacent reserve," though he died a Roman Catholic.

[130] Chief Waibenessieme / Webinesimi (c1800-1867). Waibenessime was invited by Superintendent Ironside to be part of the Manitoulin delegation to meet the Prince of Wales in Sarnia in 1860. Waibenessieme signed the 1862 treaty.

[131] This account of the treaty is compiled from the author's translations of LAC, RG 10, 292, pp. 195661-673, and SPPC, 1863, Documents de la Session (No. 63) (Protestation des Indiens de Wikwemikong, 15 Nov. 1862).

[132] "This is what happened on Sunday night. There was a trader named Miskomanitans there. He had some firewater. He brought it to drink. Well, he was the one who brought it. A son of Assiginak brought it to his elder brother Itawashkash to drink, saying to him at the same time, to cede this land that we own together. But he did not listen, while he had awareness. But then having lost awareness, being inebriated, it seems that then he said: I cede. ... He was inebriated all night until daybreak. When it was light, these same instruments to deceive, hurried to finish quickly." Trans. S. Pearen.

[133] *The Markham Economist*, 4 Dec. 1862, pp. 2-4.

[134] *The Markham Economist*, 4 Dec. 1862, pp. 2-4.

[135] LAC, RG 10, 284, C12,664 (Mai-she-quong-gai, 19 Jan. 1864), p. 191347.

[136] The Jesuits at the time considered the word *Anishinaabeg* to be an Ojibwe word requiring translation. French Jesuit documents written between 1844 and 1870 from Manitoulin usually used the word *sauvage*, meaning Native or Native people. The terms "Native" or "Native people" are used in this chapter to reflect the Jesuit view.

[137] Cadieux, *Letters from Manitoulin*, #35 (Choné to Scholastics of Laval, 5 June 1862), p. 198.

[138] Cadieux, *Letters from Manitoulin*, #36 (Choné to Scholastics of Laval, 12 Nov. 1862), p. 205.
[139] Cadieux, *Letters from the New Canada Mission*, part 1, pp. 276-8; part 2, p. 487.
[140] Cadieux, *Letters from the New Canada Mission*, part 2, pp. 128-34; Shelley J. Pearen and William Lonc, *Letters from the Ft. William Jesuit Mission, 1848-1862* (Toronto: W. Lonc, 2010), p. 48; *Letters from Manitoulin*, p. 181.
[141] Joseph-Urbain Hanipaux (1805-1872).
[142] Auguste Kohler (1821-1871).
[143] Joseph Jennesseaux (1810-1884) served at Wikwemikong from September 1850 until his death in 1884.
[144] Nicolas Point (1799-1868).
[145] Cadieux, *Letters from Manitoulin*, #34 (Choné to Scholastics of Laval, 21 Aug. 1861), p. 190; Lorenzo Cadieux, S.J., and Robert Toupin, S.J., "Les Robes Noires à l'Île de Manitou: 1853-1870," unpublished manuscript, 1980, lettre #34, pp. 138-39.
[146] Cadieux, *Letters from Manitoulin*, #34, pp. 191-92; Cadieux, "Les Robes Noires," p. 140.
[147] Wikwemikong Diarium, 4 Feb. 1861, trans. S. Pearen. The Diarium was a brief daily record of the mission's activities, written in French, now held at The Archive of the Jesuits in Canada, Montreal.
[148] LAC, RG 10, 258, C12,646 (Ironside to Pennefather, 5 Mar. 1861), pp. 156059-61; LAC, RG 10, 573, C13,374 (Ironside to Pennefather, 8 Mar. 1861), pp. 280-1.
[149] Cadieux, *Letters from Manitoulin*, #34, pp. 193-94; Wikwemikong Diarium, 26 May 1861, trans. S. Pearen.
[150] Wikwemikong Diarium, 22 June 1861, trans. S. Pearen.
[151] Cadieux, *Letters from Manitoulin*, #34 (Choné to Scholastics of Laval, 21 Aug. 1861), pp. 190-93.
[152] LAC, RG 10, Vol. 261, C12,648, pp. 158008-10.
[153] Cadieux, *Letters from Manitoulin*, #35 (Choné to Scholastics of Laval, 5 June 1862), pp. 198-200.
[154] *The Canadian Freeman*, 24 Oct. 1861, p. 2.
[155] Wikwemikong Diarium, 26 Nov. 1861, trans. S. Pearen.
[156] Wikwemikong Diarium, 24 Feb. 1862, trans. S. Pearen.
[157] LAC, RG 10, 292, C12,669 (Choné to Governor General, 9 Aug. 1862), pp. 195653-55 and 195674-77. Chief Mokomanish's sword was exhibited at the Ojibwe Cultural Foundation on Manitoulin Island in 2003, and was featured in the Canadian War Museum's Royal Canadian Legion Hall of Honour when the museum opened in Ottawa in 2005.
[158] LAC, RG 10, Vol. 621A, C13,392 (Tehkummah, 7 Jan. 1863), pp. 702-4.
[159] *The Quebec Mercury*, advertisement, May through Sept. 1862; *The Canadian Freeman*, 18 Sept. 1862, p. 2.
[160] LAC, RG 10, 292, C12,669 (Choné to the Superintendent of Indian Affairs, 15 Aug. 1862), pp. 195635-37, trans. S. Pearen.
[161] *The Canadian Freeman*, 18 Sept. 1862, p. 2.
[162] *The Markham Economist*, 2 Dec. 1862, pp. 2-4, from *London Morning Herald*, 30 Oct. 1862; Day, *English America*, p. 105.
[163] Wikwemikong Diarium, 4-8 Oct. 1862, trans. S. Pearen.
[164] Cadieux, *Letters from Manitoulin*, #36 (Choné to Scholastics of Laval, 12 Nov. 1862), pp. 205-15, and the French transcript of letter #36. Section/paragraph numbers evidently inserted in the text by Cadieux as he transcribed Choné's letter have been omitted here.

Choné's account to his colleagues appears to be an abbreviated version of the *Anishinaabeg* account.

[165] Cadieux, *Letters from Manitoulin*, #36 (Choné to Scholastics of Laval, 12 Nov. 1862), pp. 205-15, and the French transcript of letter #36.

[166] The terms *"Anishinaabe,"* "native" and "Indian" are all used in this chapter to reflect Peter Jacobs' heritage and life, which straddled two cultures.

[167] Peter's brothers were John Jacobs, who became a teacher and Church of England missionary to the Ojibwe at Sarnia, Cape Croker and Kettle Point, and Andrew Jacobs, who assisted at the Church of England on Manitoulin Island in 1865 before converting to Methodism and becoming a teacher. Two sisters assisted their brothers at Manitowaning and Sarnia. Peter Jacobs [Sr.], *Journal of the Reverend Peter Jacobs, Indian Wesleyan Missionary, from Rice Lake to the Hudson's Bay Territory; and Returning. Commencing May, 1852: With A Brief Account of His Life; and a Short History of the Wesleyan Mission to that Country* (Toronto: Anson Green, 1853), pp. 18-19.

[168] LAC, MG 17, A325, Colonial & Continental Church Society (hereafter C&CCS), Annual Report (Jacobs, 1857-58).

[169] LAC, MG 17, A326, C&CCS, Annual Report (Jacobs, 1861-62).

[170] LAC, MG 17, A326, C&CCS, Annual Report (Jacobs, 1861-62).

[171] Journal of the Legislative Assembly of the Province of Canada, 1858, App. 21 (Report of the Commissioners Appointed to Investigate Indian Affairs in Canada).

[172] LAC, RG 10, 263 (Jacobs to Strachan, 17 Nov. 1857), pp. 161352-53.

[173] LAC, MG 17, A326, C&CCS, Annual Report (Jacobs, 1861-62).

[174] LAC, MG 17, A217, Society for the Propagation of the Gospel in Foreign Parts (hereafter SPGFP) (Jacobs to Hawkins, 27 Mar. 1858).

[175] James Chance was born in 1829 in Worcestershire, England, emigrated to Canada in 1853, studied Ojibwe under Rev. O'Meara in winter 1853-54, was posted to Garden River in spring 1854 and was ordained in 1856 with Peter Jacobs.

[176] *The Globe*, 19 June 1862, p. 2.

[177] SPPC, 1863, App. 63 (Bartlett and Lindsey, 12 Oct. 1861).

[178] LAC, MG 17, A229, SPGFP (Jacobs, 3 Jan. 1862), p. 2637.

[179] SPPC, 1863, App. 63 (Bartlett and Lindsey, 12 Oct. 1861).

[180] LAC, MG 17, A229, SPGFP (Jacobs, 3 Jan. 1862), p. 2637.

[181] LAC, MG 17, A229, SPGFP (Jacobs, 3 Jan. 1862), p. 2637.

[182] Cadieux, *Letters from Manitoulin*, App. 2, pp. 269-70.

[183] *The Globe*, 18 Oct. 1861, p. 2.

[184] *Christian Guardian*, 6 Nov. 1861, p. 176.

[185] *Christian Guardian*, 13 Nov. 1861, p. 180.

[186] *Brockville Recorder*, 14 Nov. 1861, pp. 1, 2.

[187] *Canadian News, New Brunswick Herald, and British Columbian Intelligencer* [London, England], 7 Nov. 1861, Upper Canada correspondent's report of 21 Oct. 1861.

[188] *The Globe*, 24 Apr. 1862, p. 2 (copy from *Huron Signal* editorial).

[189] *The Globe*, 5 Mar. 1862, p. 2 (Shan to the editor, 10 Feb. 1862).

[190] *The Globe*, 5 Mar. 1862, p. 2 (Shan to the editor, 10 Feb. 1862).

[191] *The Globe*, 21 Mar. 1862, p. 1 (William Gibbard to the editor, 17 Mar. 1862).

[192] *The Globe*, 7 Apr. 1862, p. 1 (William Keating to the editor, 27 Mar. 1862).

[193] *The Globe*, 24 Apr. 1862, p. 2 (William Gibbard to the editor, 8 Apr. 1862).

[194] LAC, RG 10, 280, C12,662 (Chance to Spragge, 27 Jan. 1863), pp. 189398-99.

[195] Day, *London Morning Herald*, 30 Oct. 1862, reprinted in *The Markham Economist*, 4 Dec. 1862.

[196] Day, *English America*, pp. 91-97.

[197] LAC, A324, C&CCS, Annual Report (Rev. James Chance, 1865), p. 64.
[198] Day, *London Morning Herald*, 30 Oct. 1862, reprinted in *The Markham Economist*, 4 Dec. 1862.
[199] LAC, MG 17, A230, SPGFP (Jacobs, 9 Oct. 1862), p. 11071.
[200] LAC, MG 17, A230, SPGFP (Jacobs, 9 Oct. 1862), p. 11071.
[201] The first quotation from Choné is in Cadieux, *Letters from Manitoulin*, p. 209; the second is from LAC, RG 10, 292, p. 195663 (Protestation des Indiens de Wikwemikong, 15 Nov. 1862), trans. S. Pearen.
[202] *The Globe*, 16 Oct. 1862, p. 2.
[203] *The Markham Economist*, 16 Oct. 1862, p. 2, and 23 Oct. 1862, p. 2.
[204] *The Quebec Mercury*, 23 Oct. 1862, p. 3, quoting the *Huron Signal*. The *Signal*'s publication date is unknown but obviously before 23 Oct.
[205] *Canadian News, New Brunswick Herald, and British Columbian Intelligencer* [London, England], 6 Nov. 1862 and 13 Nov. 1862.
[206] *The Markham Economist*, 30 Oct. 1862.
[207] *The Canadian Freeman*, 6 Nov. 1862, p. 2.
[208] *St. Catharines Constitutional*, 23 Oct. 1862, p. 2.
[209] *St. Catharines Constitutional*, 20 Nov. 1862, p. 2.
[210] *Christian Guardian*, 19 Dec. 1862, p. 198.
[211] *The Markham Economist*, 11 Dec. 1862.
[212] *The Daily Spectator and Journal of Commerce*, 17 Nov. 1862, p. 2.
[213] *The Globe*, 3 Dec. 1862, p. 2.
[214] *The Markham Economist*, 4 Dec. 1862.
[215] Day, *London Morning Herald*, 30 Oct. 1862, reprinted in *The Markham Economist*, 4 Dec. 1862.
[216] *The Canadian Freeman*, 29 Jan. 1863, pp. 2, 3. This is another translation of the French account in LAC, RG 10, 292, pp. 195661-73 and SPPC, 1863, Documents de la Session (No. 63) (Protestation des Indiens de Wikwemikong, 15 Nov. 1862).
[217] *Hamilton Evening Times*, 4 Feb. 1863, p. 2.
[218] *The Canadian Freeman*, 19 Feb. 1863, p. 2.
[219] *Kingston Daily News*, 11 Feb. 1863, p. 2; *Canadian News, New Brunswick Herald, and British Columbian Intelligencer* [London, England], 6 Mar. 1863, p. 6. The newspapers published only the short letter to the governor, not the entire report of the negotiations.
[220] *The Quebec Mercury*, 23 Feb. 1863, p. 2, and 19 Feb. 1863, p. 2.
[221] *The Globe*, 4 Mar. 1863, p. 2.
[222] LAC, MG 17, A231, SPGFP (Jacobs, 2 Apr. 1863), p. 5448.
[223] Chiefs Louis Taibosegai, J.B. Atagiwinini and Michel Cainooshimague succumbed to the agent's demands of loyalty to the Crown, but their sons Louis Taibosegai, Jr., Jako Atagiwinini and Tomah Kinojameg remained strongly opposed to any further land surrenders. Michel Cainooshimague died before the treaty was signed and his son replaced him as chief.
[224] The Archive of the Jesuits in Canada, Montreal, D-4-3, s1-7,4 (draft letter, Choné to Moyle, 23 Oct. 1862).
[225] LAC, RG 10, 331, C9581 (Choné to Cazeau, 1 Dec. 1862), pp. 28-31, trans. S. Pearen.
[226] Wikwemikong Diarium, 17 Nov. 1862, trans. S. Pearen.
[227] The Archive of the Jesuits in Canada, Montreal, D-4-3, s1-7,14 (Wiquemikong, 3 Nov. 1862, 3-page document in Ojibwe). They also complained that, on 28 Oct., Wabiwiokwan had sold wood from his wharf and not paid them for it. Summarized by

Alan Corbiere, M'Chigeeng, Manitoulin Island. It is not known if this document was translated into French or sent to the governor.

[228] LAC, RG 10, 292, pp. 195661-73, trans S. Pearen. This petition was printed in French in SPPC, 1863, Documents de la Session (No. 63) (Protestation des Indiens de Wikwemikong, 15 Nov. 1862), but does not appear in the English Sessional Papers of 1863. See Chapter 2, "*Odawa Minising* and *Ogimaa* Itawashkash," for Pearen's translation of the *Anishinaabeg* account of the treaty; and Chapter 5, "Reaction to the Treaty," for *The Canadian Freeman*'s translation, published on 29 Jan. 1863.

[229] LAC, RG 10, 574, C13,374 (Dupont to Spragge, 18 Dec. 1863), p. 34, re: 18 Nov. expulsion.

[230] LAC, RG 10, 292 (protestation, 15 Nov. 1862), pp. 195671-72, trans. S. Pearen.

[231] LAC, RG 10, 621A, C13,392 (Jan. 1863 depositions before Dr. Layton), pp. 702-13.

[232] SPPC, 1863, No. 18 (Megwance, 15 Jan. 1863).

[233] LAC, RG 10, 567, C13,372 (Ironside to Spragge, 18 Nov. 1862), pp. 69-71; LAC, RG 10, 615, C13,387 (Ironside to Spragge, 16 Jan. 1863), pp. 212-13; LAC, RG 10, 522, C13,348 (Walcot to Ironside, 5 Jan 1863), p. 97.

[234] SPPC, 1863, No. 18 (depositions of 15 Jan. 1863).

[235] LAC, RG 10, 288 (Gibbard to Commissioner of Crown Lands, 9 Dec. 1862).

[236] LAC, RG 10, 258 (Ironside to Pennefather, 12 Mar. 1861), pp. 156169-71; LAC, RG 10, 573, C13,374 (Ironside to Indian Dept., 17 July 1861), and LAC, RG 10, 2050, file 9444, 26 Nov. 1896. The discipline was probably intended as temporary; unfortunately, it continued for decades, until 1896.

[237] SPPC, 1863, No. 63 (Choné to Cazeau, 14 Oct. 1862). A slightly different translation is found in LAC, RG 10, 280 pp. 189802-7.

[238] LAC, RG 10, 521, C13,348 (Spragge to Cazeau, 10 Nov. 1862), pp. 479-81.

[239] Archives of Ontario, F968, MS159, Can. 1 – XV 35 (Kohler to Becks, 20 Nov. 1862), trans. S. Pearen.

[240] SPPC, 1863, No. 5, App. (J.S. Dennis, report of 31 Dec. 1862).

[241] LAC, RG 10, 615, C13,387 (Ironside to Spragge, 3 Jan. 1863), pp. 205-7.

[242] SPPC, 1863, No. 5, App. 44 (Report from Indian Department appended to Report of Commissioner of Crown Lands).

[243] Narcisse Belleau made several references in the Legislative Council to the existence of petitions against the McDougall treaty from the Indians of Sheshegwaning, Michigiwatinong and Atchiwaigunning. The Wikwemikong *Anishinaabeg* noted in a letter to the governor general of 1 Dec. 1863 that four protests against the treaty had already been sent.

[244] LAC, RG 10, 615, C13,387 (Nesahwahgwud to Tabahsega, 20 Feb. 1863), pp. 208-10; LAC, RG 10, 291, C12,668 (Ironside to Spragge, 4 May 1863), p. 195945. The letter is not in Hanipaux's handwriting. It is probably a translation made by Ironside or his son. The suggestion to appeal to the governor if they were dissatisfied with the treaty would be a natural recommendation, and was an action later recommended by the Protestant minister.

[245] LAC, RG 10, 615, C13,387 (Ironside to Spragge, 20 Mar. 1863), pp. 231-33.

[246] LAC, RG 10, 292, C12,669, pp. 196060-63, trans. S. Pearen.

[247] LAC, RG 10, 292, C12,669, pp. 195914-15 in English, pp. 195983-84 in French, and pp. 195985-87 in Ojibwe.

[248] SPPC, 1863, No. 18, 24 July 1863.

[249] LAC, RG 10, 292, C12,669, 17 May 1863, English trans. pp. 195804-14. Document written in Ojibwe, then in French, then in English.

[250] Cadieux, *Letters from Manitoulin*, App. 2, p. 270.

[251] LAC, RG 10, 299, C12,674 (Taylor to Russell, 22 May 1863), p. 201016.
[252] LAC, RG 10, 296, C12,672 (Rafferty to McDougall, 9 Nov. 1863), p. 198621.
[253] *The Globe*, 10 Jan. 1863, p. 2.
[254] Journal of the Legislative Council of the Province of Canada, 1863: 6 Mar., 18 Mar. and 22 Apr. 1863; SPPC, 1863, No. 63 (Returns of 6 and 18 Mar. 1863, and 22 and 23 Apr. 1863); SPPC, Documents de la Session (No. 63), 1863 (Protestation des Indiens de Wikwemikong, 15 Nov. 1862).
[255] *The Quebec Mercury*, 9 May 1863, p. 2.
[256] *The Globe*, 20 May 1863, p. 2.
[257] *The Canadian Freeman*, 27 Aug. 1863, p. 3. Kohler claimed that Gibbard made the remarks onboard the steamboat *Ploughboy* in 1859, and admitted and confirmed them in June 1863.
[258] The McKenzie family of Cove Island and Wikwemikong made a profit of $10 per barrel on fish shipped via Chicago and the Midwest in 1859. In 1861 the family had sales of $3,645 in fresh and salted trout, whitefish and pike. "Report of William Gibbard, Fishery Overseer for the Division of Lakes Huron and Superior for 1859," SPPC, 1860, No. 12.
[259] *The Globe*, 21 Mar. 1862, p. 1, and 24 Apr. 1862, p. 2. See also Chapter 4.
[260] SPPC, 1863, No. 18. Unless otherwise noted, all quotations and information from Gibbard on the fishing incident are from this source. Gibbard had leased the island to non-Natives previously, but his superiors acknowledged Manitoulin was one of the traditional fishing islands and had cancelled the lease.
[261] *The Globe*, 7 Aug. 1863, p. 2; SPPC, 1863, No. 18; LAC, RG 10, 292, p. 195893 (*Anishinaabeg* version).
[262] LAC, RG 10, 292, p. 195877; see also pp. 195873-98. Unless otherwise noted, all quotations from the Wikwemikong *Anishinaabeg* are from this source, trans. by S. Pearen when required. The lessees were Pinimon (Philemon Proulx) and Shagwawimanitons (Charles de Laronde).
[263] SPPC, 1863, No. 18.
[264] Copies of their letters were translated and printed in *The Canadian Freeman* on 6 Aug. 1863.
[265] *The Globe*, 30 July 1863, p. 2.
[266] *The Quebec Mercury*, 12 Aug. 1863 (de Lamorandière to the editor, 3 Aug. 1863). Although the *Mercury* published a copy of this letter, I have not found it in *The Globe*.
[267] *Le Journal de Québec*, 1 Aug. 1863, p. 2, trans. S. Pearen.
[268] *Le Journal de Québec*, 4 Aug. 1863, p. 2, trans. S. Pearen.
[269] *The Globe*, 3 Aug. 1863, p. 2.
[270] *The Morning Chronicle and Commercial and Shipping Gazette* [Quebec], 1 Aug. 1863, p. 2.
[271] *The Morning Chronicle and Commercial and Shipping Gazette* [Quebec], 3 Aug. 1863, p. 2.
[272] *St. Catharines Constitutional*, 6 Aug. 1863, p. 2.
[273] *The Irish Canadian*, 5 Aug. 1863, p. 2.
[274] *The Globe*, 24 Aug. 1863, p. 2 (Kohler to the editor, 4 Aug. 1863); *The Canadian Freeman*, 27 Aug. 1863, p. 3; *The Irish Canadian*, 26 Aug. 1863, p. 2. *The Globe* published Kohler's letter with an editorial that accused him of being "lively, hot-headed, not blessed with much judgement, and sadly lacking in prudence, a zealot for his church, and not very particular about the means he employs for advancing its interests."
[275] LAC, MG 17, A231, SPGFP (Jacobs, 30 Mar. 1864), p. 60671.
[276] LAC, RG 10, 281 (Cooper to McDougall, 11 Aug. 1863), pp. 190185-203. The letter

is signed R. Cooper, Manitowaning parsonage. Cooper is possibly a relative of Rev. Jacobs' wife Susan Cooper, or the Rev. Richard S. Cooper of Paisley, Bruce County, who was a colleague of Rev. Jacobs.

[277] SPPC, 1863, No. 18 (Whitcher to McDougall, 24 Aug. 1863).
[278] *The Quebec Mercury*, 29 Aug. 1863, p. 2.
[279] *The Canadian Freeman*, 3 Sept. 1863, p. 2.
[280] "Yesterday's Leader," *The Irish Canadian*, 2 Sept. 1863.
[281] *The Quebec Mercury*, 27 Aug. 1863, p. 2.
[282] *The Quebec Mercury*, 31 Aug. 1863, p. 2.
[283] *Hamilton Evening Times*, 15 Sept. 1863.
[284] Louis Carrez, S.J., who was in Canada from 1858 to 1868.
[285] Cadieux, *Letters from Manitoulin*, #39 (Carrez to Scholastics of Laval, 12 Sept. 1863), p. 223.
[286] British Library, India Office Records, IOR/L/MIL/9/179/268-74.
[287] A summary of the Supreme Court's criminal sessions regarding Gibbard's trial for murder, as well as the Calcutta newspapers' "disquisitions" on the "dreadful case," can be found in *The Asiatic Journal and Monthly Register for British and Foreign India, China, and Australasia*, Vol. 33 New Series (Sept.-Dec. 1840), (London: Wm. H. Allen, 1840), pp. 104-6 and 274-76; see also Vol. 40 New Series (Jan.-Apr. 1843), pp. 421-22.
[288] Journal of the Legislative Assembly of the Province of Canada, 1864, App. (No. 5), William Gibbard to the Select Committee on the Working of the Fishery Act, 27 Apr. 1863.
[289] LAC, RG 10, 281, C12,663 (Choné to McDougall, 1 Sept. 1863), pp. 190161-63.
[290] LAC, RG 10, 280, C12,662 (Choné to Governor General, 16 Sept. 1863), pp. 189795-800; LAC, RG 10, 292, C12,669, French version on pp. 195916-19.
[291] Journal of the Legislative Assembly of the Province of Canada, 1863, 1 Oct. 1863, p. 216; SPPC, 1864, No. 53 (Return of 22 June 1864 to an Address of 12 Oct. 1863). Note the 12 Oct. 1863 request for copies of protests against the McDougall treaty addressed to the governor general in January and May from the Indians of Sheshegwaning, Michigiwatinong and Atchiwaigunning; the whereabouts of a copy of the latter petition is unknown.
[292] *The Quebec Mercury*, 29 Aug. 1863, p. 2.
[293] Cadieux, "Les Robes Noires," p. 173, and Cadieux, *Letters from Manitoulin*, #39 (Carrez to Scholastics of Laval, 12 Sept. 1863), p. 235.
[294] Charles Thomas Dupont (1837-1923) was joined on Manitoulin by his brother John Ahern Dupont, a merchant/trader who set up a shop in Little Current about 1864. Charles later worked as an excise officer in Windsor, Ontario before heading west to Vancouver and Victoria, British Columbia, where he was a successful land speculator.
[295] J.W. Keating and McGregor Ironside expressed interest in the position.
[296] LAC, RG 10, 283, C12,664 (Dupont to Spragge, 26 Sept. 1863), pp. 191217-21.
[297] Wikwemikong Diarium, 27 Sept. 1863, 4 Oct. 1863 and 12 Oct. 1863.
[298] *The Canadian Freeman*, 21 Jan. 1864, p. 3.
[299] LAC, RG 10, 284, C12,664 (27 Dec. 1863), p. 191282. Dupont noted "This is written judging from the handwriting by Choné."
[300] LAC, RG 10, 284, C12,664 (Dupont to Spragge, 7 Dec. 1863), p. 191285.
[301] LAC, RG 10, 284, C12,664 (Dupont to Spragge, 8 Dec. 1863); LAC, RG 10, 615, C13,387 (Hobson to Dupont, 14 Jan. 1864), p. 356.
[302] LAC, RG 10, 574, C13,374 (Dupont to Taibosegai, 11 Jan. 1864), pp. 37-38.
[303] LAC, RG 10, 284, C12,664 (Dupont to Spragge, 16 Jan. 1863 [i.e., 1864]), pp. 191319-21.

[304] LAC, RG 10, 523, C13,349 (Spragge to Dupont, 9 Jan. 1864), pp. 120-21.
[305] LAC, RG 10, 523, C13,349 (Spragge to Hanipaux, 11 Jan. 1864), pp. 124-25.
[306] LAC, RG 10, 281, C12,663 (Choné to Spragge, 2 Feb. 1864), pp. 190110-13.
[307] LAC, MG 17, A231, SPGFP (Jacobs, 30 Mar. 1864), p. 60671.
[308] LAC, RG 10, 574, C13,374 (Dupont to Spragge, 18 Jan. 1864), pp. 39-43; LAC, RG 10, 284, C12,664 (Ojibwe document signed Charles Wabigijik, ka massinakising, Wikwemikong 1864 kikinonowin), pp. 191283-84.
[309] LAC, RG 10, 574, C13,374 (Dupont to Spragge, 18 Jan. 1864), pp. 39-43.
[310] LAC, RG 10, 615, C13,387 (Choné to *surintendant*, 17 Jan. 1864), p. 358, trans. S. Pearen.
[311] LAC, RG 10, 284, C12,664, pp. 191346-48; LAC, RG 10, 615, C13,387, pp. 347-51.
[312] LAC, MG 17, A231, SPGFP (Jacobs, 30 Mar. 1864), p. 60671.
[313] LAC, RG 10, 284, C12,664 (Dupont to Spragge, 23 Jan. 1863 [i.e., 1864]), p. 191344.
[314] LAC, RG 10, 292, C12,669, pp. 195859-63. A faint note in the margin says "Indian Dept. 31 March 1864."
[315] LAC, RG 10, 281, C12, 663 (Choné to Campbell, 7 May 1864), p. 190174.
[316] LAC, RG 10, 281, C12, 663 (draft, Campbell to Choné and Cazeau, 10 June 1864), pp. 190165-70.
[317] LAC, MG 17, A231, SPGFP (Jacobs, 30 Mar. 1864), p. 60671.
[318] LAC, RG 10, 574, C13,374 (Dupont to Givens, 20 Sept. 1864), pp. 93-96.
[319] Jabez Waters Sims (1831-1869) was born in Basingstoke, England and came to Canada as a teacher about 1856 with his wife and son. He was befriended by Rev. F.A. O'Meara, the former Church of England missionary to Manitoulin Island, who encouraged him to become an Anglican priest and later to take on the Manitoulin mission. Sims is also this author's great-great grandfather.
[320] Day, *English America*, pp. 115, 118-19.
[321] LAC, RG 10, 615, C13,388 (Spragge to Choné, 6 May 1865), pp. 797-99.
[322] LAC, RG 10, 322, C9577 (Choné to Commissioner of Crown Lands, 8 May 1865 and 18 May 1865), pp. 215526-34.
[323] LAC, RG 10, 711, C13,401 (licence, 10 June 1865), pp. 411-14; LAC, RG 10, 567, C13,372, p. 363.
[324] LAC, RG 10, 282, C12,664 (Choné to Campbell, 18 Feb. 1865), pp. 190843-52.
[325] LAC, R4176-0-0-E [formerly MG 24, J51] (Journal of the Reverend Jabez W. Sims, 26 June 1865), pp. 202-3.
[326] LAC, RG 10, 426, C9627 (Petition, 15 July 1865), trans. Allen Salt, Christian Island interpreter, 13 Nov. 1865, pp. 399-404; and in Ojibwe with translation in LAC, RG 10, 307, C12,679, pp. 206163-71.
[327] LAC, R4176-0-0-E (Journal of the Reverend Jabez W. Sims, 14 July 1865).
[328] Wikwemikong Diarium, 15 July 1865, trans. S. Pearen.
[329] LAC, RG 10, 331, C9581 (Dupont to Spragge, 12 July 1865), p. 42.
[330] LAC, RG 10, 331, C9581 (Dupont to Spragge, 31 July 1865), p. 65.
[331] LAC, RG 10, 525, C13,350 (Spragge to Dupont, 16 Oct. 1865), pp. 78-79.
[332] LAC, RG 10, 331, C9581 (Dupont to Spragge, 12 July 1865), pp. 41-44; LAC, RG 10, 574, C13,374, pp. 225-26.
[333] LAC, RG 10, 524, C13,350 (Spragge to Dupont, 22 July 1865), pp. 457-58.
[334] LAC, RG 10, 524, C13,350 (Spragge to Dupont, 1 Aug. 1865), pp. 477-78.
[335] LAC, RG 10, 525, C13,350 (Spragge to Dupont, 16 Sept. 1865: land reserved for one year from Sept. 1865), pp. 11-12; LAC, MG 17, A232 (Report of Bethune and O'Meara, 1 Nov. 1865).

[336] LAC, RG 10, 331 C9581 (Dupont to Spragge, 15 Oct. 1865), pp. 185-92; LAC, RG 10, 574, C13,374 (Dupont to Spragge, 24 Aug. 1865), pp. 234-35.
[337] The Indian Dept. applied to the Governor General for permission to issue petroleum licences on behalf of the *Anishinaabeg*, and permission was granted by Order in Council. LAC, RG 10, 525, C13,350 (Spragge to Dupont, 16 Sept. 1865), p. 12.
[338] LAC, RG 10, 525, C13,350, pp. 12, 86, 87, 128.
[339] LAC, RG 10, 336, C9584 (Férard to Dep. Comm. Crown Lands, 9 Jan. 1866), p. 263.
[340] LAC, RG 10, 357, C9594 (31 Jan. 1866), pp. 172-74; *The Globe*, 17 Feb. 1866, p. 1.
[341] LAC, RG 10, 336 (Férard to Spragge, 31 Mar. 1866), pp. 318-19.
[342] LAC, RG 10, 307, 12,679 (Bartlett to Spragge, 16 Mar. 1866), pp. 206632-35.
[343] LAC, RG 10, 332, C9582 (Dupont to Spragge, 4 Aug. 1866), pp. 489-98.
[344] LAC, RG 10, 332, C9582, pp. 34-36.
[345] LAC, RG 10, 333, C9582 (Ojibwe petition and English translation), pp. 78-105.
[346] LAC, RG 10, 333, C9582 (Dupont to Spragge, 6 Sept. 1866), pp. 74-79.
[347] Memorandum of 26 Jan. 1866, approved of by the Governor General in Council on 9 April 1866. Regulations approved on 4 May 1866. LAC, RG 10, 711 p. 223; LAC, RG 10, 616 C13,388, p. 36. An initial sale date of 24 May was postponed until 18 June 1866.
[348] LAC, RG 10, 333, C9582 (Charles de Lamorandière to Deputy Superintendant General Indian Affairs, 9 Aug. 1866), pp. 2-3.
[349] LAC, RG 10, 616, C13,388 (Spragge to Dupont, 8 Aug. 1866), p. 129.
[350] LAC, RG 10, 372, C9600 (Sims to Samuel Henry Strong, Nov. 1867), pp. 294-96. Lawyer Strong had been sent to Manitoulin Island to investigate the charges brought by Sims against Dupont.
[351] LAC, RG 10, 372, C9600 (Pahbamasay to Samuel Henry Strong, Nov. 1867), p. 306.
[352] LAC, RG 10, 372, C9600 (Maishequongai, Nov. 1867), pp. 315-16.
[353] LAC, RG 10, 371, C9599 (Obetosaway to Spragge, 25 Aug. 1865) pp. 24-25.
[354] LAC, RG 10, 1950, C11121, file 4713; LAC, RG 10, 1950, C11110, 1915, file 2670, 1873 letters.
[355] A total of 6,561 acres of farmland at 50 cents per acre, and 2,208 acres of oil and mineral lands at one dollar per acre. LAC, RG 10, 722, C13,412, p. 350; LAC, RG 10, 711, p. 430 (Order in Council approved on 31 May 1867).
[356] LAC, RG 10, 527, C13,351 (Langevin to Plummer, 28 Sept. 1868), p. 470; LAC, RG 10, 528, C13,351 (Langevin to Plummer, 15 Jan. 1869), p. 101.
[357] LAC, RG 10, 379, C9603 (Plummer to Howe, 31 May 1870), p. 258; RG 10, 529, C13,352, p. 560.
[358] LAC, MG 17, A234, SPGFP (Appeal, 22 June 1867) p. 9697.
[359] LAC, MG 17, A235, SPGFP (Sims, 30 June 1868), p. 9473.
[360] LAC, RG 10, 358, C9594 (Férard to Howe, 1 June 1870), pp. 363-64.
[361] LAC, RG 10, 380, C9603 (25 July 1870), pp. 263-64.
[362] LAC, RG 10, C11159, 2105, file 19,303.
[363] *Official Report of the Debates of the House of Commons of the Dominion of Canada, 8 Mar. 1886* (Ottawa: MacLean, 1886), p. 64.
[364] LAC, RG 10, 2050, file 9444, 26 Nov. 1896.